William Harding Carter

Horses, Saddles and Bridles

William Harding Carter

Horses, Saddles and Bridles

ISBN/EAN: 9783744662376

Printed in Europe, USA, Canada, Australia, Japan

Cover: Foto ©Andreas Hilbeck / pixelio.de

More available books at **www.hansebooks.com**

HORSES,

SADDLES AND BRIDLES.

By CAPTAIN WILLIAM H. CARTER,

SIXTH CAVALRY, U. S. ARMY.

LEAVENWORTH, KANSAS:
KETCHESON & REEVES, PRINTERS AND BINDERS.
1895.

Entered according to act of Congress, in the year 1895,

BY CAPTAIN WILLIAM H. CARTER,

in the office of the Librarian of Congress, at Washington.

PREFACE.

There is no scarcity of excellent books on the history, breeding, training, and veterinary treatment of all classes of horses, as well as on horsemanship in general.

Many of these will well repay the student for the time spent in mastering them, but none seem to meet the wants of the army, for which this book is primarily intended.

It has been my endeavor to find, and bring together in available form, some of the facts regarded as of value to those upon whom the government must depend, to a great extent, for important services when war comes upon the country.

Photography has been used as far as possible, because of the natural tendency to exaggeration in drawn illustrations. The photographs, except those of foreign services, were taken by Captain W. D. BEACH, Third Cavalry, in charge of the Department of Engineering, and to whom I am indebted for assistance and encouragement during the progress of the entire work.

I desire, also, to express my obligations to Major J. B. BABCOCK, Assistant Adjutant-General, in charge of the Bureau of Military Information, to the military attachés who kindly assisted me in obtaining valuable data, and to

PREFACE.

Lieutenant E. L. PHILLIPS, Sixth Cavalry, for several of the line drawings.

A great many publications have been consulted, and in many instances quoted. It has not been practicable to give proper credit for use of ideas and language in each instance, but a general acknowledgment is here made.

PARTIAL LIST OF PUBLICATIONS CONSULTED.

The Exterior of the Horse. (GOUBAUX AND BARRIER.)
Horses and Stables. (FITZWYGRAM.)
Diseases and Injuries of the Horse. (KIRBY.)
Seats and Saddles. (DWYER.)
The Horse in Motion. (STILLMAN.)
Parfait Marechal. (PAR DE SOLLEYSOL, Ecuyer, MDCXI.)
Principes De Dressage Et D'Equitation. (FILLIS.)
Modern Horsemanship. (E. L. ANDERSON.)
Training Cavalry Horses. (GARRARD.)
How to Buy and Sell. (HOWDEN.)
Horses and Riding. (NEVILLE.)
Riders of Many Lands. (DODGE.)
Patroclus and Penelope. (DODGE.)
Bridle Bits. (BATTERSBY.)
Records of the Rebellion.
Journal United States Cavalry Association.
Journal Royal United Service Institution (British).
Reports Quartermaster General, 1861 to 1866.
Report of Chief of Cavalry, 1863.
Report on Diseases of the Horse. (Department of Agriculture.)
Report of Board on Cavalry Equipments and Veterinary Supplies, 1884.
Report Department of Agriculture on Agricultural Grasses and Forage Plants of the United States.

WILLIAM H. CARTER,
Captain Sixth Cavalry.

FORT LEAVENWORTH, KANSAS,
January, 1895.

CONTENTS.

CHAPTER I.—INTRODUCTORY.

CHAPTER II.—THE CAVALRY HORSE.

Purchase of Cavalry Horses.—Importance of Careful Inspection.—Remarks on Judging Horses.—Nomenclature of the Horse.—The Skeleton.—The Superior Muscles.—The Exterior Regions.—Examination of the Horse.—Relations Between Dimensions of Certain Parts.—Examination in Detail as to Form.—The Head; Neck; Withers; Shoulders; Back; Ribs; Chest; Fore Legs and Feet; Hind Quarters; Tail; Body.—Examination for Soundness .... 17 to 55

CHAPTER III.—AGE OF HORSES.

Period of Longevity or Extreme Age.—Mares Live Longer than Horses.—"Rising" and "Past" a Certain Age.—Age as Indicated by the Teeth.—Wolf's Teeth. - Temporary Teeth.—Permanent Teeth.—The Marks or Cups.—Angle Which Incisors Make in Coming Together.—The Tusks.—Rasping Off the Corners of Incisors.—Bishoping ... 56 to 73

CHAPTER IV.—ENDURANCE OF HORSES.

Influence of the Weight of the Pack.—Necessity for Husbanding Strength at First.—Preliminary Hardening Valueless Unless Horses Are Kept Supplied with Forage.—Abuse of Horses.—Marching Gaits. —Endurance Varies with Treatment, Size and Shape.— Causes of Losses of Horses in War.—Cavalry Raids.—Losses of Horses in Various Campaigns.—The Establishment of the Cavalry Bureau, and What It Accomplished.—Frontier Service .... 74 to 95

CHAPTER V.—FRAMEWORK OF THE HORSE MECHANICALLY CONSIDERED.

Center of Motion.—Center of Gravity.—Base of Support.—Relative Positions of Centers of Motion and Gravity.—Equilibrium.—Effect of Head and Neck on Center of Gravity.—Artificial Balance of Saddle Horse . . . . 96 to 105

CHAPTER VI.—GAITS OF THE HORSE.

Motion Implies Displacement of Center of Gravity.—Natural Gaits.—Stride and Step.—The Walk.—The Trot.—The Hand Gallop.—The Gallop; True, False, Disconnected.—Fatigue Somewhat Dependent on Motion of Center of Gravity.—The Jump . . . . 106 to 121

CHAPTER VII.—BITS.

Classified as Bar, Snaffle and Curb.—The Mouthing: Pelham; Whitman.—Bit and Bridoon.—Horse's Mouth Structurally Considered: Curb Groove; Jaw Bone; Tongue Channel; Bars.—Temperament of Mouth: Normal; Tender; Hard; Spoiled.—Dimensions Considered in Fitting Curb Bits; Width of Mouth; Width of Tongue Channel; Height of Bars.—The Curb Bit: Its Action as a Lever; Proportions of Upper and Lower Branches; Falling Through; Standing Stiff; Angle at which Reins Act on Bit; Position of Curb Chain; Width and Length; Form and Proportions of Mouth-Piece; Attachment of Headstalls.—American, British and European Cavalry Bits . . . . 122 to 152

CHAPTER VIII.—BITTING AND TRAINING.

End and Aim of Bitting.—Principle Governing All Bitting.—Importance of Knowledge of Subject.—Effect of Head and Neck.—How Bit Should Be Regarded.—Rational Treatment.—Training.—Horse Made Familiar with New Surroundings.—Equipped with Snaffle Bit—"Dumb Jockey."—Riding School and Track.—Establishing Gaits.—Jumping.—Use of Longe; Training Halter; Running Rein.—Saddle.—Use of Saber and Fire-Arms.—Selecting and Fitting Curb Bit.—Mouth Gauge.—Trial Bit.—Hard and Tender Mouth.—Effect of Seat of Rider.—Riding with One Hand.—Guiding by Pressure of Rein on Neck . . . . 153 to 171

CONTENTS. 7

CHAPTER IX.—SADDLES.

Value of Knowledge of Construction and Adjustment.—Under Surface: Shape; Size Proportioned to Weight Carried.— Upper Surface: Size Proportioned to Bulk Carried.—Importance of Shape of Seat.—Where to Put the Weight in Saddle.—Position of Saddle on the Horse.—Materials for Construction.—Military Saddles.—Side Bars: Length; Shape; Adjustable.—Experiment to Show Proper Adjustment of Pack.—Padding: Pads; Blankets.—Cruppers.—Breast Straps.—Rules for Selection and Arrangement of Saddle and Pack . . . . 172 to 183

CHAPTER X.—CAVALRY SADDLES AND PACKS.

Designed to Carry Heavy Loads.—Weights of Saddles and Packs.—Disadvantages of Heavy and Bulky Packs.—American Cavalry: The Saddle; Field Equipment; Pack; Field Uniforms.—British Cavalry: Service Orders; Saddle; Field Equipment; Pack; Remarks.—German Cavalry: Arms; The Saddle; Pack; Remarks.—Russian Cavalry: Arms; Saddle; Pack.—Belgian Cavalry: Arms; Saddle Equipments; Pack.—Austrian Cavalry: The Saddle; Pack.—Observations . . . . 184 to 242

CHAPTER XI.—SEATS.

Variety of Seats.—Value of a Well Balanced Seat.—Safest and Best Seat.—Balance, Friction and Stirrups.—Seat Depends Upon Purpose In Riding.—Long or Chair Seat; Tongs-across-a-wall" Seat; Fork Seat; Military Seat . . . . 243 to 264

CHAPTER XII.—FORAGE.

Allowance to Public Animals.—Standard Weights.—Hay: Upland; Lowland; Wet Meadow; Good; Inferior; Mow-Burnt.—Dust in Hay.—Haystacks.—Grasses in General: Timothy; Red Top; Bermuda Grass; Orchard Grass; Kentucky Blue Grass; Clover; Alfalfa; Buffalo Grass; Gramma Grass; Gietta Grass; Blue Stem; Blue Joint; Fodder or Roughness.—Weight and Measurement of Hay.—Oats.—Corn.—Barley.—Bran . . . . 265 to 289

CHAPTER XIII.—STABLE MANAGEMENT.

Herding.— Stables.— Ventilation.—Water.— Feeding.— Stable Routine.— Grooming.— Shoeing.— Nursing Sick Horses: Discharges; Hand Rubbing; Sponging; Hot and Cold Applications; Steaming; Poultices; Bandages; Pulse; Temperature; Blankets; Removing Shoes; Balls; Drenches; Injections.—Supply Table of Medicines.—Instruments.— Explanation of Medicines.—Prescriptions . . . . 290 to 324

CHAPTER XIV.—DISEASES AND INJURIES.

Common Cold.— Influenza.— Strangles.— Glanders.— Pneumonia, or Lung Fever.— Lampas.— Constipation.— Spasmodic Colic.— Flatulent Colic.— Diarrhea.— Lockjaw.— Profuse Staling.— Retention of Urine.— Bloody Urine.— Poll Evil.— Sore Back.— Mange.— Scratches.— Spavins.— Curb.— Capped Hock.— Broken Knees.— Splint.— Ringbones.—Wind-galls.— Interfering.— Swelled Legs.— Pricking of the Foot.— Punctures of the Frog.— Corns.— Quittor.— Sand Cracks.— Seedy Toe.— Thrush.— Navicular Disease.— Laminitis.— Side Bones.— Calking.— Flesh Wounds: Gun Shot; Stabs; Cuts; Lacerations and Contusions . . . . 325 to 368

HORSES, SADDLES AND BRIDLES.

CHAPTER I.

INTRODUCTORY.

Although the relative importance of the horse as a factor in the progress of civilization has been materially reduced by the introduction of steam and electricity, it must not be forgotten that he has been the constant companion of the Caucasian race in all its migrations, an indispensable ally in all its conquests, and one of the most efficient agents of its civilization. There is no history that is not interwoven with his, and if by some convulsion of nature he should cease to exist, it would then be realized how very necessary he still is for pleasure, war or business.

A knowledge of all that pertains to the horse and his equipment is very valuable and necessary to the officers of the army, for the government expects them to have the animals under their charge kept in health and training, so that when called upon they will be able to render a good account of themselves, and if required to go to the limit of endurance and even of life itself, the fatal moment may be deferred until the desired end has been attained.

It is presumed that only that service which is within the limit of human and animal power will be imposed.

Theoretical knowledge is of value in any profession; it comes with study and not by instinct. In no other subjects, however, is it more necessary to have theory and practice go hand in hand, than in those treated of in these pages. Books alone cannot convey a knowledge of the powers and endurance of commands under varying conditions of service, for often, as in Indian campaigns, the capacity is judged by the weakest members, owing to the inhumanity of abandoning a comrade in a species of warfare in which the taking of prisoners is confined to the civilized combatants.

Actual experience on the march is the only method of testing the value of saddles and other equipments, and the capacity of horses to carry their riders and packs without breaking down.

Even those familiar with war have little appreciation of the enormous numbers of horses and mules required to replace those used up by armies during actual field service.

The Quartermaster General in his report for the year ending June 30, 1864, says:

"It appears, therefore, in practice, that the quartermaster's train of any army requires, on the average, one army wagon to every twenty-four or twenty-five men, and the animals of the cavalry and artillery and of the trains will average one to every two men in the field."

A knowledge of horses, saddles and bridles is of more importance to the cavalry officer than to any other rider, because good bitting, saddling, packing and riding, are what make up the efficiency of cavalry, and provide for an economical administration of that important arm.

Ignorance as to the great expense necessary for the proper maintenance of this arm became so apparent during the first two years of the Civil War, that in an order establishing the Cavalry Bureau, published by the Secretary of War at the close of the Gettysburg campaign, the following paragraph occurred:

"The enormous expense attending the maintenance of the cavalry arm, points to the necessity of greater care, and more judicious management on the part of cavalry officers, that their horses may be constantly kept up to the standard of efficiency for service. Great neglects of duty in this connection are to be attributed to officers in command of cavalry troops.

"It is the design of the War Department to correct such neglects, by dismissing from service officers whose ineficency and inattention result in the deterioration and loss of the public animals under their charge."

Under the circumstances the establishment of the Cavalry Bureau was an urgent necessity. It at once became a potent factor in the conduct of the war, systematizing and improving the remount purchases for the large body of cavalry in the field, and materially aided in making possible their succession of victories during the last eighteen months of the war.

The Cavalry Bureau not only enforced a better system of inspection, but by the establishment of several immense depots, under competent officers, it was enabled to receive a large number of broken down horses for recuperation, and ultimately return more than fifty per cent of them to duty. Many of the others were sufficiently recuperated to be sold to farmers, and thus bring about a release of better cavalry horses for sale to the government. Thousands of horses were returned to the ranks after a few months' rest, which would have been abandoned, or if kept in the ranks would have seriously impaired the efficiency of the cavalry.

Cavalry officers frequently present arguments in favor of granting authority to each regiment to buy its own horses, and enlist its own recruits. A thorough and candid examination of the recorded experience of the Civil War will convince any unprejudiced individual, that the purchase of horses under contract is a perfectly logical system. Every attempt to gratify the wishes of cavalry officers resulted in increasing the price of horses, and the unreasonable requirements of many of the inspectors so discouraged horse owners and traders, that a return to the contract system was deemed necessary.

In time of peace the manner of purchase is not so important, except that a system should be adhered to which will need no change in time of war. The present practice has resulted from authority contained in appropriation bills, and should be made a permanent army regulation. This provides for the purchase of horses under contract by the Quartermaster Department, subject to inspection by a veterinary surgeon or other person employed by that department, as to soundness; then to be submitted to the inspection of a *cavalry* or *artillery* officer, to determine whether or not the animal is suitable, and adapted to the particular service required of him.

For many years subsequent to the war horses were bought by boards composed of three officers detailed from the regiment to be supplied. A return to this system is not believed to be desirable. It is more satisfactory to detail one officer to inspect the horses, for knowing he will be criticised concerning his acceptance of each and every horse which does not turn out well, he will be particularly careful.

In time of war it would not be practicable to buy for individual regiments, but there would be no difficulty in finding enough capable cavalry officers to supply one to each purchasing point where contractors would be required to deliver.

By having a competent cavalry officer of high rank to inspect remounts sent to depots from time to time, it could be determined whether any of the inspectors were negligent or inefficient, in either of which cases they should be relieved.

It cannot be expected that every officer will become perfect in so difficult a matter as the inspection of horses, but any good officer with the interest of the service at heart can learn to perform this duty, and he will improve with experience and persistent work.

Several European governments provide horses for their cavalry from their own breeding establishments, or by acquiring first rights of purchase through the grant of free service of the stallions retained by the government for that purpose. This system has been repeatedly urged for adoption in America, but there are so many good reasons for not doing so that it is safe to conclude that the horses required for public service will continue to be purchased from private breeding farms.

With so unlimited an agricultural country, there should never be any lack of suitable horses of any class for which there is an active demand at fair prices.

In a conflict of such dimensions as the Civil War the number of animals required could not have been furnished by a reasonable number of government farms.

It is not necessary to breed a high class of horses for cavalry, but to train a large number of officers to the duty of inspecting and selecting the best produced on American farms.

The horse, if selected with care and properly used, is capable of rendering long and valuable service. A knowledge as to how to develop his full capacity for making hard marches while still retaining his health and vigor does not come intuitively, but as a matter of experience and keen observation. The merest lout who can ride fairly light may take a horse over an immense distance in a single ride, but he will in all probability expend the entire vital force of the animal, and leave him a broken down, spiritless wreck at the end of his journey.

In the American service there are no regular riding

masters, and few who pretend to any other knowledge than that which has come through hard service and long experience.

Short service men cannot be trained to perfection. Some men, and horses also, are very slow to acquire that individual instruction which is so essential to correct maneuvering in large bodies.

The trained horse of the high school is not regarded as the ideal animal for service, but great stress is laid upon the value of the riding school as a means of bringing all the men and horses to an average state of efficiency.

The cavalry composes a class of riders from which a great degree of uniformity is demanded. The necessity arises from the existence of a special and narrowly defined object to be attained. The possibility of accomplishing it exists only when both men and horses are selected with reference to this object. Some men are born riders, and if taken in service young soon adapt themselves to cavalry riding. Such men are usually of a peculiar build, which combines strength and vigor, with lightness and dexterity, and possess that peculiar temperament which enables them to train horses to perfection.

All men are not so gifted, and in order to train this large majority, the officer should acquaint himself with everything that pertains to the horse. The presence in the ranks of untrained riders is bad in peace and criminal in war, but every army has them. In order to neutralize the effect of their ignorance, good, well-fitted saddles and bits are prime necessities. It is the pain and excitement caused in young, nervous horses, by powerful bits in the hands of thoughtless or bad riders, which make them degenerate into plungers and bolters. Curb, spavin, broken knees, and other injuries may frequently be traced to the same cause. Horses thus injured are condemned and sold for a mere trifle, and the indifferent rider is placed on another animal, not infrequently to repeat the same experience through ignorance.

No more costly or humiliating lessons were learned during the Civil War than those relating to cavalry service. The enthusiasm, patriotism, intelligence and courage of the American cavalrymen were proven on many fields, but bitter experience taught them that those desirable qualities do not alone command success. Training, discipline, and patient work are more potent than patriotism, coupled with ignorance and lack of experience.

There is an infinite amount of hardship and drudgery connected with service in the ranks of any cavalry. It is necessary, therefore, to have not only ability to ride and intelligence to reconnoitre, but capacity in both man and horse to sustain long continued exertion of the most arduous character. If either man or horse becomes exhausted or loses spirit, the effect is soon felt by the other. The necessity, therefore, for training inspectors of horses is too apparent to require argument.

CHAPTER II.

THE CAVALRY HORSE.

Purchase of Cavalry Horses.—Importance of Careful Inspection.—Remarks on Judging Horses.—Nomenclature of the Horse.—The Skeleton.—The Superior Muscles.—The Exterior Regions.—Examination of the Horse.—Relations Between Dimensions of Certain Parts.—Examination in Detail as to Form.—The Head; Neck; Withers; Shoulders; Back; Ribs; Chest; Fore Legs and Feet; Hind Quarters; Tail; Body.—Examination for Soundness.

Horses for cavalry service are purchased under the contract system by the Quartermaster Department. The examination for soundness is conducted by professional veterinarians employed for the purpose. Only the horses which pass this examination are submitted to further scrutiny of officers detailed to duty in connection with the inspection and purchase under each contract. It will therefore be seen, that the knowledge required by the inspecting officers is such as will enable them to form a correct judgment concerning the adaptability of the animal for service, as shown by his conformation and breeding.

The duty is a very important one, and the care with which it is performed has a marked effect on the efficiency of the service. As surgeons occasionally err in accepting recruits, so mistakes must occur in judging horses; but the former are much more leniently regarded than the latter.

With proper care in the inspection and purchase of cavalry horses, sound and healthy animals are generally procurable. When young horses are received from farmers, and placed in warm city stables pending inspection, the change of air and surroundings is very apt to produce colds, influenza, or strangles. Particularly the last named trouble may exist in a latent form until the animal is shipped upon cars or boats, when the continual draughts to which they are exposed cause the rapid development of the trouble. Upon arrival at the distributing point or destination, the animals may be found in an unserviceable condition, although apparently well when inspected.

For the above reason, in time of active field service it is much better to buy horses not less than six to eight years of age. When only garrison service or moderate field work is expected, horses from four to six years of age are preferable, for although more subject to disease, they can be more satisfactorily trained than old horses.

Every one does not judge a horse in the same manner, and the opinions of some are not as judicious or reliable as those of others. Those sometimes called upon to decide the good points or defects of horses may not be naturally endowed with the peculiar qualifications necessary for the solution of the problem. Those whose duty may *require* them to perform this work, may by intelligent observation, education, and experience, attain a satisfactory degree of proficiency, especially if possessed of natural aptitude, and not swayed by prejudice and fashion.

The faculty of judging implies not only attention, but a well balanced ability for comparison. The points of a horse are observed more quickly when he is brought beside an animal selected as a model.

The price usually paid by the government for horses is fixed by the lowest bidder. It is not, therefore, to be expected that ideal animals will be presented for inspection, but only such as the contractor can procure at a lower price than he himself receives. There will be a few first-class, many fair, and a superabundance of indifferent and mediocre horses presented. The government will be best served by rejecting all the latter.

The form of a horse determines to a great extent his fitness for service, and enables a fair prediction to be made as to his various qualities, provided he is sound. It requires judgment, much instruction, and long practice, to correctly estimate the relative value of various points, and to determine whether the good qualities counterbalance existing or probable defects. Some men seem able to see at a glance all the points of an animal, but conformation requires study, and those who have obtained practical knowledge only are not infrequently swayed by prejudice rather than controlled by sound judgment.

Good points in a horse are not mere matters of beauty, but shapes which, on mechanical principles, are likely to answer the required ends. However, shapes which may be objectionable for one class of work, are not necessarily so for another. Thus small "chunky" or pony-built horses are better for continuous work in the mountains, than larger and longer coupled horses.

While useless to search for perfection, it is well to study all the points of the ideal horse, in order to promptly recognize them when seen. The points taken together constitute the *form*, which must not be confounded with particular attitudes assumed by the horse, for an animal whose conformation is perfectly adapted to service, will frequently assume such awkward positions while standing in a stall, or at the picket line, as to entirely deceive any but a well trained eye.

As soon as a horse is found which is a suitable model, he should be retained at hand for comparison, but contractors are entitled to a fair construction of their contracts. In other words, if the government pays only $125.00 per animal, the contractor should not be expected to put in horses whose value is $200.00.

In conducting an examination of horses, he who possesses a perfect knowledge of the anatomy and physiology of the animal, will have a great advantage over one who does not.

It is absolutely necessary to know the names of the various parts of the horse, and it is presumed that those who read this book will wish to understand the construction of the skeleton and the superficial layers of muscles.

The nomenclature of these parts is given, as far as

possible, in plain language, but some technical names are used because there are no popular names for the parts mentioned.

THE SKELETON OF THE HORSE.

PLATE I.

The animal here represented is the celebrated racehorse "Eclipse," pronounced by the highest veterinary authority to be perfect. The form of the horse is indicated in outline. The nomenclature of the skeleton is as follows:

1. Zygomatic arch.
2. Eye cavity.
3. Face bones.
4. Incisor teeth.
5. Molar teeth.
6. Lower jaw.
7. Atlas, 1st vertebra of neck.
8. Axis, 2d vertebra of neck.
9. Cervical vertebræ (5).
10. Spinal processes of back.
11. Dorsal and lumbar vertebræ.
12. Sacrum.
13. Tail bones.
14. Shoulder blade.
15. Acromion process.
16. Hollow of shoulder blade.
17. Upper end of arm bone.
18. Arm bone or humerus.
19. Elbow bone.
20. Cartilages of the ribs.
21. Ribs.
22. Haunch.
23. Haunch bone.
24. Great trochanter.
25. Small trochanter.
26. Thigh bone.
27. Ischium.
28. Radius or fore-arm bone.
29. Carpal or knee bones.
30. Trapezium.
31. Cannon bone.
32. Pastern bone.
33. Sesamoid bone.
34. Small pastern bone.
35. Upper end of leg bone.
36. Stifle joint.
37. Leg bone or tibia.
38. Point of hock.
39. Hock joint.
40. Head of small metatarsal bone.
41. Cannon or metatarsal bone.
42. Coffin bone.
43. Fetlock joint.
44. Patella, or stifle.
45. Fibula.

SUPERIOR MUSCLES OF THE HORSE.

The illustration (Plate II) shows the exterior muscles of the horse as they appear with the skin of the animal removed. Some of the deep seated and powerful locomotive muscles are not shown, and the one over the ribs is omitted.

The principal muscle for consideration in the plate is the long muscle, or system of muscles of the back. It fills the angular space on each side of the spinous processes, giving roundness to the back. It is very broad and thick over the loins, and in addition to other connections, it is strongly attached to the hip bone. It is attached forward to all the spines of the vertebræ, as far as the neck, and to a strong tendon-like membrane that is firmly fastened to the same bones.

Special interest attaches to this muscle and tendon, because the saddle must rest upon it in such a way as not to interfere with the muscular action of the fore and hind quarters.

PLATE II.

The names of the muscles are all of a technical character to indicate location, or action, and are omitted because knowledge of them is only necessary for a scientific study of the physiology of the horse.

NOMENCLATURE OF THE EXTERNAL REGIONS OF THE HORSE.

PLATE III.

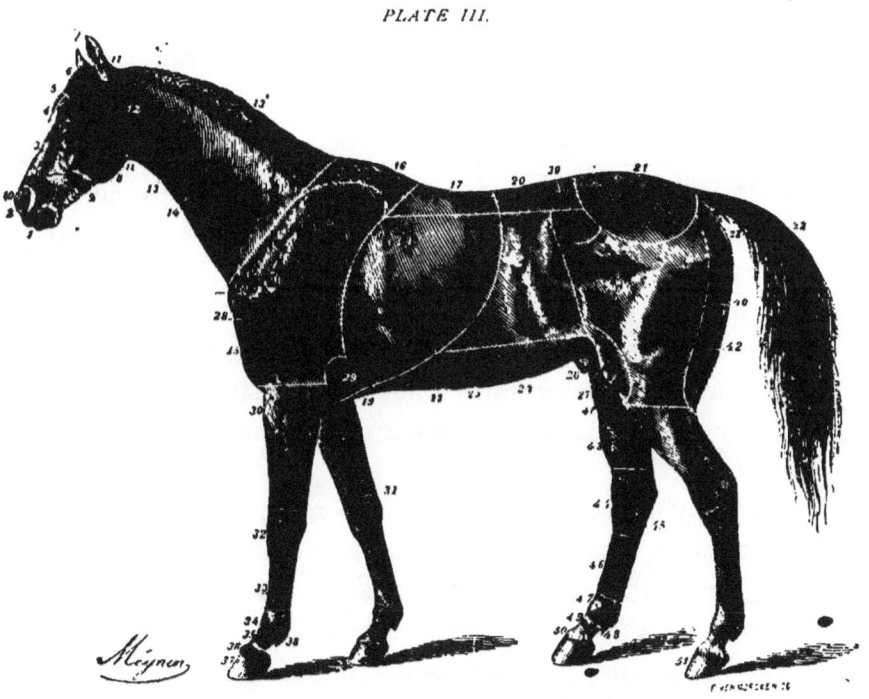

The plate, copied from "Mégnin," is numbered so as to locate by name the external regions of the horse. It is absolutely necessary to commit to memory this nomenclature in order to describe horses as well as to understand what is referred to by others when mentioning the parts.

1. Lips.
2. Nose.
3. Face.
4. Forehead.
5. Eyebrows.
6. Forelock.
7. Ears.
8. Lower jaw.
9. Cheek.
10. Nostril.
11. Poll.
11¹ Throat.
12. Parotid gland.
13. Neck.
13¹ Mane.
14. Jugular channel.
15. Chest.
16. Withers.

17.	Back.	27.	Testicles.	35.	Pastern.	45.	Chestnut.
18.	Ribs.	28.	Shoulder	36.	Coronet.	46.	Cannon or
19.	Girth.		and arm.	37.	Foot.		shank.
20.	Loins.	29.	Elbow.	38.	Fetlock.	47.	Fetlock joint.
21.	Croup.	30.	Forearm.	39.	Haunch.	48.	Fetlock.
22.	Tail.	31.	Chestnut.	40.	Thigh.	49.	Pastern.
23.	Dock.	32.	Knee.	41.	Stifle.	50.	Coronet.
24.	Flank.	33.	Cannon or	42.	Buttock.	51.	Foot.
25.	Belly.		shank.	43.	Gaskin.		
26.	Sheath.	34.	Fetlock joint.	44.	Hock.		

If many horses are to be examined, copious notes should be retained by the officer for self-protection, and every horse passed should be branded with a number on the hoof for identification on the descriptive list, and also have the brand common to all public animals put on in the presence of the inspectors. Blemishes existing at the date of inspection should all be noted carefully on the descriptive lists.

It may happen at times that officers will be called upon to examine horses without the assistance of a veterinary surgeon. The "examination for soundness" and the chapter on the more common diseases and injuries will give the student sufficient knowledge to conduct fairly well the examination for soundness, provided he systematically applies the information contained therein to the cases available for his observation in service from day to day.

If unable to decide upon any question arising during the examination, the government should be given the benefit of the doubt. Such action will leave no cause for future regret.

It is seldom possible for inspecting officers to quietly

view the animals in their stalls, before being presented for examination, because contractors are compelled to go over a great deal of country to collect such animals as in their opinion will be accepted by the government.

Contractors sometimes arrange to have a representative of the government accompany them when gathering horses, in order to avoid the heavy expense incurred by buying those which are sure to be subsequently thrown on their hands for various defects.

Whenever possible to see animals in their own stalls, it should be observed carefully if they kick or crib, which can be easily told by the appearance of the stall and manger.

If a horse points a toe, or shows other signs of weakness or lameness, it can be more easily discovered at this time than when crowded in public stables or sheds with large numbers of other horses.

Few of the stable vices can be cured, and unless horses are badly needed for immediate field service, animals known to have them should be rejected.

Some stable vices may be acquired from other horses, and it is therefore very desirable to avoid introducing into cavalry stables animals which may spoil others compelled to stand near them.

In addition to kicking and cribbing, which are about the worst habits a troop horse can have, may be mentioned weaving or the swaying motion so common to caged animals, wind sucking, continual pawing, pulling back when tied, and biting.

The wind sucker takes hold of the manger, picket line or halter strap, arches his neck and draws back with a grunting noise. The horse may be deterred temporarily from acting in this way by painting or smearing the objects in his vicinity, but he will resume the practice at the first opportunity.

Pulling back is very destructive of halters, and should be cured when possible by passing a piece of small and new hemp rope under the tail as a crupper, the rope being knotted on the back and the ends passed through the halter and tied to the manger, so that when the animal pulls back to break loose, the rope tightens and lacerates his tail. One or two applications of this rope crupper will in most cases affect a permanent cure.

The line of demarcation between blemishes and defects is sometimes very dim. Under the first named come all abnormal conditions of the various parts of the horse which do not affect his serviceability, such as scars, splints so placed as to be of no consequence, and similar things.

Under the head of defects come peg splints and those very close to the knees, ring bones, side bones, false quarter, quarter cracks, sit-fasts, and any trouble, local or constitutional, which may tend to shorten or render unsatisfactory the service of the animal. These will all be treated in detail later for the guidance of the inspector, as well as with a view to amelioration and cure when they occur in animals already purchased.

Horses should be examined, if possible, in the open air. When this is not practicable, an open passageway or shed should be selected, where plenty of light may be had. When the horse is led out, he should be examined in profile from in front and behind, from the right and left, and obliquely forward and backward, careful attention being given to his temperament and attitudes in the meantime.

View the horse in all possible aspects, to determine the general harmony of his whole conformation. View the formation of the feet and legs separately and in pairs; the shape, expression and size of the head generally and in detail; the shape of the back and withers, with reference to carrying a saddle.

The examination should be made on unshod horses, but if any animal is presented shod, special attention is necessary to see if shoes have been put on for the purpose of correcting defects.

A good horse is one with many good, few indifferent, and no really bad points. One radically bad point neutralizes any number of good ones. Excess of power or development in one part of a horse may not only be useless, because the strength of the animal is limited by the weakest point, but it may be a positive source of evil. For example, a strong, powerful forehand is not an advantage if the hind quarters are light, because the strain on the hind legs will be unduly great. Similarly, if the fore legs are weak they may suffer from excessive propulsion communicated by powerful hind quarters, whilst they might have lasted a long time if all were proportionately developed. In a well formed horse there must be not only no weak point, but no part with excessive development, as compared to the others.

Outward forms are mainly dependent on the formation of the bony skeleton. In a well bred horse the tendons, ligaments and muscles are generally in keeping with the bones; that is, large bones usually give attachment to large, powerful muscles, tendons, etc. The processes of the bones are better developed, and give a greater mechanical advantage to the muscles than in the case of common country horses.

The power of a horse increases with his size, provided the relative proportion of the parts and the general compactness are maintained. This, however, is rarely the case. There is a certain size beyond which the parts do not seem to grow in due proportion to each other. Very large horses are seldom fit for saddle purposes.

Without good structural formation strength must not be expected, and even with it, do not expect all the desirable qualities.

There are some relations between parts of the horse which it is well to consider as an aid in training the eye. In this way it may be decided at a glance if a horse approaches the average form accepted as most suitable for service.

RELATIVE PROPORTIONS.

The horse shown in Plate IV was selected to be photographed because of his well earned reputation as an all-around cavalry horse and weight carrier.*

The position is not constrained; it is the natural and free position assumed by the horse without assistance or interference. It will be observed that the frontal line of the head is nearly or quite parallel to the slope of the shoulders.

Now taking the head, measured from the poll to the extremity of the upper lip, as a unit, it will be found to enter as a factor quite accurately into several important measurements. The head should be measured as a shoemaker does the foot, and not with a tape-line.

This length of the head AB is almost exactly equal to the distance: 1. From the top of the withers to the point of the shoulder CD; 2. From the lowest point of

---

*The horse, "Deadwood," pictured in Plate IV, is thirteen years old, and has been in service since August 7, 1886. He is fifteen hands high, appears perfectly sound, moves at a walk, trot and gallop without any stiffness or peculiarities of gaits, and is a clean-cut, strong and enduring cavalry horse. At the time this photograph was taken the horse was very fat.

He was ridden by the orderly for the quartermaster of the Eighth Cavalry on the march from Fort Davis, Texas, to Fort Meade, South Dakota, in 1887, a distance of about nineteen hundred miles. As the orderly accompanied the quartermaster in looking for camping ground, purchasing forage, and riding back and forth to the wagon train, it is a low estimate to place the distance covered by this animal at twenty-five hundred miles. He has done steady duty in field and garrison ever since, and he has undoubtedly been enabled to do this because his form is perfectly adapted to the weight-carrying requirements of cavalry service.

the back to the abdomen *EF;* 3. From the point of the stifle to the point of the hock *IJ;* 4. From the point of the hock to the lower line of the hoof *JK;* 5. From the shoulder blade to the point of the haunch *LM.*

PLATE IV.

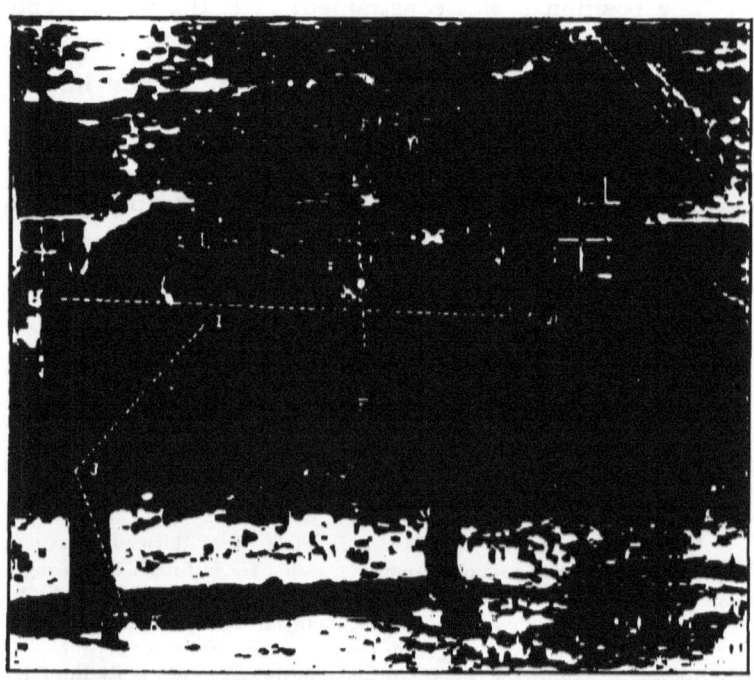

Two and one-half times the head gives: 1. The height of the withers *C* above the ground; 2. The height of the top of the croup above the ground; 3. Very nearly the length from point of the shoulder to point of buttock *DH.*

Do not expect every horse to fill these conditions, but

remember that a small fraction of the length of the head added to his height or length, will at once give the animal an abnormal appearance. The length or height of a horse will seldom or never equal three head lengths.

If proportions are satisfactory, examine the muscles in a general way to form an estimate as to the probable endurance of the animal. Firm, dense, compact and clearly defined muscles are requisite for weight carriers.

The examination should next take a more detailed character, remembering always, that although race horses may run and win in all forms, cavalry service demands a marked degree of uniformity, and the higher the grade of excellence secured the more economical and enduring will be the results.

Before proceeding with the examination, the age and height of the animal should be taken, to determine whether these come within the limits specified in each contract or letter of instructions. Perfection of form is usually found to a greater extent in horses under fifteen-and-a-half hands high, than in those of greater height.

The Head.—When carefully observed, a great variation is seen to exist in the size and shape of the heads of horses. A wide forehead is nearly always accompanied by large nostrils, well situated eyes, ears small and widely separated, distance from the eye to the angle of the jaw great, large space under and between the jaws, head short and not of great volume. On the contrary, a narrow forehead is accompanied generally by small nostrils, eyes but partly open and appearing small, ears large and close together, and with but small space under and between the jaws.

The head first described is the one best adapted to the saddle horse, for the second or coarse head acts like a heavy weight at the end of a long lever, bringing forward the center of gravity, and making the horse heavy in hand.

The nostrils should be large, and occupy nearly the whole of the lower part of the facial structure, because the horse breathes entirely through his nostrils, and not partially through his mouth as man does.

Fig. 1.

The coarse horse has contracted nostrils with overlapping borders, and the entrances are beset with bristly hairs.

The mouth should be small, with thin, firm lips. The eyes should be large and mild, with fine eyelids. The ears should be delicate and pointed, and should move backward and forward with a quick, firm motion, without the least appearance of flabbiness.

The eyes and ears indicate fairly well the temper of the horse.

Figures 1 and 2 represent two entirely different types of good heads. The first has the depression in the frontal line known as "dish-faced," and an unusual depth from the eye to the point of the jaw. The second is the head of a very fine saddle animal, characterized by docility and intelligence, and perfection as to gaits.

Fig. 2

The Neck.—The neck should be examined as to its form, length, carriage, and mode of attachment to the head. The neck is called straight when its borders are rectilinear; arched, when its upper border is more or less convex throughout; ewe-necked, when its upper border is concave.

The long neck accords well with extreme speed, the short neck with power, and the medium neck for all around saddle purposes, and in which class there is a wide range of intermediate forms (Figs. 1, 2, and 3). Very long necks are too mobile, while very short ones are not supple enough. Very long necks also have the disadvantage of over-weighting the forehand by bringing forward the center of gravity. The volume of the neck should not be too large, but harmoniously proportioned to the other parts of the body.

The class of neck possessed by a horse is not altered by the addition of fat. A fine, silky mane characterizes well-bred horses; and coarse, long and stiff manes, common horses.

The Withers.— The withers comprise the region between the shoulders in front of the back, and in consequence of their prominence and anatomical complexity are exposed to wounds of variable gravity. As many of the muscles, ligaments and tendons which control the motion of the forehand are attached here, a considerable degree of elevation is necessary in order to afford good leverage, as well as to give due length to the shoulder. Horses with very fine, high withers, while pleasant to ride, are unsuited for hard service with packed saddles. Elevated withers are usually accompanied by long, sloping shoulders and a rather deep chest. High, thin withers are usually accompanied by flat muscles about and in rear of the shoulder blade, where the front end of the side bars of military saddles are calculated to rest; this flatness allows the saddle to slip unduly forward, which is very objectionable. (Fig. 3.)

Horses with low withers, not well defied or outlined, are not suited for heavy, packed saddles, because such a formation permits the saddle to slip forward and bruise the parts near the top of the shoulder blade, and this displacement also causes cincha sores close to the fore legs.

Fig. 3.

The Shoulder.—The shoulder should be sloping and comparatively long. (Plate IV.) If the shoulder blade is long, broad and well sloped, the saddle will sit properly in its place; while if short and upright, the saddle will have a tendency to work forward on the withers. Upright or straight shoulders are very undesirable in saddle horses, although perfectly suitable for purposes of draught. Undue thickness through the shoulders increases the weight of the forehand, and consequent wear on the fore legs, without any compensating advantages.

While all authorities agree that a sloping shoulder is essential in a good saddle horse, and many speak of it in an off-hand way, it will be found most puzzling to determine exactly how to class shoulders in fat horses.

In examining this part, it is proper to consider not only the portion occupied by the shoulder blade, but also the short bone (humerus) connecting the shoulder blade with the upper bone of the leg. This short bone slopes backward and downward, and as the shoulder blade is better placed the more it slants; this short bone, on the contrary, is considered best when it slopes the least. It is the degree of slope of this short bone that causes the difference in the appearance in various horses as to the way the fore leg is set on; in some animals it seems to spring from the front line of the chest, and in others several inches back of that part. If the shoulder is very straight, and the horse be otherwise acceptable, the best plan is to mount him; if he is, as he ought to be with such a shoulder, very rough, reject him.

The Back.—The back may be straight, convex or roach-backed, or concave or sway-backed. The straight back is a sign of strength, and with this conformation the saddle will rest in a good position. The roach-back, while strong, is unsightly, and contrary to free and rapid motion. The sway-back may be congenital or acquired, and is the most faulty of all for saddle purposes, because the weight is

Fig. 4.

almost entirely sustained by the ligaments, and the saddle is certain to bore into the muscles of the back.

Sometimes the line of the back is oblique from front to rear or rear to front. These forms entail an unequal distribution of the weight of the body upon the four extremities. The center of gravity is carried towards the fore limbs when the horse is higher behind than in front.

The back should not be over long. Short, straight backs are the strongest for weight carriers, but a certain amount of length is essential to much speed; moreover a horse with a very short back is apt to overreach.

The Ribs.—The ribs should have a well defined convexity from above to below. This curvature, taken with full development of length, and definite separation from each other, constitute three desirable points of excellence. Flatness, shortness and nearness together are undesirable, because they limit the volume of the chest, and characterize the horse as short-winded and deficient in power.

The Chest.—The chest should have great capacity in depth without excessive width, and should be plump in front. Narrow-chested horses lack endurance. The capacity of the lungs is marked by the size of the chest at the girth. While excessive width in front is not desirable for rapid gaits, such form is well adapted to carrying great weight. The fore legs should spring from the chest perpendicularly as viewed from in front. Fig. 4 is a front view of the horse shown in Plate IV.

Fig. 5.

The Fore Leg.—The upper bone of the leg should be long in proportion to the lower or cannon bone. This bone cannot well be too large or too fully supplied with muscles.

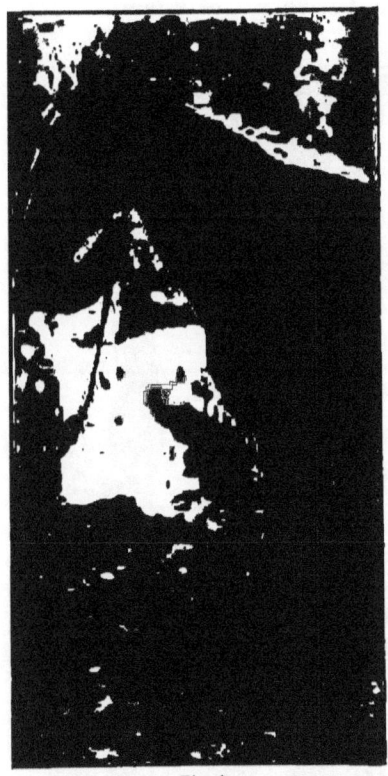

Fig. 6.

When the horse is examined in profile this bone should be vertical, and when viewed from in front parallel to the median plane of the body. The knee should be wide from side to side, and thick from before to behind. The vertical direction of the upper bone, and cannon or lower bone, should be maintained at the knee. (Fig. 4.)

While a contrary condition may be congenital, and therefore not an unsoundness, since it does not interfere with firm and free movements, still a horse over in the knees, or knee-sprung, is not desirable for service. (Fig. 5.) The opposite condition, known as "calf" or "buck" knees, is decidedly objectionable, owing to the undue strain brought on the ligaments and tendons.

The leg just below the knee should not be very small

or "tied in," which indicates a weakness of the part, but should be as large as the other portions of the limb in that vicinity. (Fig. 6.)

The large or cannon bone, between the knee and fetlock, cannot be too short or too strong. It should be straight, as any deviation from a straight line is both a sign and cause of weakness. The fetlock, consisting of the upper and lower pastern bones, should be of moderate length. If the fetlocks are very long, they are necessarily weak, and there will be undue strain on the ligaments and tendons; if they are short, the horse will be unpleasant to ride on account of the concussion to which the upright formation gives rise.

Fig. 7.

The feet should be of medium size, due regard being had to the size and shape of the horse, and there should be no visible difference in the feet as to size and form. They should be neither very upright nor too flat. The front feet being on the same line, the distance between them should generally be equal to the width of one foot from quarter to quarter.

The introduction of draught blood in many parts of the country has brought into the market a great many medium sized horses with large feet. Ordinarily a large foot is an indication that the horse has been reared on moist, soft pastures, and such feet are almost sure to deteriorate rapidly when put to service on hard roads at any but a slow gait.

Fig. 8.

Horses whose hoofs are naturally small and hard are better prepared to withstand the effects of warm, dry stables, or long marches over rough or dry country. They have less bulk and weight to lift at each step; their action under the saddle is more nimble and pleasant, and the pounding received by the feet is not so apt to be severe, because horses of this class usually travel close to the ground, while horses with large or flat feet generally lift their feet high.

A contracted foot must not be mistaken for a naturally small foot.

Some horses toe in (Fig. 7) and some turn out their toes (Fig. 8). Both are objectionable in cavalry horses. Sometimes a horse toes in more with one foot than another, and breaks down first on the one which turns in most. The horse which turns out his toes is apt to "paddle" when in motion, and his hocks are likely to turn in too much.

The hind feet are usually more upright than the fore feet, and are much less subject to disease, injury or mal-direction. The same remarks as to size and condition of the fore feet are applicable in general to the hind feet. If the toes show signs of striking the shoes of the front feet, producing in motion the sound called "clicking," the horse will not be satisfactory for marches at a trot under a heavy weight.

Fig. 9.

The Hind Quarters Generally.—The hips should not be ragged. High hips are not only unsightly, but are apt to be weak, for the reason that their prominence may be due to narrowness of the loins. The loins should be large, well arched, and fully furnished with muscle. The thighs should be deep and full, but with sufficient interval to prevent friction. The absence of muscular development known as "split up behind" is very objectionable. Fig. 9 is a rear view of the horse shown in Plate IV as a typical weight carrier.

Fig. 10.

The upper bone of the hind quarters, which articulates at the stifle with the upper bone of the hind leg, should be long and lie obliquely forward; the upper bone of the hind leg should lie obliquely back so as to bring the hocks into their proper place. The stifle should be prominent and well defined; it should lie close to the abdomen, and be slightly deviated outward.

The hock should be neatly outlined, wide and thick. Large bones are usually accompanied by strong tendons and ligaments. The leg below the hock should incline but little if at all under the body; if inclined too much the liability to strain on the ligaments and tendons becomes great. If the leg below the hock is perpendicular, the conformation is favorable to speed, because the foot on arriving on the ground is strongly flexed upon the leg, which gives the hock energetic impulsion, and admits of long strides. If the lower part of the leg be inclined under the body, it not only affects the speed by diminishing the step, but increases the weight borne by the hind quarters, and causes a considerable part of the muscular effort of impulsion to be expended in lifting the body, instead of carrying it directly forward.

The hocks should also be viewed from behind with reference to their parallelism to the median plane of the body. The hocks may turn towards one another behind, giving

Fig. 11.

the horse the appearance called "knock-kneed" in man, and "cow-hocked" in the horse (Fig. 10). If the points of the hocks are turned out, the appearance is similar to bow legs in man. Both forms are objectionable for many reasons.

Doubts sometimes arise as to whether certain forms of curby hocks and spavins (Fig. 11) are really to be regarded as unsound; in all such cases the inspector should reject the animal for saddle purposes if the veterinarian does not feel justified in doing so.

The Tail.—The dock should be large and muscular. The tail should be carried firmly, and well away from the hind quarters. The tail is usually set on much higher and is more ornamental in well bred than under bred horses. The hair of the former is fine and scanty; in the latter it is frequently thick, coarse or curly. When the horse has considerable slope at the croup and his tail is set on low down he is characterized as "goose rumped."

The Body.—If from want of proper length and convexity of the ribs the circumference decreases rapidly from the forehand to the rear (Fig. 3), the cincha, and consequently the saddle, will slip back to such an extent as to necessitate breast straps. Such horses are very unsatisfactory, and no amount of good points compensates for this defective girth. This form does not possess an aptitude for retaining flesh under short rations and hard work, very essential qualifications in cavalry horses.

Upon completion of this examination, have the horse

led at a walk on a hard road bed, and view his action from in front and behind. Repeat this at a trot, viewed as before. Now have a saddle and bridle put on the horse, and note the disposition of the animal while this is being done. Have a rider mount and gallop the horse, so that he may be viewed as at a walk and trot. It is usual at this time to have the horse galloped fast for several hundred yards to enable the veterinary surgeon to examine his respiration and wind.

The entire examination should be made without whips, noise or excitement of any kind. This is difficult to enforce at public stock yards and stables, but should be insisted upon.

In examining the horse in motion it should be observed if his movements at all gaits are regular, free and natural. The artificial gaits of the trained saddle horse are not only of no value to cavalry, but are an absolute disadvantage, for when animals with these gaits are ridden by guides it is impossible to regulate by them. It should be demanded that the horse walk, trot and gallop without defects or peculiarities of gaits.

If the horse is lame in the slightest degree, even from an apparently fresh and insignificant wound, the examination should not be continued.

If the horse throws his feet out of the vertical plane at a walk and trot—usually called "paddling"—or if he interferes sufficiently to cut himself, he should not be accepted. A horse which interferes when in good condition without a load is apt to be worse when thin in flesh and fatigued from packing a heavy weight on the march. The "paddling" movement is not only unsightly, but occasions fatigue and an unnecessary waste of energy.

Some horses, apparently sound and without vice or fault, will still be far from desirable cavalry horses. If, for instance, a horse appears clumsy and rough, especially at a trot, the inspector should mount him and give him a thorough trial, else he may pass into the ranks a rough animal whose harsh gaits will cause more discontent than he is worth.

Disappointment may come because an animal whose form justifies the highest expectations may prove without the courage or ability to perform according to nature's gifts, but there will be some satisfaction in the knowledge that those whose forms indicated unfitness have not been made a burden upon the government.

The principal points of the horse, affecting his adaptability for cavalry service, are all that it has been attempted to portray. A more complete theoretical knowledge may be obtained from many scientific books on the subject, but it is best not to overburden the memory at first. To apply theoretical knowledge, examine the same horse repeatedly and at intervals; seek opinions and advice of those who already have acquired practical knowledge.

In examining horses your attention will always be called to the fine points, of which most horses possess some. After the eye has become trained, a horse whose defects of detail predominate will at once show a want of harmony of the whole. If, on the other hand, his defects are few, the impression conveyed will be harmonious. It is then only necessary to determine if any of the defects of form are such as to be a source of weakness when the horse is put to the use for which he is to be bought.

It has been the main object in this chapter to give the young officer a knowledge of the various forms of horses, and of the relative value of different points. Something more is desirable, for it is not always practicable to have the professional assistance of a veterinarian. Cavalry officers and quartermasters especially should be able to make an examination of the horse for soundness without assistance, except as to certain occult forms of disease. The method prescribed herein is in accordance with the best practice of veterinary surgeons, and if closely followed will generally give satisfaction.

In all examinations of animals for public service, it should be kept in mind that endurance is limited by the weakest part, and that while in private life such care may be bestowed upon a horse as to cause a weak member to last as long as the more sound ones, this must not be expected in actual service.

EXAMINATION FOR SOUNDNESS.

1. Examine the animal as he stands in his stall to see if he points either fore foot, or favors any leg. Observe the position of the posterior extremities when standing;

move him from side to side and notice whether he steps upon his toe. Observe whether he cribs the wood work; holds on to the manger or halter ropes or straps, to suck wind; bites or kicks; weaves; or whether he exhibits any glaring unsoundness forbidding further examination. Notice the pupils of the eyes.

Fig. 12.

2. Lead the animal out into the light, and observe if both pupils contract evenly; if not suspect defective vision. Stand in front and compare the eyes, as to whether one is smaller than the other; whether there exist any signs of an operation having been performed; any signs of ophthalmia, white specks in the corner, torn eyelid, warts or

other abnormal conditions. Wave the hand gently to and fro in front of the eye; if the animal does not instinctively close the eye upon the approach of the hand, proceed carefully to determine whether or not sight has been lost. Examine the ears for cuts and slits made by sticking the head into barbed wire fences. If the ears hang flabbily, or do not move quickly and rigidly at intervals, something is wrong; observe carefully the base of the ear and vicinity for canker. Look the horse squarely in the face to see if there is any abnormal development about the head. Look for evidences of ulcerated teeth, as indicated by offensive odors, and swelling in the vicinity of the facial sinuses and of the bones of the lower jaw. Open the animal's mouth, and observe if all the teeth, molars as well as incisors, are intact. Examine carefully for parrot mouth, lacerated tongue, abscesses, bit bruises on the bars, and the teeth to determine age. Examine the nostrils for polypi, healthy color, ulcers indicating glanders, and for offensive discharges. Feel under the jaw for enlargement

Fig. 13.

of the lymphatic gland. Examine the region of the parotid gland for evidences of inflammation, and also for fistula of its duct. Look for farcy buds on the neck and sides of the face. Raise the jugular vein to see if it is intact; observe if any inflammation of the vein exists.

Fig. 14.

Pass the hand from the face down the neck to the withers for evidences of poll evil, bruises, or abscesses. Place the ear to the trachea, to observe if the sound of breathing is clear and even.

3. Pass to the left side of the animal and examine the withers for fistula (Fig. 12), and the back for sit-fasts, or saddle sores. Observe the shoulder for signs of wasting

away of the muscles, enlargement of the joint, heat or tenderness. Feel the point of the elbow for capped elbow. Examine the near fore leg with the hand, looking at the off leg also for broken knees (Fig. 13), speedy cut, splints (Fig. 14), side bones, ring bones, brushing, sand cracks, seedy toe, false quarter, scratches, grease, wind galls, heat about the fetlocks or coronet, and scars from wire fence wounds. Take up the foot and examine for indications of laminitis, contraction, quittor or flatness; to see if the bars have been cut away; whether there is any offensive odor of the frog, and to see if there is any peculiarity about the shoe, made necessary by the form of the foot, or the action of the horse. See if there is any appreciable difference in the size or shape of the feet. Examine the tendons for evidences of sprains.

4. Listen to the heart to determine if its beats are regular. Observe the breathing to determine if the inspirations and expirations are equal. If inspiration is accomplished with one effort, and expiration with two, called "double breathing," the horse is unsound. This may be observed by watching the abdomen. Examine the abdomen for hernia. Pass the hand along under the chest and abdomen to feel for cincha sores and shoe bruises occasioned by a faulty method of lying down. Have an attendant hold up a fore foot while an examination is made of geldings to see if castration has been properly performed, and that no signs of scirrhous cord exist. Examine the stifle joint, and pass the hand along down the near

hind legs to the hocks, comparing at the same time the relative size of the hocks; examine for bone and bog spavin, thoroughpin, capped hock, curb (Figs. 11 and 15), and skin disease in the hollow of the hocks (sallenders). Examine the lower limb and foot as in the case of the fore leg, except that some injuries of the fore are never found in the hind leg. The inside of the thigh should be examined for farcy buds. Pass behind and compare the hips, quarters and buttocks; feel the tail, and observe the anus and vicinity for injury or disease.

5. Proceed to the off side and repeat such part of the examination as may be necessary for that side. Observe during the entire examination whether any parasites are attached to the skin.

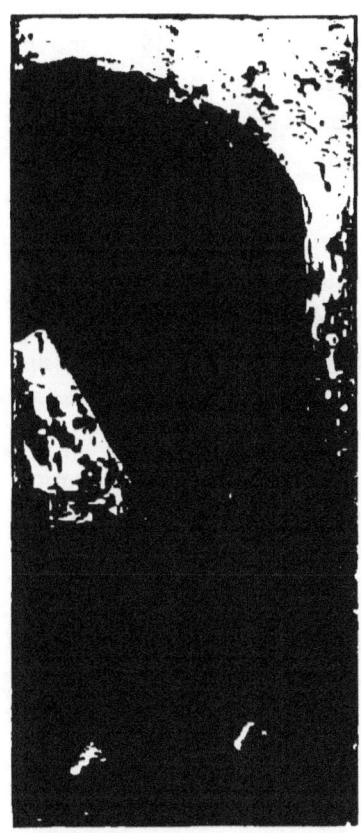

Fig. 15.

6. Go to the horse's head, take hold of the bridle and back him suddenly; if the tail is elevated and the hind legs do not respond, or the animal should partially sit

down, or elevate one of his limbs suddenly, he is unsound. Turn him around suddenly and look for the same symptoms. The horse should be led at a walk, and then at a trot, his action being carefully noted for any inequality of movement, which, if discovered, must be critically examined.

7. Saddle the horse and observe if he gives in the loins when mounted, or shows any signs of weakness or flinching. Have him ridden at a walk, trot and gallop, and watch for indications of lameness and peculiarities of motion. Have him galloped rapidly, up hill if practicable, and then have him halted suddenly; put the ear close to his nostrils, and listen to his respiration for roaring, whistling or broken wind, and also observe if respiration subsides promptly to normal or not.

Opinions vary as to whether grunting is an indication of unsoundness, and many practical horsemen believe this trouble changes into roaring. To be on the safe side, regard it as evidence of unsoundness. To detect it, strike the horse a sharp blow with a whip or stick, and make believe to strike again, when the horse will grunt if affected with the ailment. It may also be detected by halting suddenly from a rapid gait.

CHAPTER III.

AGE OF HORSES.

Period of Longevity or Extreme Age.—Mares Live Longer Than Horses.—"Rising" and "Past" a Certain Age.—Age as Indicated by the Teeth.—Wolf's Teeth.—Temporary Teeth.—Permanent Teeth.—The Marks or Cups.—Angle Which Incisors Make in Coming Together.—The Tusks.—Rasping Off the Corners of Incisors.—Bishoping.

The probability of a horse's reaching an advanced age does not depend so much upon race and breeding as upon his care and surroundings. Bad treatment, food insufficient in quantity and poor in quality, alike tend to shorten the duration of the horse's service. In this way one horse may be old and worn out at twelve or fourteen, while another may continue to render satisfactory service at from twenty to twenty-five years of age.

The oldest horse, at present in service known to the author was about seven years old in 1875, at which time he participated in a march from Kansas to Arizona, a distance of nearly fifteen hundred miles. He was ridden for many years regularly, but is no longer fit for hard marches. He is now about twenty-six years old. There were several horses used in the Fort Leavenworth squadron during the past year which were more than twenty years of age.

There are numerous instances to substantiate the statement that horses live to be thirty-five or forty years of age. It will be sufficient to cite the case of "Belle Mosby," whose photograph is shown in Fig. 16, with her owner, JOSEPH R. PHILLIPS, Company "F," Eighteenth Pennsyl-

Fig. 16.

vania Cavalry, and the celebrated army mule, "Mexique," which died about 1866.*

---

*The mare was stolen by a negro boy from a Confederate camp near Newmarket Creek, Va., in March, 1865, and was brought across the creek to the camp of the Eighteenth Pennsylvania by means of a single twelve-inch plank walk thrown across the abutments of the recently burned bridge. She was purchased from the negro by Lieutenant YOUNG in exchange for an overcoat. She soon after became the property of her present owner, who used her in service for several months, and then sent her home to his farm. She has never weighed more than 950 pounds, and was worked until about six years ago. Her teeth showed her to be five years old when brought into camp, which makes her present age thirty-five.

A few years ago a petition was sent to the War Department by the offi-

It is usually claimed that mares live longer than horses, and small horses longer than large ones, but it is difficult to prove such statements because all animals do not receive the same treatment. Some animals lead a quiet existence with good hygienic surroundings, and attain great age, whereas, had they been used in a city on stone pavements, or subjected to hard campaigning with its consequent exposure and semi-starvation, they would probably have fallen victims before attaining even moderate age.

It is very generally accepted as a fact that horses which mature slowly live longer than those which mature rapidly, provided, of course, they receive like treatment and are not put to hard service until full grown.

The difference in general appearance between young

---

cers stationed at Mount Vernon Barracks, Ala., stating that a white mule which had been in service at that post for forty-five years was about to be sold as unserviceable, and requesting authority to purchase him, to be kept at their own expense, because of his long and faithful service. The petition was endorsed by General SHERMAN as follows:

"I have seen that mule, and whether true or false, the soldiers believe it was left at Big Springs, where the Mount Vernon Barracks now are, at the time General JACKSON's army camped there—about 1819 or 1820. Tradition says it was once sorrel, but now it is white from age. The Quartermaster's Department will be chargeable with ingratitude if that mule is sold, or the maintenance of it thrown on the charitable officers of the post. I advise it to be kept in the department, fed and maintained until death. I think the mule was at Fort Morgan, Mobile Point, when I was there in 1842."

The Secretary of War thereupon made the following order: "Let this mule be kept and well cared for as long as he lives."

Secretary LINCOLN's order did not arrive until after the sale, but "Mexique" was bought in and kept by the officers until he died, about two years later. There was no documentary evidence, but the history of this animal was traced far enough to make him quite forty years of age, while less reliable information made him much older.

and old horses is very marked. It requires but little familiarity with horses to detect the extremes of age and the contrary condition. After maturity, however, more reliance is to be placed upon the indications afforded by the teeth, than upon outward signs.

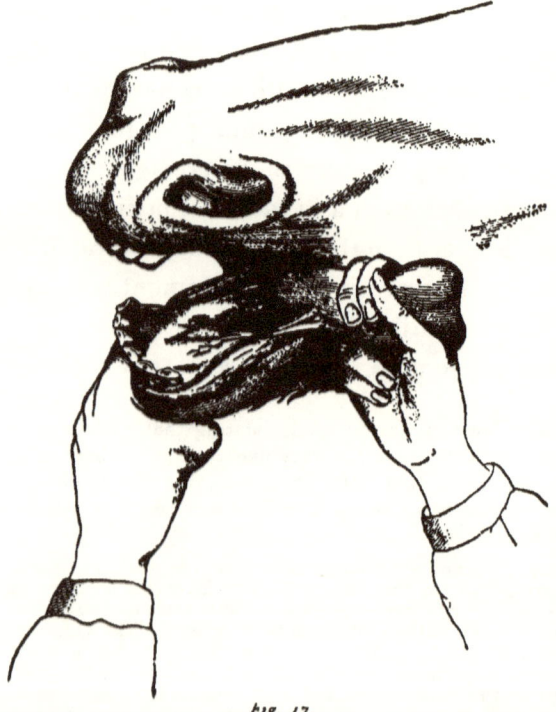

Fig. 17.

In order to examine the mouth, the left hand should be placed upon the horse's nose quietly, while the right is introduced into the mouth to seize the tongue, which is gently drawn out on the left side. If necessary, the lower lip may be held with the left hand. (Fig. 17). If the horse resists, a fore foot may be held up, and, in rare cases, a twitch applied to his ear. In the majority of cases the incisor teeth may be examined by simply inserting the fingers in the sides of the mouth, and pressing the lips apart in front with the thumbs.

Before examining the teeth in detail, the lips should be parted, and the angle at which the upper and lower incisors come together observed. This angle is obtuse in young, and acute in old horses. (Figs. 18 and 21.)

A horse is said to be *coming* or *rising* to a certain age when his mouth is at the point of presenting the characters of the age to which reference is made; he has the age when all the characters exist; he is *past*, when the characters begin to disappear; thus rising four, four, a four year old past.

Age as Indicated by the Teeth.—Structural alterations take place in the teeth every year up to the sixth; hence there can rarely be any question as to the real age of a horse up to that time, as indicated by the teeth.

After the horse has obtained his full set of teeth the age can be approximately determined by the effect of wear in altering their shape, by the receding of the gums, and by other such signs.

Many circumstances, however, often contribute to modify the effect of wear on the teeth, and also to increase or decrease the action of time in other respects; hence a correct estimate of age can only be formed by those who have given to the subject considerable study.

The young foal usually has two, and sometimes three, temporary molars in each jaw. When about twelve months old another molar, a permanent tooth, appears, and before completion of the second year a fifth molar, also a permanent tooth, shows itself.

At about two-and-a-half years of age the two anterior temporary molars are replaced by permanent teeth, and at between three and four the remaining or third temporary molar is replaced. At about the same time the last or sixth permanent molar begins to appear. Thus when the mouth is completed there are twelve permanent molars in each jaw, or twenty-four in all.

These structural changes afford a good index of the age of the horse up to the period when they are completed, namely, four years. These molars, however, are seldom referred to, because their position at the back of the mouth renders their examination inconvenient, and often very difficult. Nevertheless, it is well to be acquainted with the changes in the molars, in case there should be any doubt as to the true age as indicated by the incisors, up to and including four years.

A supplementary molar, known as "wolf's tooth," sometimes appears in either jaw. Such teeth seldom cause any inconvenience. If they do so, they can easily be removed by the pincers, as they are only of a rudimentary character.

The incisors are six in number in each jaw when the mouth is complete, and in the immediate rear of these, on each side, but at a variable distance from them, appears a pointed tooth, called tusk. These begin to appear at about four years, but are not fully developed until the last per-

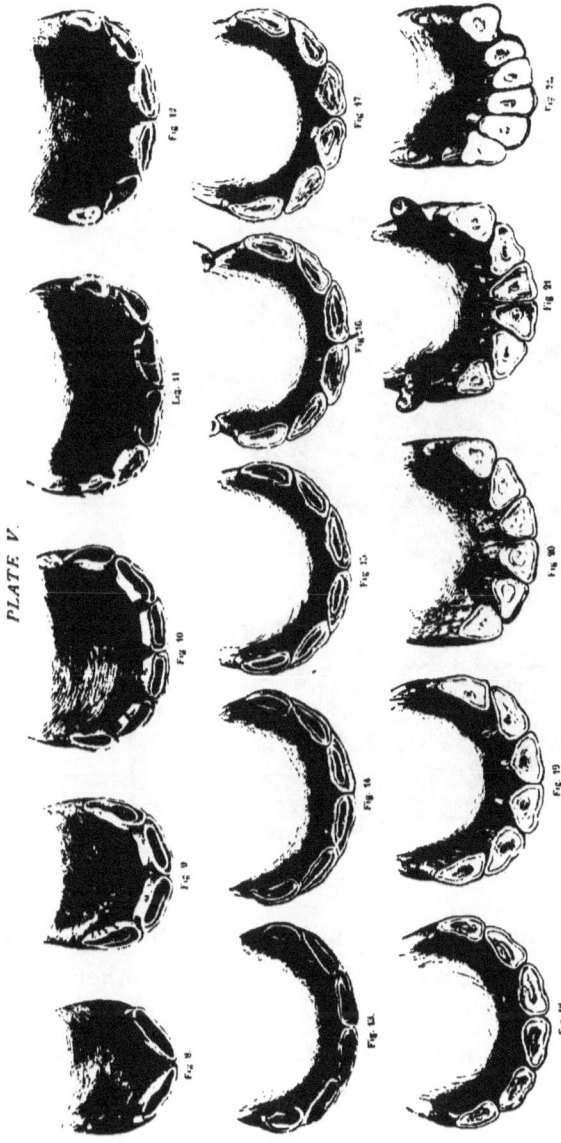

PLATE V.

manent incisor is more or less up. These tusks are rarely found in mares.

Temporary incisors, called milk teeth, are easily distinguished from permanent incisors, being smaller, whiter, and having more distinct necks. They are smooth externally, and grooved inside. Their fangs are small, and have but little attachment to the gums. The jaws are plump, fleshy and round, and the teeth are arranged in something like a semi-circle.

Permanent teeth on the other hand are larger, broader, wider in their necks, grooved externally, and smooth inter-

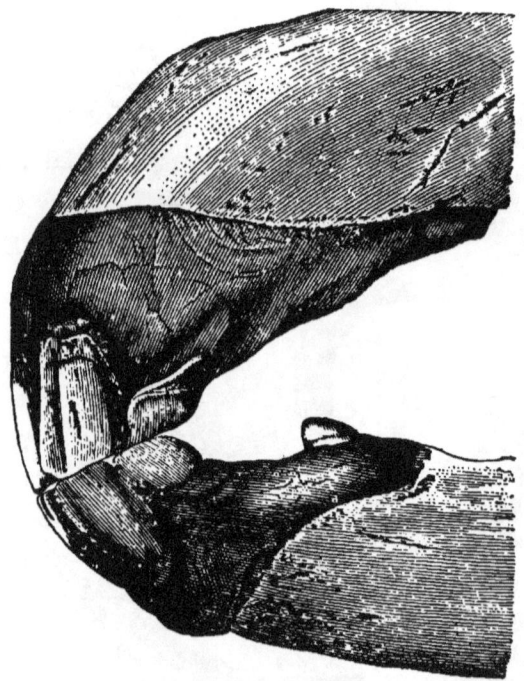

Fig. 18. (Four years.)

nally, and more discolored than milk teeth. This discoloration is due to the lodgement of the juices and other matters connected with the food in the grooves. The plumpness and circularity of the part of the jaw containing the incisors is less than in the younger animal, and it gradually decreases, until in old age the teeth are arranged in nearly a straight line.

Temporary or milk teeth (incisors) are in the gums in a rudimentary state when the foal is born, and they appear from time to time during the first year, at the end of which period the yearling mouth is complete in all six incisors. Up to this time the foal may be distinguished by his woolly tail. The teeth are very close together, and show no signs of wear. The corner teeth are mere shells. (Figs. 8, 9, 10, Plate V.)

At two years of age the inner wall of the corner teeth has grown up level with the outer wall. The center teeth show considerable signs of wear, and all the teeth appear somewhat smaller than they did in the yearling. They also appear somewhat wider apart at their necks on account of the gradual growth of the jaw in width.

A few months before three years old the horse sheds the two center milk teeth, which are replaced by permanent incisors. Thus at three years the jaw contains two center permanent and two milk teeth on each side. (Fig. 11, Plate V.)

A few months before four, the next two milk teeth are shed and replaced by permanent teeth, the jaw now containing four permanent and two milk teeth. (Fig. 12, Plate V, and Fig. 18, page 63.)

The tusks appear in that part of the lower jaw, on each side, between the incisors and molars, at about four, and continue to grow until the horse is five years old or past.

The new tusk is quite sharp at the point when it first appears, and at five there is a slight bend inward, forming a hook at the top. This gradually wears off, and each succeeding year the tusk becomes rounder and more blunt, and its upper portion wears off.

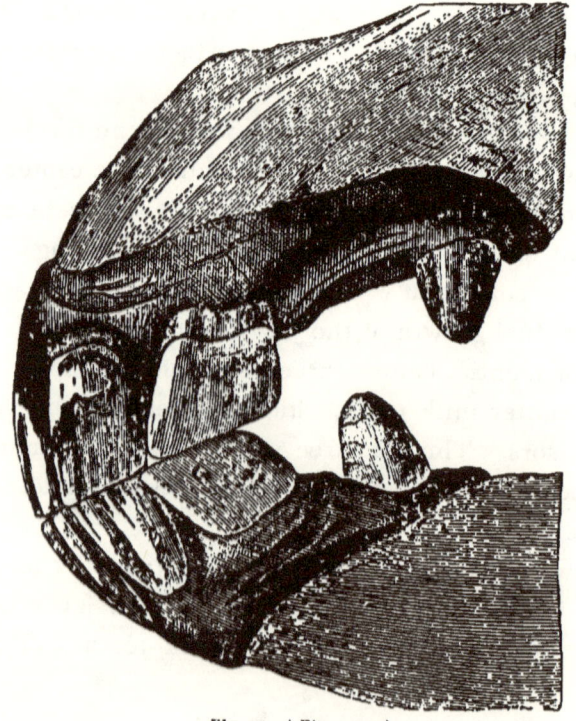

Fig. 19 (*Five years.*)

Although the opposing tusks do not meet, they undergo changes from the effect of mastication, and thus become additional aids in determining age. In general terms, the young horse may be known by the sharp pointed tusk, and the old horse by the flat top tusk, which in the latter case is usually much discolored.

A few months before five the horse sheds the two remaining milk teeth, which are replaced by permanent ones. The jaw now has a full set of six permanent incisors, but the corner teeth have no inner walls. This absence of internal wall distinguishes the five from the six-year-old mouth. (Fig. 13, Plate V, and Fig. 19, page 65.)

A few months before six the inner wall of the corner teeth has grown up level with the outer wall, but in some cases this inner wall is entirely absent. (Fig. 14, Plate V.)

The mouth is now complete in incisors, and no further structural changes take place in them. As a general rule the upper temporary teeth fall out a little before those in the lower jaw. Up to six years, owing to structural changes, there can seldom be any doubt as to the age of the animal.

High feeding encourages the growth of the teeth in common with the rest of the frame, and may give a colt a very forward appearance for his age.

The Mark.—The mark is a very peculiar hollow extending when the teeth first come up, about half an inch down in the temporary, and rather deeper down in the permanent incisors.

When an incisor first comes up the hollow affords lodgement for the debris of the food and the juices expressed from it, and therefore soon looks black. As the tooth wears down the hollow of course disappears. The dentine immediately below the original hollow being of a somewhat soft material, has become stained for some distance down; thus there is still a black mark. With the further wear of the tooth the stained portion wears away, and the mark disappears. The time required for the mark to wear out varies according to circumstances.

Between three and five years the marks are very plain in all the permanent incisors.

At six the marks, or cups as sometimes called, are wearing out of the two center teeth, which come up at three years. They are plain in the two adjacent, and fresh in the two corner teeth. (Fig. 14, Plate V.)

At seven the marks have disappeared from the center teeth, are wearing out of the two adjacent, and are distinct and plain only in the corner teeth. (Fig. 15, Plate V.)

At eight the marks have disappeared from all but the corner teeth, in which they are becoming indistinct. (Fig. 16, Plate V.)

At nine the marks are not usually to be seen in any of the teeth (Fig. 17, Plate V), but for about two years after the mark has disappeared in each tooth there may still be seen a trace of the enamel which lined the bottom of the original hollow, and which underlies it for some depth. This of course decreases in size with the wear of the teeth.

At about twelve or thirteen the last traces of the enamel have usually disappeared. The lower incisors all show a rounded section, and the dental star is quite central, and very apparent throughout. (Fig. 18, Plate V.)

From the age of fourteen years (Fig. 19, Plate V) to that of seventeen years (Fig. 20, Plate V), the teeth assume a triangular form; the center ones, or pincers, at fourteen; the middle at fifteen, and the corners at from sixteen to seventeen.

At about eighteen (Fig. 21, Plate V) the triangles formed by the teeth lengthen and become laterally contracted, so that at twenty or twenty-one years (Fig. 22, Plate V) the teeth are biangular.

Many circumstances may cause a deviation in a slight degree from these rules. The time required for the mark to wear out will vary in different horses according to the hardness or softness of the teeth, and the nature of the food on which the animal is fed. Horses raised on the fresh, green pastures of well cultivated farms retain their marks longer than range horses of the West which graze upon the dry and tough, but nutritious native grasses of the arid region.

Sometimes there are causes affecting the marks in particular cases to be taken into consideration. The most common of these are cribbing and "parrot mouth." In the first case the teeth are worn off rapidly by the constant gnawing of the animal, and in the second no wear of the incisors takes place because the upper teeth project over and in front of the lower.

The upper incisors are larger and longer than the lower, and the hollow is nearly twice as deep. The marks or cups therefore remain visible a much longer time than in the lower teeth.

At seven years (Fig. 20) the lower corner incisors, being narrower than the upper, commence to wear the surface of the upper incisors into a well defined angle, which becomes more marked at eight, and at nine appears as a deep notch. This notch is sometimes absent, but rarely so unless the corners have been rasped off with intent to deceive. This notch is particularly useful to those unable to decide upon the appearance of the tables or top surfaces of the lower incisors.

At eight years the dental star appears in the form of a yellowish, transverse line, most marked in the two center incisors, and indistinct in the others. From this time on the dental star must be considered, for after the ninth year the determination of age by the teeth becomes very difficult. After the twelfth year the age can be only approximately determined. After the sixteenth year all is confusion, for there are no positive means of ascertaining the age from the appearance of the teeth with even approximate ac-

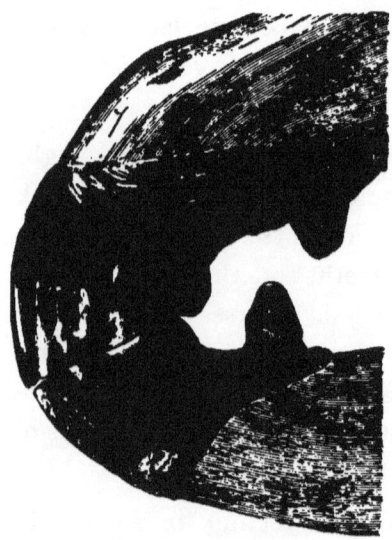

Fig. 20. (Seven years.)

curacy. It is safe then only by careful examination of the shape of the teeth, condition of the gums, appearance of the head and frame, to announce that the animal is old or very old; to say *about* sixteen, eighteen, twenty, or twenty-five, indicates better judgment and more accurate knowledge than to look at the mouth of an old horse and say he is "rising seventeen" or "nineteen past."

The dental star, mentioned as long at eight, gradually changes its appearance, until at fifteen it appears distinct and round in all the lower incisors, and is found near the center of the tables or tops of the teeth.

Fig. 21. (Nineteen years.)

When a horse has passed twelve, especially if weakened by hard service and poor food, his tongue begins to project over the bars.

In general the tables of a young horse's teeth are broad in the direction of the jaw; those of an old horse are round or broad in a direction perpendicular to the jaw.

The teeth of a young horse come together in front at a

very obtuse angle, or almost in a line. (Figs. 18 and 19.) Those of an old horse, on the contrary, come together at

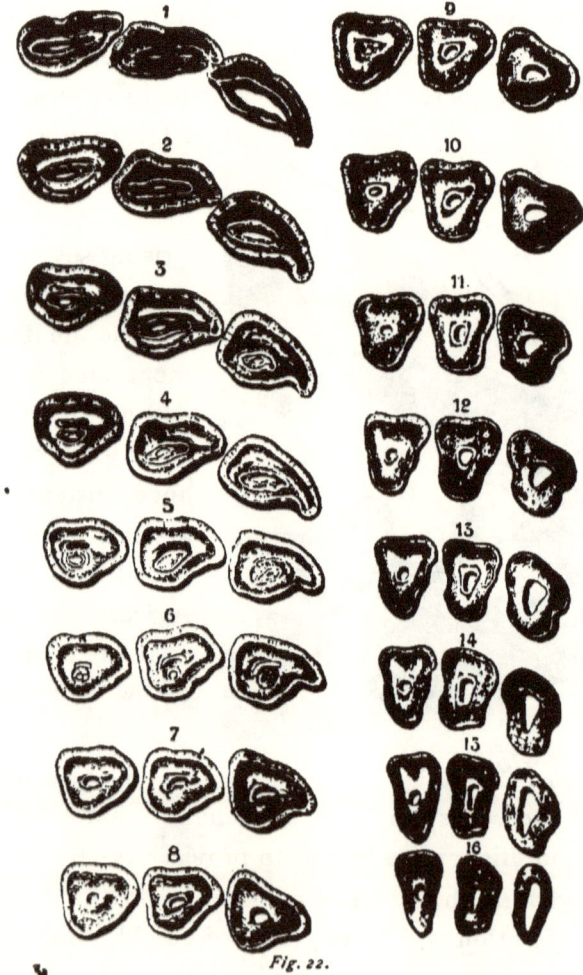

Fig. 22.

such a small angle that sometimes the lower teeth seem to be in the prolongation of the jaws. (Fig. 21.)

The changes of form in the top surface of the incisors arise from wear, but this may be illustrated in another way. Fig. 22 represents a series of cross-sections cut from the three right lower incisors of a five-year-old horse. It will be seen upon examination that at the top the sections are long in the direction of the jaw, 1 and 2; oval in the next few sections, 3, 4 and 5; rounded forms in 6, 7, 8 and 9; triangular or long from front to rear in 10, 11, 12, 13, 14, 15 and 16. The first shapes characterize the young, and the last the very old horse.

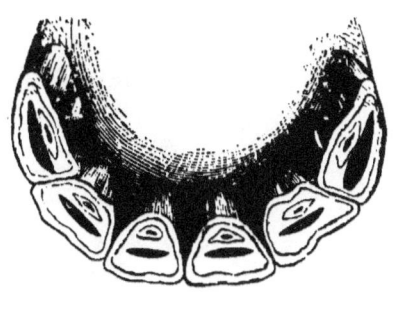

Fig. 23.

There are several fraudulent ways of giving a horse's mouth a more youthful appearance than nature has provided for his years. These are generally confined to rasping off the corners of the notches in the upper incisors, and burning new cups or marks in the lower incisors—a process called "bishoping."

To detect such frauds it is necessary only to remember that the shape of the teeth in young and old horses is entirely different, and that when the natural mark exists it is surrounded by a border of enamel which is in relief above the dental table. On the contrary, when an artificial hole is made, not being surrounded with hard enamel, the edges are not in relief. (Fig. 23.)

The fraudulent operation is very troublesome, the chance of detection is great, and ordinary horses are not sufficiently valuable to justify the labor or the risk attendant upon the operation. The ages of valuable horses are matters of record, and cannot, therefore, be falsified.

CHAPTER IV.

ENDURANCE OF HORSES.

Influence of the Weight of the Pack.—Necessity for Husbanding Strength at First.—Preliminary Hardening Valueless Unless Horses Are Kept Supplied With Forage.—Abuse of Horses.—Marching Gaits.—Endurance Varies With Treatment, Size and Shape.—Causes of Losses of Horses in War.—Cavalry Raids.—Losses of Horses in Various Campaigns.—The Establishment of the Cavalry Bureau, and What It Accomplished.—Frontier Service.

For the few brief charges upon the field of battle, into which the excitement of the moment may carry the sick and the lame, there must be months and years of patient and laborious work in reconnaissance, patrol, advance and rear guard, outpost duty, and route marches with horses loaded down with heavy and unwieldy packs.

Few men upon first entering the service can realize how accurate a balance is required for the large amount of baggage and kit placed upon the horse.

Experience gradually teaches the trooper that the more he packs on his horse the greater will be the chance of breaking him down, but stringent orders are necessary with all recruits on service to compel them to leave in camp or quarters all but the necessary and authorized articles.

While the weight of the pack does not appear, under ordinary circumstances, to diminish the rate of speed upon the march, it necessarily augments the fatigue of the horse, and ultimately tends to reduce his length of service. When it becomes imperative to march at a faster gait than a walk for several days, it is customary to reduce the weight of pack to its lowest limit, and to secure that remaining in such a manner as to prevent it from swaying about.

On long marches, where grain is hauled in wagons and there is no danger of being suddenly ordered to abandon the train, it is advisable always to save up the horses by loading the bulky portions of the packs in the wagons as the grain is fed out.

It is not, however, always the pack and the legitimate work of cavalry which breaks down the horses and renders them unserviceable. Many fat horses are started on the downward road by being galloped about in an excited manner by couriers, who form exaggerated ideas of the importance of the messages they bear. This applies especially when ordered to take the field suddenly after prolonged garrison service.

All soldiers of experience know well the value of carefully husbanding the strength and wind of horses at the start. Many men have been compelled to lead broken down horses, or pack their saddles and equipments into camp on foot, because of uselessly worrying fresh horses when getting ready for the march.

It is folly to imagine that horses can be put through any preliminary training or hardening process which will enable them to undergo the hardships of campaigning, unless provided with sufficient food and properly cared for on the march.

Various instances are recorded where the horses, not of pickets and vedettes, but of large bodies of cavalry, were kept saddled and bridled for days at a time in anticipation of immediate service. This practice cannot be regarded as otherwise than criminal in a properly instructed command.

A few saddles removed at a time, the horses allowed to roll and then groomed, the saddle blanket shaken out and refolded, and finally a good brisk hand rubbing of the legs, would not be dangerous to the command if vedettes were properly posted; to the tired horse it would be just such a boon as comes to the invalid when his bed is aired and made over after a serious illness.

The greater part of cavalry marching is done at a walk. When riding in the enemy's country it is necessary to give time for the advance parties to send scouts out in all directions, and allow the foraging details to collect supplies and bring them to the line of march. When traveling with convoys a faster gait than a walk would leave the trains unguarded.

When circumstances do not prevent, however, the present plan in the American service is to alternate the march at a walk with the trot. This brings the command to the end of the journey in much less time, and admits of the heavy weight being removed entirely from the horse, so that he may rest and graze. This method obtains in other services, and experiments made in marching at various gaits indicate that the combination of walk and trot is the best for cavalry.

The endurance of horses varies, not only with the treatment accorded to them, but also with regard to their size, shape and adaptability for service.

The loss of animals in all wars is very great, and occasionally the average is much increased by occurrences of an unusual nature. The situation at Chattanooga, when the Army of the Cumberland was besieged after the battle of Chickamauga, may be placed under this category. There was absolutely no forage for the animals; they ate bark, wagon bodies, one another's manes and tails, and those not used for food by the half-starved troops finally succumbed to starvation at the picket lines.

The losses of horses in service arise from a variety of causes; gun-shot wounds, starvation, epidemics, stampedes, over-exertion, improper shoeing, rope burns, sore backs, and exposure to inclement weather all have their influence.

Some of these causes appear on the surface to be preventable, but when large numbers of animals are assembled, as was the case in the Army of the Potomac, where every pound of supplies had to be brought by sea or rail from Northern farms, it is not difficult to understand how it happened that many detachments, even regiments, were left unprovided for at times.

Constant exposure in rain and mud caused much disease; at one time nearly all the cavalry horses were laid up with scratches and grease heel, brought on by unsanitary surroundings.

The records of the Civil War as to the loss of animals are not available in a complete form, but enough is known to establish the fact that the expense of keeping up cavalry in the large volunteer army was very great, and arose from a multiplicity of causes, which were and always will be inseparable from raw levies of mounted men.

In the early part of the war the demand for horses to mount the newly organized cavalry regiments was very great, and as the majority of people supposed that the war would be of short duration, considerable carelessness prevailed in the selection of horses.

Thousands of animals utterly unfit to take part in the fatigues and exposure of campaigns were hurried into service, with the very natural result that they soon died or became a burden upon the government.

The cavalry service was unsatisfactory to the ambitious officers who saw the possibilities open to that arm of the service if well drilled, disciplined and mounted. It was apparent that the results obtained were not commensurate with the expense lavished on that arm, and every effort was put forth to discover wherein the service could be improved and the horses made to last longer.

The records of the volunteer cavalry during the Civil War are not sufficiently accurate to base any conclusions or comparisons as to the endurance of trained animals in the hands of regular soldiers, such as exist in large numbers in European armies. They do, however, give an idea of just what may be expected whenever a large number of volunteers are put into the field upon untrained horses in America.

General MEIGS commented upon this subject in his report as Quartermaster-General in 1862 as follows:

"Ignorance and carelessness of raw soldiers waste our horses, but it is believed that the quality of the animals supplied is quite as good as in any other army.

"After every battle and every considerable march great numbers of horses are turned into the depots as disabled, and urgent requisitions are made upon the department for remounts, as essential to the efficiency of the troops. Of the disabled horses many die; many prove on inspection to be incapable of recovering in such time as to be worth the expense of keeping them; these are sold. Those which by good feeding and careful attention can be recruited are kept in the depots, and issued for use in the army when again fit for the service.

"The reports and returns received from the *new and inexperienced officers, who, from necessity, have been employed in this department*, are too irregular and imperfect to give, at this time, a perfectly accurate statement of the number of horses and mules purchased and issued to the army during the fiscal year. The consumption of horses has been very great."

When it is considered that each cavalryman in the Confederate army was compelled to supply himself with a horse, without recourse to the government, the number supplied to the Federal army surpasses all belief.

There were purchased during the fiscal year ending June 30, 1864, 188,718 horses; captured from the enemy and reported, 20,308. Leaving out of consideration those captured and not reported, it is observed that the army required 500 horses each day for remounts; and this is the measure of destruction of horses during the same period.

Notwithstanding his opinion, that "as the cavalry has improved in discipline and knowledge, it is believed the horses last longer," the Quartermaster-General again called attention to the great loss of horses in the following language:

"During the first eight months of the year 1864 the cavalry of the Army of the Potomac was supplied with two remounts, nearly 40,000 horses.

"The supply of fresh horses to the army of General SHERIDAN during his late campaign in the valley of the Shenandoah has been at the rate of 150 per day."

Such data as can be obtained leads to the conclusion that much of the loss of horses in the Army of the Potomac during the first two years of the war was brought about by mistaken ideas as to the proper use of cavalry. The amount of picket duty performed by mounted men was out of all proportion to their numbers or to the necessities of the service.

Worn out troopers, lounging in muddy and frozen saddle kits, on half-starved horses, characterized the outpost duty of the army during the winter of 1862 and 1863.*

Cavalry raids were inaugurated by the Confederates for the purpose of carrying the war into the territory of the enemy, thus cutting lines of supply and forcing undesirable concentrations of troops. These raiders lived off the country, and returned to their lines laden with booty, and accompanied by a plentiful supply of fresh horses gathered from the enemy.

As the Federal cavalry became trained to its work, raiding columns were sent into various parts of the South; many of them, particularly those penetrating to the rear of LEE'S army, found it was very different from Confederate raids, for there was nothing left in the country, and it was more like starving than living off the enemy.

These raids tested the powers of endurance of the horses to the utmost limit, and were responsible for an immense loss of animals.

Raiding became accepted as a thing of recognized value in the art of war, and the full accomplishment of mighty ends was regarded as value received for the thousands of dead horses that marked the routes of march.

Although the weight of packs carried on these raids was always fixed as low as possible under the extraordinary circumstances surrounding them, the horses were weighted

---

*The sixth regiment of regular cavalry was encamped near Falmouth, Va., for four months performing outpost duty, and when ordered to march on the resumption of the campaign, April 13, 1863, it was necessary to leave 300 men in the dismounted camp, notwithstanding strenuous exertions had been made to keep the regiment mounted. It is probable that like proportions obtained in other regiments in that army.

beyond their capacity, ridden beyond their powers of endurance, fed mostly on green corn fodder or "roughness," and used up generally in the accomplishment of the great ends for which the columns were set in motion.*

The loss of horses alarmed the government for fear it would be impracticable to keep up a numerous and well equipped cavalry, and the organization of new cavalry regiments was discouraged. It required the utmost efforts of the Cavalry Bureau to remount the regiments already enlisted in the early days of the war.

In this connection it appears proper to cite a few instances from the experience of other nations, in order to show that the loss of horses during the Civil War was not the result of wanton waste, but was what should have been expected in accordance with the teachings of history.

As has been stated, the loss of horses arises from a variety of causes, those killed in battle being but a small percentage of the whole. Forced marches, periods of great privation, and epidemics, occur at intervals to raise the ordinary average, and these causes must always be counted upon as exercising a marked effect in every campaign, no matter where the theater of operations may be.

---

*Although WILSON'S expedition to Selma, Ala., with a body of 13,000 horsemen, was through much of the South which was depended upon to furnish supplies to the Confederate armies, each trooper was ordered to carry, in addition to his ordinary kit, five days' rations, twenty-four pounds of grain, 100 rounds of ammunition, and two extra horseshoes. This enabled them to pass across a strip of country which had been devastated by both armies. The raid was entirely successful, and culminated in the capture of ex-President JEFF DAVIS.

THE RUSSIAN CAMPAIGN. 1812.

During the Russian campaign the French crossed the Niemen in June, 1812, with cavalry, artillery and train horses to the extent of 187,121; about 60,000 of these pertained to the cavalry.

Up to this time it had been very hot, but an unprecedented rainfall commenced; in a few days the weather turned cold, the roads became almost impassable, and there was little or no food for the horses. Ten thousand horses were left dead between the Niemen and Wilna.

At this time the only food to be had for the large number of animals with the army consisted of young, growing crops of wheat, rye and barley. Such food is calculated to produce weakness, and intestinal troubles of a grave nature, and this was without doubt the cause of most of the loss.

MURAT states that half the cavalry perished around Moscow in their search for supplies. It was not the horrors of the icy retreat which used up the animals, for NAPOLEON caused BERTHIER to write to VICTOR on November 6th that the cavalry was unhorsed; in all 92,000 horses had succumbed before the first fall of snow.

On December 13th the remnant of the invading army re-crossed the Niemen with 1,600 cavalry. In six months the horses had all disappeared, and there is ample evidence that this was not the result of cold, but of starvation, aggravated, perhaps, by cold towards the end of the campaign.

RETREAT ON CORUNNA—PENINSULA WAR.

This retreat was carried out in rain, ice and snow, over mountain roads. The food supply was not abundant, but the chief cause of loss was want of horseshoes and nails. There was plenty of iron, but no time to perform the work of making shoes by hand.

After all the perils and suffering of the retreat, those horses which survived and reached Corunna were put to death on the beach to prevent them falling into the hands of the enemy, there being no room for them on the transports. About 2,300 horses constituted the loss.

WELLINGTON'S RETREAT FROM SALAMANCA.

When WELLINGTON retreated from Salamanca to Ciudad Rodrigo, a distance of 240 miles, the horses were verging on starvation, having no other food than the bark of trees and wild brier. Incessant rain, stony and heavy ground, together with the want of food, caused the loss of 280 horses, or more than one for every mile of road.

MASSENA'S RETREAT FROM PORTUGAL.

MASSENA retreated from Portugal with 8,000 horses. During the ten days occupied by the retreat the total loss was 1,955, or 195 each day, being over twenty-two per cent. of the whole number.

AFGHAN CAMPAIGN. 1838–39.

There was not a large number of cavalry horses employed in the first Afghan War, but the loss was nearly sixty per cent. The loss of pack animals from starvation was very heavy, and has caused the Bolan Pass to be well remembered in the British service. The animals were worn out by a long march and bad water, and being entirely dependent upon grazing for food, the loss amounted to 20,000 animals before reaching Candahar, and more than 30,000 for the campaign.

In the second Afghan War (1878) the loss of pack animals during a period of six months was 9,496 out of a total of 13,840 on the returns.

CRIMEA. 1855.

All sorts of excuses have been made for the losses in this campaign, but the melancholy fact remains that the horses were starved to death. During a period of six months the loss of transport horses was thirty-eight per cent., and out of 5,048 cavalry and artillery horses there remained at the opening of spring 2,258.

ITALIAN CAMPAIGN. 1859.

During the campaign in Italy the Emperor, NAPOLEON III, ordered a cavalry commission to investigate the circumstances which had reduced the cavalry to a comparative state of inefficiency. It transpired that on May 20, 1859, the French cavalry had 9,008 effective horses, which number was subsequently increased by the arrival of a brigade; so that on the 24th of June, the date of the battle of Solferino, the total number of horses borne on the returns was 10,206.

On the day of the battle it was found that only about 3,500 horses were in the ranks fit for duty.

The remainder had been disabled by less than a month's marching, and an immense proportion of these had been rendered unserviceable by the saddle and other portions of the equipment.

BOHEMIA. 1866.

During the brief campaign of a few weeks in Bohemia in 1866 the Prussian cavalry suffered a loss of 4,226 horses, that being about seventeen per cent. of the whole number in the campaign.

FRANCO-GERMAN WAR. 1870.

The official returns of the German army only show the loss of horses in action; that is, killed, wounded and missing. No returns are given of those which died from diseases, but as the army received a supply of 38,000 horses during the campaign, besides the animals captured or impressed by detachments to replace broken-down horses, and not reported, the loss from disease may be assumed at not far from 30,000. The number killed, wounded, etc., was reported at 14,595.

EGYPTIAN CAMPAIGN. 1885.

The total strength of horses for all branches of the service landed in Egypt was 5,000, of which one-eighth died or were destroyed. The loss in the cavalry was one-fifth. The number of sore backs treated during this campaign was very large, being more than 500.

No nation has within the present century had anything like the experience of Americans with mounted men in a protracted war. In order to show the magnitude of cavalry operations it is only necessary to present a brief sketch of the Cavalry Bureau and of one of its remount depots.

In these brief references to the experience of other nations, enough has been shown to emphasize the fact that heavy losses of horses must be expected in service, and are absolutely inseparable from *active* and *successful* campaigning. This is said advisedly, for it would be courting disaster to teach any such doctrine as that the saving of horses from injury and death is of such importance as to permit it for a moment to hazard the full success of any campaign.

The whole object of this book is to place a few facts about horses in such a light as will cause young officers to give the matter their best thoughts, with a view to their future service to the government. If, therefore, by giving the subject attention in all its details, they are enabled to understand why one cavalry commander, by impressing his knowledge upon a large body of horsemen, is enabled to accomplish great results at small cost to the country, while another can only accomplish the same results by breaking down all his horses, a great end will have been accomplished.

That patriotism alone cannot immediately bring forth good cavalrymen there is ample evidence in the many fruitless efforts of the first two years of the war.

The unsatisfactory results and continued complaints about the class of remounts, finally caused the subject to receive careful attention, but not until an enormous amount had been invested in unsuitable animals.

It took two years of a great war to bring about the establishment of the Cavalry Bureau; the result of this action was so beneficial to the troops in the field, as a whole, that it appears proper for future reference to insert here a brief sketch of some of the operations under this bureau.

It may here be noted that it was found advisable when regiments had been subjected to very hard service and severe losses to send them to the nearest depot to be remounted and equipped, transferring to other regiments in the field such serviceable horses as were fit for immediate use.

The Cavalry Bureau was charged with the organization and equipment of the cavalry forces of the army, and with the duty of providing for the mounts and remounts.

The purchase of all horses for the cavalry service was directed to be made by officers of the Quartermaster's Department, under the direction of the Cavalry Bureau, and the inspection of all horses for the cavalry service was required to be made by cavalry officers.

Depots were ordered to be established for the reception, organization and discipline of cavalry recruits, and for the collection, care and training of cavalry horses; the depots to be under the general charge of the Cavalry Bureau.

The principal depots for public animals established by authority of this order were located at Giesboro, D. C.; St. Louis, Mo.; Greenville, La.; Nashville, Tenn.; Harrisburg, Pa., and Wilmington, Del.; all of which contributed much to the efficiency of the service, especially in the matter of affording facilities for the recuperation of broken down animals.

A general order was promulgated on July 28, 1863, containing instructions intended to promote the efficiency of the cavalry service, and Major-General GEORGE STONEMAN was announced as Chief of the Cavalry Bureau in Washington.

On January 2, 1864, Brigadier-General KENNER GARRARD was assigned to the charge of the bureau, and also instructed to assume the direct command of the cavalry depot at Giesboro, D. C., but he was relieved on the 26th of the same month by Brigadier-General J. H. WILSON, who continued in charge until April, on the 14th of which month the following instructions were promulgated from the War Department:

"I. That the Cavalry Bureau shall be under command of the Chief of Army Staff, who shall perform the duties of Chief of the Cavalry Bureau prescribed by existing orders, and the officers of that bureau, respectively, will report to him.

"II. All the duties relating to the organization, equipment and inspection of cavalry will be performed by a cavalry officer specially assigned to that duty.

"III. The duties in relation to purchase and inspection of horses, the subsistence and transportation of horses purchased, will be performed by and under the direction of an officer of the Quartermaster's Department specially assigned to that duty."

The principal depot for horses was located on the farm known as Giesboro Manor, situated on the northern bank of the Potomac, nearly equi-distant between Washington and Alexandria. This site, consisting of about 625 acres, was selected by General STONEMAN after an examination of various places in the vicinity.

The government took possession of the estate on August 12, 1863, and paid to the owner a monthly rental at the rate of $6,000.00 per annum from that date until August 31, 1866. Immediately after taking possession the erection of stables and other buildings was commenced under the general supervision of Lieutenant-Colonel C. G. SAWTELLE, Chief Quartermaster of the Cavalry Bureau, and Colonel CHARLES R. LOWELL, Sixth U. S. Cavalry, was assigned to duty as commanding officer of the depot.

Within three months after the commencement of operations provision was made for 15,000 animals, and at the end of the next three months arrangements had been completed for the proper care of 30,000 animals, although 21,000 was the largest number ever on hand at any one time.

Stables, corrals, stock yards, forage houses, storehouses, shops, mess houses, quarters, a grist mill, chapel and three wharves were constructed. The wharves afforded facilities for loading three steamers of the largest class at the same time. The hospital stables had accommodations for 2,650 horses.

All of the stables and buildings were abundantly supplied with water, and also with fire apparatus. A steam fire-engine was kept in constant readiness for use, and its services were required only once during the existence of the depot, when principally through its agency a large amount of forage was saved.

Many of the horses were kept in open sheds and yards, but there were thirty-two stables, capable of accommodating more than 6,000 horses, besides the hospital and smaller stables.

The stock yards covered about forty-five acres. Each yard was provided with troughs and hay racks, and the horses had free access to the river.

A steam feed mill, with a capacity to grind and mix grain for 13,000 full rations each day, was erected at a cost of $26,500.00.

During the progress of construction about 5,000 men were employed, but this number was reduced after the buildings were completed, and was never after above 1,500.

The estimated cost of the Giesboro depot was $1,225,000.

As an illustration of the magnitude of the operations carried on under the Cavalry Bureau, the following report from the Giesboro depot is of interest:

On hand October 1, 1863, cavalry horses,	4,281
Received to December 31, 1863,	36,932
Total,	41,213
Issued,	22,204
Sold,	1,651
Died,	1,637
Total,	25,492
On hand January 1, 1864,	15,721
Received by purchase, January 1, 1864 to June 30, 1866,	5,326
Received from other depots for issue,	59,507
Received for recuperation,	85,980
Received by transfer from artillery,	4,120
Total,	170,654
Issued to armies in the field,	96,006
Issued to officers after June 30, 1865,	1,574
Issued for sale or sold at depot	48,721
Died,	24,321
Total,	170,632
On hand June 30, 1866,	32

This does not take into consideration the twelve or thirteen thousand artillery horses handled at this depot.

This report closes with the abandonment of the depot, but it is to be remembered that nearly all the volunteer cavalry was mustered out immediately after the surrender of General LEE's army the preceding year, so that nearly all the horses were handled during a period of eighteen months.

When it is understood that there were six large horse depots, and this one handled horses principally for the

Army of the Potomac, which contained but about onetenth of the cavalry in service, the magnitude of the labor imposed on the bureau charged with the remount duties may be comprehended.

That this work was well done during the last two years of the war must be conceded by all who have any knowledge of the deeds accomplished by the cavalry corps of the Army of the Potomac. The herculean tasks performed by this body of horsemen under SHERIDAN have not been approached by any cavalry in Europe since, and while Americans are justly proud of the results, the officers who for several years had been improving the system of remounts, and those who had been building up the troops, regiments and brigades into well disciplined and trained bodies of horsemen, should not be forgotten, for it was the harmonious whole, resulting from their long continued efforts, which made SHERIDAN'S career in Virginia a possibility.

For many years the cavalry traveled incessantly to and fro over the plains, mountains and deserts of the great Western frontier, with varying degrees of fortune.

Much of this occurred prior to the settlement of the country, and hence many of the long and arduous marches were accomplished with difficulty, often accompanied with actual suffering and disaster.

As early as the Mexican War, a cavalry column marched from Fort Leavenworth, Kan., to San Diego, Cal., a distance of more than 2,000 miles, passing through a hostile country, and fighting several severe actions, before arriving at its destination.

The nature of the service in the past has been such as to frequently demand the sacrifice of large numbers of horses. It often happened, however, that pursuit of hostile Indians had to be abandoned while many horses were capable of going on, because troopers whose horses had failed in strength could not be abandoned on the trail, and subjected to the risk of capture by merciless savages.

Scattered through the records are many reports of losses from stampedes, caused by storms or savages. This was a favorite mode of warfare with Indians, and was a most effective means of crippling an enemy far from the base of supplies.

Glanders has at various times caused the destruction of the horses of entire troops.

Upon one occasion, while proceeding by sea from New York to Galveston, after the close of the Civil War, a cavalry regiment was compelled to lighten ship, during a violent storm off Cape Hatteras, by throwing overboard many of the horses.

During the Sioux campaign of 1876 a brigade under General CROOK lost about 600 horses, a great many being killed for food, upon which the entire command subsisted for some days.

During the same campaign the Seventh Cavalry, operating with another command, lost more than 300 horses killed in action and from other causes.

During the autumn of 1879, while in action against the Utes, all the animals of Major THORNBURG'S command were killed, as well as those of a troop which made a forced march of eighty miles to aid beleaguered comrades.

Instances of endurance, forced marches, and losses by field and flood might be indefinitely multiplied from records of service upon the frontier, but the few cited are sufficient to illustrate the varied character of service, and the severity of its demands upon both men and horses.

CHAPTER V.

Framework of the Horse Mechanically Considered.

Center of Motion.—Center of Gravity.—Base of Support.—Relative Positions of Centers of Motion and Gravity.—Equilibrium.—Effect of Head and Neck on Center of Gravity.—Artificial Balance of Saddle Horse.

The skeleton forms the basis of the animal machine, and it is necessary to have some understanding of it from a mechanical, as well as anatomical point of view. The principles involved are familiar, relating chiefly to levers and equilibrium, or such a distribution of weight, with reference to its supports, as to insure stability. The principal weight to be carried is the rider and packed saddle.

Looking at the spine, or framework of the back on which the rider's weight is to be carried, it will be seen that the under line of the vertebræ is nearly straight, although not horizontal, since it inclines somewhat downwards towards the forehand. The spinous processes of the first thirteen vertebræ, reckoning from the point where the neck is attached, incline backwards; the fourteenth, fifteenth and sixteenth are nearly upright, and the remaining dorsal and all the lumbar vertebræ incline forward.

Regarding the entire backbone as an arch, it is evident

that the keystone is at the point where the vertebræ stand upright, that is, about the fifteenth, or between the fourteenth and sixteenth. It is obvious that this inclination of the processes towards a central point is intended to and does limit the motion of the back downward and upward, so that the center of motion of the horse's body, the point about which the several movements of the fore and hind legs are performed with varying degrees of rapidity, lies near the fifteenth vertebra.*

This is further shown by the distribution and points of attachment of the muscles of the back and adjacent parts

---

*Considerable discussion having arisen from time to time as to the fourteenth vertebra being the most upright, the author addressed a communication in regard to this point to one of the recognized veterinary authorities in America. The careful consideration given the subject justifies the publication of the reply:

AMERICAN VETERINARY COLLEGE, May 23, 1894.
Captain W. H. Carter:
 DEAR SIR:—To answer your letter of the 18th inst. I have made researches which I send you, but which I am afraid will not permit a definite solution of the problem.
 The veterinary anatomies that I have consulted do not seem to agree as placing the fourteenth dorsal vertebra in the light presented by Major DWYER's book. For instance, STRANGEWAY says that the thirteenth, fourteenth and fifteenth are nearly upright, and the sixteenth oblique forward. For STEEL, it is the sixteenth. For RIGOT, the sixteenth and seventeenth are about upright. CHAUVEAU and FLEMING say the sixteenth and seventeenth are about upright, the eighteenth bent forward. Others, like PERCIVAL and BLAINE, make no mention of the difference.
 Amongst the cuts that I have (Cuyer and Alix, Leisering) the fifteenth seems the most upright.
 Out of three skeletons that are in the museum of the college (French and American), two natural and one artificial, the fifteenth is the most upright of all.
 Evidently from these, taking an average, it appears that the upright conditions of the superior spinous process is more generally admitted as existing in the fifteenth and sixteenth than in the fourteenth.

*   *   *   *   *

I remain yours very respectfully,
A. LIAUTARD.

of the fore and hind quarters. Putting, therefore, the progressive movement of the animal out of the question, as being equally applicable to all its parts, the motion of the several parts of the body increases in proportion to their distance from the center of motion.

The same rule is applicable to burdens placed on the horse's back, especially that of a rider, whose frame is also subject to its own peculiar motions, some of which are caused by the progressive movement of the animal.

If the rider be placed over the center of motion, a point equally removed from the four points of support, he will occupy, as it were, the summit or apex of a more or less regular pyramid, and should have greater stability, and be less disturbed by the horse's motion, than if placed at any other point.

The determination of the center of gravity of living bodies whose parts are of various density and subject to constant displacement by locomotion, change of attitude, and by action of the organs themselves, is a very difficult matter when compared to its determination in bodies of geometrical form and homogeneous construction. The practical value of its determination in the horse lies in the knowledge thereby acquired as to the proper distribution of load in order to retain the normal position of the center of gravity, and thus prevent one set of limbs being used up before the others.

The position of the center of gravity and the distribution of the weight of the body on the legs vary with the conformation of the animal, particularly as to the size and shape of the head and neck. In consequence of the projecting position of these parts, a somewhat greater proportion of its total weight falls on the fore legs than on the hind ones, and causes the forehand to average about one-ninth heavier than the hind.*

A great many experiments have been made to determine the exact position of the center of gravity of the horse, and the best authorities agree that it lies at or near the intersection of a vertical line (AB, Plate I) passing just behind the posterior extremity of the sternum, or breast bone, and a horizontal line (EF) cutting the lower third of the body from the upper portion. This intersection will generally lie in the median plane of the body.†

The usual method of determining the center of gravity is to use two weighing machines, so placed that the anterior extremities rest upon the middle of one, and the posterior extremities upon the middle of the other. By this same method the effect upon the center of gravity is found as the horse raises or lowers his head; when the saddle and load are shifted forward or back; also, when the rider throws his weight into the stirrups, or leans forward, back, or to either side.

It has been stated that the center of motion is situated in a perpendicular line cutting the vertebræ at or near the fifteenth (CD, Plate I), and the center of gravity on a line

---

*General MORRIS's "Essai Sur l'Extérieur du Cheval."
†"The Exterior of the Horse," by GOUBAUX and BARRIER.

cutting the vertebræ nearer the shoulder (*A B*, Plate I). A horse in a natural state goes with the two centers in the relative positions described, and can do so with a rider; the horse can also go, when either trained or weighted, so that the center of gravity falls to the rear of the center of motion, as in certain styles of school riding.

For all general purposes, however, the perpendiculars falling through these two centers should be made to coincide; for correct military riding this condition is particularly desirable, owing to the necessity for turning sharp curves at all rates of speed while heavily weighted.

The polygon, formed by lines joining the four points touched by the horse's feet standing at rest, is called the base of support. In motion this base of support becomes sometimes a triangle, at others a line, and finally, as in the run, a mere point.

The equilibrium is of course more stable as the base of support becomes larger, and the line of gravitation nearer the center of the base, and unstable under the contrary conditions. A broad or "square built" horse will have a condition of stable equilibrium greater than a narrow-chested horse, whose legs are close to the median plane. Both being at rest, the rectangle forming the base of support in the latter case will fall within the rectangle of the former, the length being the same.

While at rest all the legs are regarded as bearers, but when in motion the fore legs are the bearers, and the hind legs act essentially as propellers. To a certain extent, however, the fore legs assist propulsion, as the hind legs also assist in sustaining the weight.

Many of the conditions governing a horse's attitude in a state of rest continue to be equally imperative after action has commenced, and some even more so. It is more dangerous to the horse to lose his balance when in motion, especially at high rates of speed, than when standing still.

It is an established fact that race horses are favored in their stride by putting the jockey well forward, and the converse of this is true; that is, by weighting back there is a loss of propelling power, owing to the hind legs also becoming bearers. While speed is gained for short distances by adjusting the load forward, it will not do for service because of the rapid breaking down which occurs in the fore legs.

A mounted horse is said to be in equilibrium when he is capable of obeying the hands and legs of the rider without unnecessary effort, and with perfect freedom of the muscular groups whose action is necessary to produce the desired movements.

What has been shown to be true by actual experiments with live horses on proportion scales, may be illustrated in another way by a simple diagram.

Suppose the head and neck of the horse to occupy the position DA in Fig. 24; the relative weight would then be represented by the distance from N to I on the line DE, or IN. If the head and neck be lifted to the position DB, the relative weight will be represented by IN', and if still more elevated, to DC by IN''. The relative overhanging weight of the head and neck is diminished in proportion as their position is brought nearer to that represented by DC, and the further effect of this is to throw the center of gravity of the animal to the rear of its former position; that is, if the center of gravity is at F when the head and neck occupy the position DA, it will be moved to G when the head and neck are raised to the line DB, and further

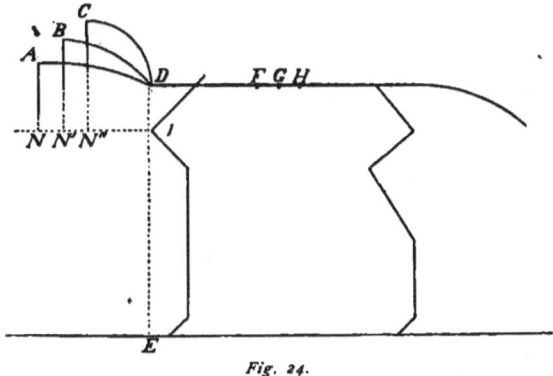

Fig. 24.

back to H when the head and neck are raised to the position DC.

A horse's neck is flexible to a certain extent, and the head which forms no inconsiderable portion of the overhanging weight, can be bent at various angles to the neck. It is therefore practicable to diminish the preponderance of these members by altering their relative position as described above, and to diminish the distance at which the perpendicular falls outside the base line DE, by bending the neck, and also by causing the head to assume an acute angle with the neck, whether the latter be straight or curved.

The application of this knowledge renders it possible, in connection with proper bitting and saddling, to train cavalry horses to maintain their equilibrium at all gaits while carrying on their backs about one-fourth or more of their own weight.

In the foregoing the movement of the center of gravity has been considered only in a vertical direction. It also has a marked horizontal motion, its oscillations to the right and left at a walk and trot being quite regular, and constantly traveling in the direction of the fore foot which is about to support the weight.

In riding on curves, as in the riding school or circus, the horse and rider both lean towards the inside to bring the center of gravity in that direction, otherwise the animal would lose his balance and fall.

As a matter of fact the horse not only leans toward the inner side of the curve, but also turns his head in the same direction.

It has been shown that the center of gravity lies somewhat nearer the shoulders than the center of motion. It is a very natural question, therefore, as to whether the load should be adjusted so as to leave the center of gravity where nature placed it, or to move it further back.

That the horse instinctively changes the location of this center himself is shown in the way a loose horse travels. Horses on the range moving along at a walk almost invariably hang their heads down slightly, and on a march they do the same thing. When they strike into a trot every head will go up at once. If anything causes the herd to break into a gallop, so long as they remain at a hand gallop their heads may continue as at a trot, but as soon as the stride becomes lengthened into a fast gallop or run, the heads will be straightened out and lowered again. Either straightening out or lowering the head brings forward the center of gravity.

If there were no other conditions to be met than those involving progress in a forward direction, no reason would exist for any alteration of the horse's natural balance; but there are many things which have to be taken into consideration which influence the fixing of an artificial balance of the saddle animal, particularly the cavalry horse.

It is necessary to establish the horse in such equilibrium that he may execute all the movements of drill with promptness and accuracy, and with a minimum of fatigue to himself and rider. This involves quick turns without decreasing the gait, which latter the horse in nature nearly always does.

To use a saber on horseback it is necessary to have the horse balanced more with a view to quick turns on the hind rather than the forehand.

One reason exists for throwing the balance of the horse somewhat to the rear, which alone makes it expedient to do so. This is the necessity for preventing the front feet and legs from becoming prematurely ruined. It is not a matter of theory merely, but a well known result of actual experience, that horses carrying weights upon their backs become broken down in front, as a rule, long before they suffer any deterioration of the hind legs.

The date of breaking down is much hastened by saddling far forward over the withers, and by an improper use of the stirrups, which will be explained later.

CHAPTER VI.

GAITS OF THE HORSE.

Motion Implies Displacement of Center of Gravity.—Natural Gaits.—Stride and Step.—The Walk.—The Trot.—The Hand Gallop.—The Gallop; True, False, Disconnected.—Fatigue Somewhat Dependent on Motion of Center of Gravity.—The Jump.

The movement of the horse's body over the ground implies displacement of the center of gravity, which compels the legs to form new bases of support. The more unstable the equilibrium at any gait, the greater the speed for that particular gait. This arises from the simple fact that the more insecure the equilibrium is the quicker will the new base of support have to be formed.

The speed with which the body moves forward is in proportion to the speed with which the limbs are straightened out. Any excess of muscle beyond that required for the due working of the limbs is an impediment rather than an aid to speed.

There are four natural gaits, the walk, amble, trot and gallop; and several artificial gaits, being more or less variations of the natural gaits. Amongst these may be mentioned the running walk, a cross between the walk and trot; the single foot, distinguished by the posterior limbs moving in the order of the fast walk and the anterior ones in that of a trot, being an irregular gait, the characteristic rhythm of the footfall of which, once learned, will be easily recognized, even in the dark; and, finally, the common canter, in which the horse is said to gallop in front and trot behind.

Marches, drills and maneuvers are performed at varying degrees of speed, but the only authorized and desirable gaits are the walk, trot and gallop. Especially should officers' horses be trained to perform these gaits at the regulation rate of speed per mile. Nothing else is so trying to the temper of, or so productive of discomfort to the men in ranks, as an officer leading the column on a horse with a running walk instead of a square walk, or a single foot instead of a trot.

It may be remarked that in the analysis of the gaits it will be found that no two animals will show the same imprints at any particular gait, and the same horse even will be found to vary greatly in a few strides.

By stride is understood the distance from the print of one foot to the print of the same foot when it next comes to the ground, in contradistinction to step which relates to the forward or backward movement of one limb only.

These modifications depend entirely upon the conditions in which the animal is placed, for the horse instinctively alters the position of his supports to accommodate his

108   HORSES, SADDLES AND BRIDLES.

PLATE VI.

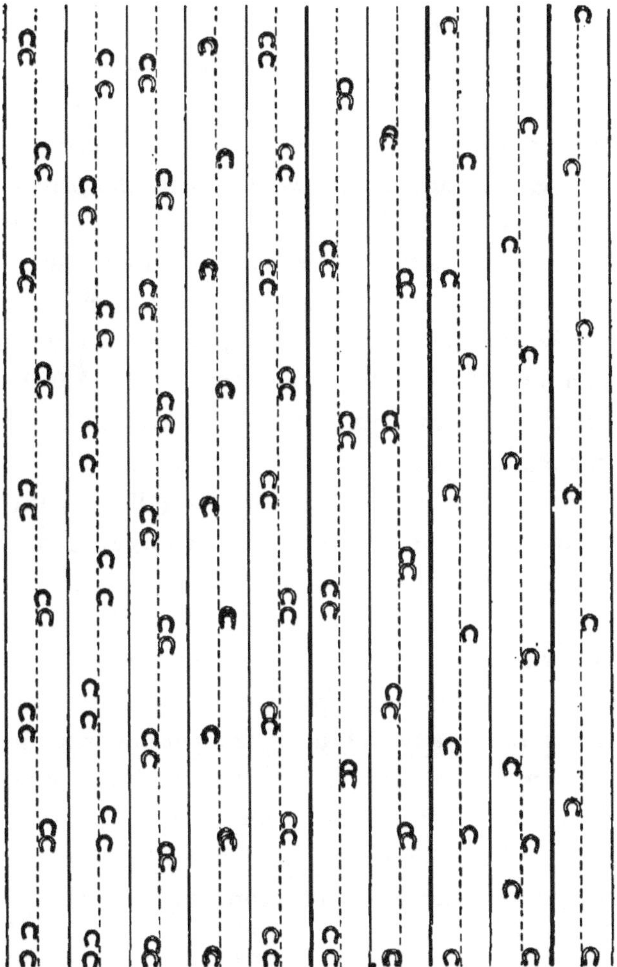

A   B   C   D   E   A'   C'   A''   C'''   A'''

equilibrium, which may be slightly but continually varied by his rider. This is especially noticeable in the line of footprints made at a gallop. In this case the horse is supported by one limb at a time, and it is essential that the variations of the center of gravity from side to side should be promptly met by corresponding variations of the points of supports, as well as the variations in a forward direction.

In Plate VI the dark shoes represent the prints of the hind feet. A, B and C represent the trails made by three good cavalry horses taken from the troop stable, and walked over a prepared track. D and E are trails drawn on the same scale, to illustrate the superposed imprints, and the case of a horse which steps short with his hind feet.

A' and C' are the trails made at a trot by the horses used for A and C.

A'' and C'' are the trails made at a gallop by the same horses, and A''' is the trail made at a fast gallop or run by the same horse used for A, A' and A''.

When the horse started over C'' the track was wet near the end, which caused him to take short steps.

The Walk.—This gait is above all others the cavalry gait, since the heavy weight of trooper and pack necessitates its use to a far greater extent than all the other gaits combined. Unfortunately it is not practicable to determine the ability of the horse as a walker by his conformation. The walk of most horses is improved by service in the ranks.

A good walk is characterized by a high rather than low carriage of the head. The fore legs should be carried forward freely and directly, without undue elevation of the knees. The hind legs should act in planes parallel to those in which the fore legs move. The hoofs should be planted squarely, and remain in place without rotating inward or outward. The prints of the hind feet should appear on the ground in front of those of the fore feet, and the intervals between them on one side should be the same as on the other. External influences operate in this connection, however, for the prints of the hind feet will sometimes be found superposed upon those of the front, and at other times to fall behind them. (*A*, *B*, *C*, *D* and *E*, Plate VI.)

The walk is a gait of four flat beats, each foot being planted in regular order. If the right fore foot first comes to the ground, the left hind foot is next planted; then the left fore foot, and finally the right hind' foot. During this movement the weight is borne first by the two fore feet and the right hind foot; then by the right fore foot and the right hind foot; then by the two hind feet and the right fore foot; and lastly by the left fore foot and the right hind foot.

The theory of the horse's walk is that there should be two feet upon the ground while the diagonal ones are being advanced, and if the legs moved synchronously in pairs, there would be four feet on the ground for a brief time at each step. It is more difficult to maintain equilibrium in a slow movement than a fast, and in the walk the diagonal limbs do not act synchronously, because it is necessary for one of the reserve feet to hold to the ground until the other has the start, in order to shorten or eliminate the instant of time in which the center of gravity would have but two points of support.

The center of gravity always falls near the intersection of the lines connecting the diagonal feet, but within the triangle connecting the three feet furnishing support.

If the horse be collected between the hand and heels of its rider, the movement that results is the safest of all for rough or slippery ground. The horse has never less than two, and never more than three feet, bearing the weight at the same time, and when he quickens his movement he does not at once change his gait, but extends his strides, and makes them more uniform until further extension becomes difficult, when he will break into a trot.

The Trot.— In the trot the footfalls mark two sharp beats, and the horse springs from one pair of diagonally disposed legs to the other pair, and is entirely free from the ground between each step, except in the short trot. If the trot depends simply upon this united action of a fore leg and its diagonal hind leg, the pace may be very slow, but if the speed be such that the stride is too long for the fore feet to remain upon the ground together, the true trot results, and the horse goes into the air from each pair of diagonal bearers alternately. The jog trot is a hybrid gait, and is not performed this way.

The theory of the trot is the same as the walk, but adapted to a higher rate of speed. It differs from a walk, in that the horse has always two feet upon the ground at a walk, while at the trot there is always a space of time in which all the feet are off the ground.

The weight is borne by the diagonally disposed limbs alternately, and the step being supposed to be a constant quantity in the fast trot, the stride can be extended only by increasing the space which the body passes over with its center of gravity unsupported. In the ordinary trot this distance is small, but in the fast trot it exceeds that in which the body is supported.

In the ordinary trot the imprints of the hind feet are superposed upon those of the front feet, but many horses, especially young and untrained ones, bring their hind feet more or less ahead of the prints of the fore feet. This is easily seen by hoof-marks on moist ground. (A' and C', Plate VI.)

There are other horses that instead of overstepping, come short of the track of the fore feet with the hind ones.

Those that overstep will usually be found to be such as are overweighted on the forehand, whilst those that step short are usually such as are overweighted behind or that have some weakness or other defect in their hind quarters.

While the trot is not designed by nature to be the fastest gait, it is the one in which the average horse is capable of traveling farther in a day's journey, with less fatigue, than any other. It is now adopted as the maneuvering gait for cavalry, and has grown much in favor as a marching gait, for the reason that, when not too heavily weighted, the horse completes the march in a shorter time, is then entirely relieved of his load, and given more time for rest and feeding.

A moderate trot is less fatiguing to horses than any other gait on account of the diagonal pairs of legs being used as bearers and propellers alternately. Some horses will, however, when ridden, break into a canter, because the alternate shifting of their own and rider's weight from right to left becomes more fatiguing than the constant use of each pair of legs for the same purpose.

Horses overweighted on the forehand and hurried in a trot, being unable to support the weight thrown more and more rapidly on their fore legs, break into a canter or gallop.

Hand Gallop.—The difference between the slow gallop and the fast gallop, or running gait, is sufficient to cause them to be mentioned separately. The hand gallop is a gait in which if the weight is received upon the left hind foot, it next falls upon the right hind and left fore, and then upon the right fore foot. It is a gait of three beats, inasmuch as the second period of contact is marked by the diagonally opposite hind and fore feet coming down together.

The trail made by the horse at this gait is entirely different from that at the fast gallop, but in passing from one to the other the rider does not perceive any disunited or violent action akin to that which takes place in passing from a trot to a gallop, and the reverse. The horse simply extends himself, gradually if not urged, and passes imperceptibly to the gait in which a diagonal pair of feet no longer come down together, and which will be described as the gallop. The horse leads with a fore leg, which does not act with the diagonal hind leg.

The Gallop.—This is the most rapid of gaits, and is taken when the propulsion from the hind quarters becomes so vigorous as to shift the center of gravity, and prevent the balance necessary for the performance of any of the other gaits. It has heretofore been the least understood of all.

The most perfect method of quadrupedal locomotion is that in which the greatest speed is attained with the least expenditure of vital force. This is found in the horse in which the deviation of the line of motion from the horizontal is least. Perfect locomotion requires uniform support to the center of gravity and continuous propulsion. The fast gallop or run more nearly fulfills these conditions than any other gait.

The drawings (Plate VII), introduced to show the action of the horse in performing the galloping stride, are from the MUYBRIDGE photographs, as shown in "The Horse In Motion," and may be relied upon for accuracy of representation.

The center of gravity is supposed to be under the saddle. Fig. 1 of the drawings represents the rider and horse ready to start. The horse goes into the air from a fore foot (Figs. 2, 3 and 4); receives the weight upon the diagonal hind foot (Fig. 5); then plants the other hind foot (Figs. 6 and 7); then taking the weight upon the latter, extends

HORSES, SADDLES AND BRIDLES.

PLATE VII.

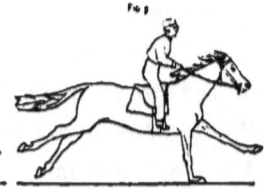

himself and plants the diagonal fore foot (Fig. 8); takes the weight upon the latter, and then plants the other fore foot (Figs. 9, 10, 11 and 12), which then alone sustains the weight until the center of gravity passes over it, when the horse again goes into the air, to alight upon the diagonal hind foot, planted in front of the spot just vacated by the last mentioned fore foot.

The imprints left upon the ground by a fast galloping horse follow each other very nearly in a straight line. This indicates a minimum size, in a transverse direction, of the base of support, and consequently great instability, as well as speed. (A'', C'' and A''', Plate VI.)

So long as the horse goes upon a straight course it matters little whether the gallop is effected upon one foot or the other, although the horse often takes advantage of a slackening in his speed to change the order of succession of his feet, most probably to ease up on a fatigued member.

It is quite different, however, when the course is curvilinear. A centrifugal force is developed, which is so much stronger as the velocity of the gait is greater, and the curve shorter. The horse is therefore obliged to incline himself towards the inner side of the trail to counteract this force. In view of a fall, which is always imminent, he must steady his equilibrium on that side by the foothold of the corresponding propelling member; the right if the course turn to the right, the left if it turn to the left.

The gallop is disunited when the horse leads with his fore feet in an inverse manner to the movement of his hind feet; that is, if he gallops to the right with his fore feet, his hind feet will move as if he were galloping to the left. The right fore foot would lead, and the left hind be the last to leave the ground, whereas in the united gallop, if the right fore foot leads, the right hind should be the last to leave the ground.

The horse gallops disunited rarely, and with great difficulty. It usually occurs when the horse tries to effect a change of lead, and is suddenly interfered with. It causes much discomfort to the rider, and cannot be continued by the horse for any length of time.

The gallop is called true when it is effected upon the right foot when the horse turns to the right. It is called false under contrary conditions, that is, when the horse gallops to the right on a curve while leading with his left fore foot.

In consequence of the regular alternation of the members at a walk and trot, the work performed by each diagonal pair is identical, but in the gallop this is not the case. In galloping to the right, the right fore and hind limbs in turn support the body for a longer period than the limbs of the other side. The hind limb on which the body falls has to sustain more than the fore limb, which supports it only before the phase of projection. It follows, that in order to distribute the work equally upon the horse's limbs, the rider should take the precaution to change his lead from time to time. This may be accomplished by bending the horse's head towards the side with which he may be leading; this will compel him to lead with the opposite side or lose his equilibrium. The horse should of course be pulled up somewhat to enable him to make the change.

The fatigue of the horse at any gait will depend very much upon the movement of his center of gravity. If this center varies but little from a horizontal line the strength is not expended as rapidly as when there is great variation, for the same amount of lifting is not required. In the first case the horse goes level, with great freedom of action, and should produce little fatigue to himself or rider. In the second case, the rider being lifted vertically through a considerable distance at every stride, the gait is not smooth; the connection between horse and rider is not closely maintained, and the horse is characterized as "rough."

If the horse be urged at any gait to continually extend himself beyond his ordinary capacity, it will be more fatiguing to him than if permitted to take the next faster gait.

The Jump.— Although leaping is a mode of progression, it is not a continuous one, and cannot be properly considered a gait. All quadrupeds in a wild state acquire a knowledge of jumping as a matter of necessity, but the horse of civilization, especially when carrying a rider, requires considerable training and good handling in order to enable him to surmount difficult obstacles.

Some horses can jump while at a trot, or even from a standing position, but the majority of horses can perform

HORSES, SADDLES AND BRIDLES. 119

THE JUMP.

Preparation.

Impulsion.

Passing the Obstacle.

Descent in front.

Descent behind.

Fig. 25

satisfactorily only at a gallop sufficiently slow to enable the animal to measure well the height of the obstruction, or length of the leap he is expected to make.

Approaching an obstruction at a run (Fig. 25), the horse betrays his anxiety by shortening his steps, advancing with both hind feet nearly simultaneously, until sufficiently near to take off. He then brings his hind feet well under the center of gravity, and instantly the fore leg on the ground is propelled upward to raise the forehand, and this action is immediately followed by energetic propulsion of the hind legs, sufficient to lift the weight to the height required, not only to surmount the obstacle, but to carry the long body of the horse entirely over.

The hind extremities from the extreme of tension on leaving the ground, pass to the opposite extreme of flexion as they go over the obstacle, and both fore and both hind as they pass are so nearly in unison that they appear together in pairs. After passing the obstacle the fore legs separate, in order not to make contact with the ground at the same time. One of the fore legs is extended to check the force of the descent, which, from the loss of horizontal motion, has little more than the momentum of gravity to deal with. This is the instant of great danger to the pastern joint and flexor tendons; but be-

Fig. 26.

fore these parts are put to the extreme test the other fore leg comes to the relief of its fellow, and immediately after the hind extremities, one after the other, are planted under the center of gravity, and by their great lifting force relieve the front limbs. All the limbs are now free to act their various parts in the gallop as before the jump.

The trail made by the horse in leaping the hedge is shown in Fig. 26.

CHAPTER VII.

BITS.

Classified as Bar: Snaffle and Curb.—The Mouthing: Pelham; Whitman.—Bit and Bridoon.—Horse's Mouth Structurally Considered: Curb Groove; Jaw Bone; Tongue Channel; Bars.—Temperament of Mouth: Normal; Tender; Hard; Spoiled.—Dimensions Considered in Fitting Curb Bits: Width of Mouth; Width of Tongue Channel; Height of Bars.—The Curb Bit: Its Action as a Lever; Proportions of Upper and Lower Branches; Falling Through; Standing Stiff; Angle at Which Reins Act on Bit; Position of Curb Chain; Width and Length; Form and Proportions of Mouth-Piece; Attachment of Headstalls.—American, British and European Cavalry Bits.

There is an endless variety of bits, many of which have been successfully designed to meet the wants of particular cases, and subsequently advertised as panaceas for all forms of restiveness arising from bad bitting. Such articles have a period of popularity more or less brief, and are then cast aside for some later innovation, which, probably like its predecessor, contains none of the essential elements of a good bit.

For the purpose of discussion, bits may be arranged under three general classes:

First. Bar bits, or bits with solid mouth-pieces without lever action, and in which a minimum of pressure on the bar, and a maximum on the tongue, is obtained. This is the lightest form of bit, and is used on driving rather than saddle horses.

Second. Snaffle bits, or those with jointed mouth-pieces, which is the oldest, most generally used, and satisfactory of all forms of bit ever devised.

Third. Curb bits, in which lever action is obtained to increase the amount of pressure brought to bear upon the bars of the horse's mouth.

Bar bits are usually made with a straight or very slightly curved mouth-piece, with a medium sized ring at either end, and sometimes with half cheek pieces also. (No. 1, Plate VIII.) They are sometimes made with cheek pieces similar to those on curb bits (No. 2, Plate VIII), but as no curb chains or straps are used, the pressure on the bars is not increased, but rather diminished, since some of it is transferred through the cheek straps to the top of the head or poll. Many of the driving bits have the mouth-pieces covered with rubber; a chain bit so covered is shown with part of the rubber removed in No. 3, Plate VIII.

Of all instruments employed in the handling, riding and driving of horses, the common smooth snaffle bit with one joint (No. 5, Plate VIII), is by far the best. For training the saddle horse it should be of the simplest form, neither too long, too thin, nor too much curved, and each half should be tapered down from the outside to the middle in such a way as to have the part which presses on the bars of the mouth about the size in diameter of the mouth-piece of the curb bit. The snaffle bit should act on the same

PLATE VIII.

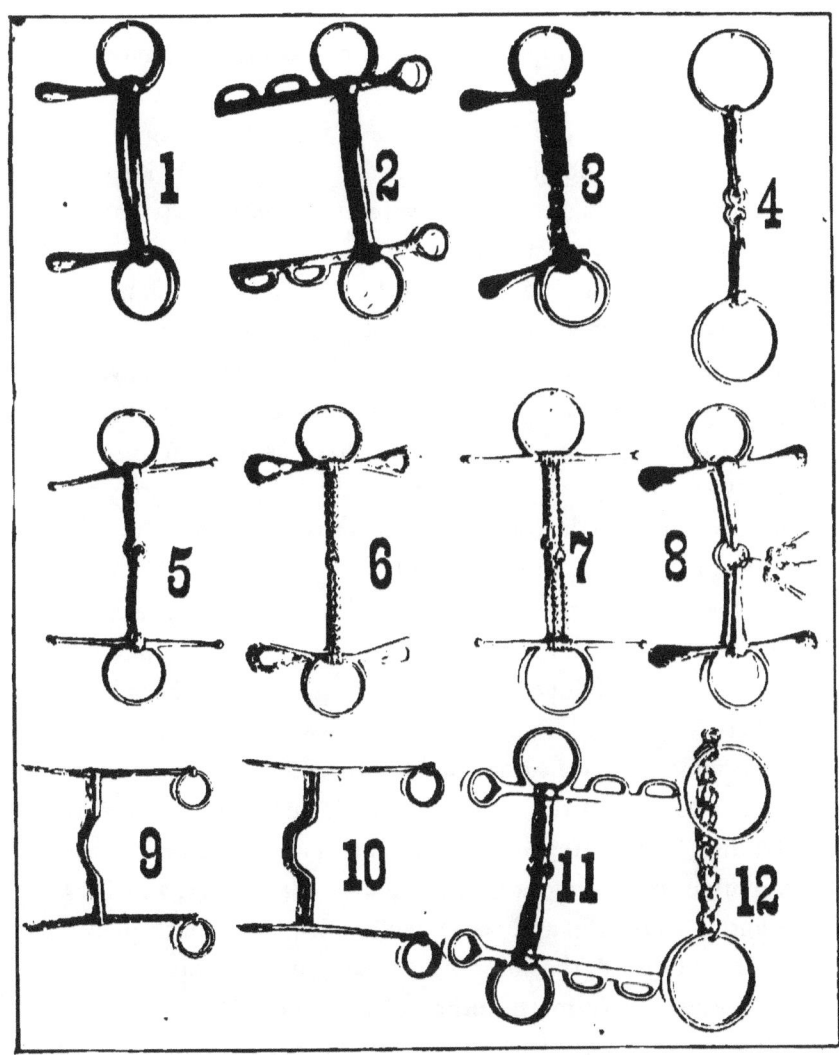

part of the mouth that the curb bit does. The horse thus acquires familiarity with, and an insight into, the means by which the rider proposes to direct and control his motions subsequently.

The action of the mouth-piece is on the tongue and bars both, and not being harsh or painful, the horse soon acquires a regular and steady feeling, known as "taking the bit." This must not be confounded with the expression "taking the bit between his teeth," which is frequently applied to runaway horses without good reason, for it is not believed a horse actually seizes the bit, but he may, by poking out his nose, bring the bit back to rest against his molars and the callous corners of his lips, thus almost entirely removing the pressure from the bars; or, he may put his lower lip outside of one branch of the curb bit, and thus prevent harsh pressure on the bars.

There is no lever action with a snaffle bit. There is a slight pincer action on the bars, but the power applied to the reins is conveyed unaltered in quantity to the horse's mouth.

Snaffle bits are often made with rings only, the cheek pieces being omitted. This form is more common with driving than riding bits. They are sometimes made with a double-jointed mouth-piece (No. 4, Plate VIII, and Nos. 3 and 4, Plate X), and occasionally with two mouth-pieces, plain or twisted, the joint of one being on the opposite side of the center from the other (No. 7, Plate VIII). Then there is the single-twisted wire snaffle bit, a very efficacious instrument for ruining the horse's mouth when used by brutal riders who pull alternately on the reins and literally saw the bars and lips (No. 6, Plate VIII); and still another contrivance called a bit, but in reality two rings connected by a chain (No. 12, Plate VIII).

Many of the so-called improvements on the snaffle bit are based entirely on the assumption that the only object of bits is to inflict pain, which is directly contrary to the principles of rational bitting. The whip and spur are the only recognized and legitimate instruments of the horseman for punishment.

The mouthing bit (No. 8, Plate VIII) is intended for use on young colts during the first period of training. The mouth-piece is very large at the outer ends, with a gradual tapering to the ring joint, to which are attached three small metal tags suspended on a thin plate. The mouth-piece being thick near the guards, is not apt to wound the tender bars and lips of the young horse. The tags hang upon and tickle the tongue, and cause the colt to champ the bit, as it is called. As the horse is incapable of many ideas at a time, it tends to keep his mind occupied while he is undergoing the process of being familiarized with strange sights and sounds. This bit is made with full cheek pieces, to prevent the rings from being drawn into the mouth.

Upon the gentle application of this and the plain snaffle to the colt's mouth, much of the future usefulness of the mature horse depends.

Curb bits are made in a multiplicity of shapes, many of which are ingeniously contrived to produce pain on the roof of the horse's mouth, as well as on the bars. These bits are known to the trade as "port bits," but this does not properly characterize the bit, inasmuch as a curb bit may in its lightest form have no port or curve of the mouthpiece.

The upper branch of the cheek piece is always straight, but the lower branches may be straight, single or double curved.

The details and principles governing the construction of curb bits will be discussed later. A curb bit with straight cheeks and a similar bit with square top port and lip strap holes are shown in Nos. 9 and 10, Plate VIII.

There is a hybrid bit, called Pelham, used both for driving and riding. The mouth-piece is jointed, either like the common snaffle bit or like a pair of compasses. This bit is called the compass canon in books on the horse of two hundred years ago. A driving Pelham is shown in No. 11, Plate VIII.

It has the cheek pieces of the curb bit, and is used with chain or curb strap. It is supposed to possess the virtues of that bit without its severity. As it is provided with guard rings, it can be used with two pairs of reins, in the one case simulating the snaffle bit, and the other the curb bit, but in both cases the action is inferior to that of the ordinary snaffle and curb bits, used separately or in combination as "bit and bridoon." It is, however, a very useful bit for some horses.

The curb bit known as the Whitman is somewhat similar to the Chifney bit, which was invented in England about the end of the last century. The upper branches of the bit are double, one set carrying the curb chain or strap, and the other being attached to the cheek pieces of the bridle. A pull on the reins acts to tighten the curb directly, without any pressure on the top of the head. This is provided for by the free motion of the mouth-piece in the circular opening in the lower ends of the upper branches of the cheek piece. The use of this bit with the halter bridle seems the most simple and serviceable arrangement possible, and a great many have been used in the service from time to time. The reins are attached to the bit, and when the bit is unsnapped from the headstall the latter becomes a

Fig. 27

halter. This does away with the bridle as an extra equipment, and is in the line of simplicity. (Plate XVI.)

The snaffle bit, called bridoon, which is used in combination with a curb bit, has a mouth-piece of smaller diameter than is generally the case when the snaffle bit is used alone, and has only rings, no cheek pieces, at the outer ends. There are two cheek straps on each side of the headstall, into which are buckled the two bits. The curb is buckled to the front straps, and the bridoon to the rear straps, and a trifle higher than the curb bit. (Fig. 27.)

If the curb bit was attached to the rear straps the bridoon would be constantly working against it, instead of on the bars of the horse's mouth.

There is little doubt but that a double-reined bridle, with bit and bridoon, is the most rational, humane and serviceable arrangement for all classes of riding which involve cross-country work and sudden changes of gaits, but it has never found favor in the American army. As simplicity is desired in all equipments, it has been deemed best to use only one pair of reins attached to a medium curb bit, arranged for average horses.

Before proceeding with the discussion of the curb bit, some points relative to the horse's mouth will be considered.

Referring to Plate I, it will be observed that the bony portions of the head are covered unequally by the soft parts—muscles, skin and membranes. The practical importance of this depends on the different degrees of sensibility to pressure that results from varieties of conformation.

The lower lip is covered with a very thick skin, underneath which lie the roots of the beard, fat and membrane, and this structure is continued up into a depression under the chin, known as the chin groove, or curb groove. The portion of bone immediately beneath the thick, and not very sensitive, skin of the chin groove, is flat and rounded off in all directions, being in fact the point where the two branches of the jaw begin to unite together. If a flat curb chain, or strap which has a proper width, act in this groove, a considerable amount of pressure may be applied without causing any pain to the horse.

Immediately above this groove, towards the angle of the jaw, the character of the bone and that of the skin covering it are very much changed; the former has sharp edges, and the latter is very thin and sensitive, so that a slight pressure of this thin skin on the sharp edges of bone causes very considerable pain. These peculiarities must be borne in mind in order to properly bit a horse, for pieces of the bone are frequently broken off, and cause suppuration for long periods.*

---

*A fine young horse has been under treatment in my troop for nearly two years for "broken jaw," caused by undue severity in the use of the Shoemaker curb bit. At the present time the opening under the jaw is still discharging, although the surrounding parts have become permanently enlarged to such an extent that there is no longer any curb groove visible. The only description found of such a case occurs in an old French book, published in 1691, entitled "Parfait Marechal par De Solleysol, Ecuyer."

In examining the horse's mouth, it is perceived that the lower jaw consists of two triangular cheek bones, whose anterior branches form a groove or channel in which the animal's tongue lies. Towards its root it is enclosed between the two rows of molar teeth; further forward, by those portions of the jaw that lie between the points where the molar teeth cease and the incisors commence.

These parts of the jaw on either side devoid of teeth, except the tusks, are called the bars, and are of interest chiefly because it is somewhere upon them that the bit must be placed. So far as the bars are concerned, or the bit itself, its location could be varied an inch or more; this, however, is limited on account of the position of the curb groove, which governs the whole arrangement.

This work also contains a most complete and illustrated dissertation on bits and bitting:

"When the bridle bears too harshly on the jaws, either through the fault of the rider's hand or otherwise, the jaw becomes wounded or broken by it. If the sore is small and the bone not broken, we should rub the parts with honey eight or ten times a day. If the bone is broken, and while passing the finger over it we find a point that pricks, or where an ulcer may be formed, take a little pledget of cotton, saturated with vitriol, and introduce it in the hole. The next and following days rub the sore with rose or common honey; the slough will fall off, and the splints of bone will drop from the bone. The slough having fallen off, put on the sore place frequently some brandy or a little sugar. * * * If there is a hole in the jaws, accompanied by a gangrenous matter and offensive odor, fill it with crushed sugar three or four times a day. The hole will close up and the jaw will heal, but we must use a simple snaffle, or other bit which will no longer hurt the horse, and lay aside absolutely the bit which has hurt him, on pain of destroying his mouth beyond recourse. If the tongue is hurt the bit must be changed, and one given him which will allow free use of the tongue.

"The bone of the jaw is sometimes strangely broken. It may be shattered under the skin of the jaw; matter forms there which rots the bone, and as nature seeks to get rid of this corrupting matter, it rots the skin at the place in the jaw, and causes a swelling or tumor with ulcerous matter, in order to give an outlet," etc.

It is self-evident that horses' mouths are not all alike; therefore each individual horse requires a bit adapted to the particular dimensions, conformation and temperament in general of its mouth.

The bit is an apparatus of restraint, which by its pressure, more or less severe, on the bars and chin, causes pain of variable intensity. The temperament is judged by the reaction in consequence of this pain.

The mouth is normal when it supports the bit with freedom, without uneasiness, pain or fear; when it neither resists nor yields too easily to the action of the hand.

The mouth is tender, sensitive, or easy, when it perceives the most delicate impressions of the hand, and responds to them with promptness.

The mouth is hard when it yields only to energetic pulls on the reins.

A spoiled mouth is one which reacts falsely to the indications of the bit, whatever may be its sensibility otherwise. Horses' mouths rendered excessively callous by bad bitting and indifferent riders usually come under this class.

Aside from the effects produced by variations of temperament in the horse, it is the bars that must be examined for an explanation of these varieties of mouth, for it is upon these more or less sensitive gums that the action of all bits fall to a greater or less extent.

While there is great uniformity in the absolute height of the bars, there is on the other hand a very great diversity in their shape and texture. Some are sharp, fine, firm and sensitive; others are broad, flat-topped, coarse and devoid of much feeling. The former characterize tender and the latter hard-mouthed horses.

As a rule well-bred horses have the first, and common horses have the second kind of bars, but it does not follow that the former all have tender and the latter hard mouths, for much depends upon individual sensibility. The first is usually found in combination with a thin tongue which just fills the channel, thus permitting the mouth-piece to exercise its proper action on the bars. The second, on the contrary, is generally found with a coarse, thick tongue, which more than fills the channel, protruding so high as to take the pressure off the bars to a great extent.

There are three dimensions of the interior of the horse's mouth, which must be ascertained before attempting to fit him accurately with a proper bit, namely:

First. The transversal width of the mouth from outside to outside of the lips, measured at the height of the chin groove.

Second. The width of the channel or groove in which the tongue lies, or the distance between the two bars.

Third. The height of the bars, or the distance between two straight edges, one placed across the bars under the tongue, and the other parallel to it, and tangent to the curb groove.

The first measures the length of the mouth-piece of the curb bit, which must fit exactly. If too short the lips are subject to injury, and if too long it slips from side to side, and allows the corners of the port to come against and bruise the bars.

The width of the mouth is a very variable quantity, depending much upon the breed, as well as the size of the horse. It varies from about three and a half to five and a half inches; the larger dimension is seldom found in good saddle horses of average size. The cheek pieces should fit snugly without pressing in the lips, and the top rings should be bent outward slightly, to allow for the double thickness of the lower ends of the cheek pieces of the bridle when buckled into them.

The second, which is the tongue channel, determines how much of the mouth-piece must be allowed for the width of the port of the curb bit, the remainder being reserved for the action on the bars. This channel has been found to be nearly always three-fourths the height of the bars, or one and one-third inches, which gives the maximum width of the port; for if the mouth-piece have the proper width, and the port be made wider than the tongue channel, one or both corners of the port would come against the bars, and produce intolerable pain to no purpose whatever. The depth of the channel should be proportional to the volume of the tongue, otherwise a vicious position of the bit, which cannot be corrected, may ensue from the overlapping portions of the tongue not being properly accommodated in the channel.

The form and volume of the tongue may be varied by the muscular action which permits of extension, retraction, elevation, etc. In a normal condition it should lie in the channel. It helps to support the bit, and receives its first action when power is applied to the reins. It is a very delicate organ, and subject to lacerations of a painful character unless care is taken to prevent such occurrences. The integrity or entireness of the tongue should receive careful attention in connection with bitting. It is no uncommon thing to find troop horses with tongue cut a quarter or half way across. A proper bit will not do this if used in a legitimate way, but almost any curb bit will do so if the horse be hitched to a post by the reins, and startled in such a way as to make him pull back suddenly.

The third, which is termed the height of the bars, is the most important, because all the dimensions of the curb bit are proportional to it. The height of the bars has been found to be quite uniform in all horses, being about one and three-fourths inches; and this measure has been accepted as the proper length of the upper branch of the cheek piece of the curb bit, measured from the center of the mouth-piece rivet to the point of the upper ring at which the curb chain or strap acts when pressure is applied; this gives a total length of the upper cheek piece of about two and one-half inches for all but very large horses.

The conditions surrounding the cavalryman demand that he shall be provided with a bit, which, while allowing him to guide his horse in the lightest possible manner, will yet provide him with ample power to bring the animal to a halt from the charge in the shortest practicable time.

A properly constructed curb bit is the only one possessing these properties.

In the curb bit the mechanical advantage of lever action is obtained. There are several kinds of levers, and it will depend on the manner in which the bit and curb chain are arranged, whether or not the lever action obtained is favorable or the contrary.

In a lever of the first order the power is applied at one end, the weight being placed at the other, and the fulcrum between the two; the power and weight move around the fulcrum in opposite directions.

In a lever of the second order the power and fulcrum are placed at the opposite extremities of the lever, the weight being between the two. The power and weight move in the same direction in rotating around the fulcrum.

Applying these mechanical facts to the bit, the cheek pieces of which represent the lever, it is observed that in the first case, the power being applied through the reins to the lower ring, the bars become the fulcrum, and the weight to be raised is represented by the curb chain. As the power and weight move in opposite directions, it follows from a pull on the reins that the curb should move forward; in other words, the stronger the pull on the reins the more the horse should stick out his nose. This is exactly what is not wanted, but which often happens.

In a lever of the second order, the power being applied through the reins to the lower ring, the tightened curb chain acting as a fulcrum, the weight is represented by the pressure on the bars, and the horse's head follows in the direction of the rider's hand, and this is the action desired.

It is evident that, as the direction in which the bit acts depends altogether on the relative amount of painful pressure exercised by the mouth-piece and curb chain, the horse's head will follow the rider's hand, even though the chain lacerate his chin, if only a greater amount of pain be applied to the bars.

It is quite possible to adjust curb bits so as to get sufficient power on the bars without undue pain on the chin groove; in this way bits of small dimensions are made sufficiently reliable in their action to insure efficiency, with a minimum of discomfort to the horse.

The important points to be determined are the length of the cheek pieces, and the relative proportions of the upper and lower branches.

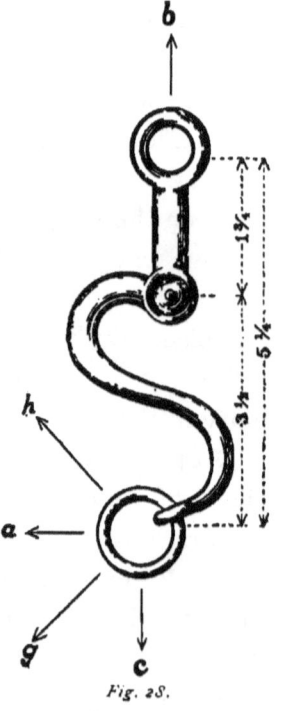

Fig. 28.

The height of the bars, or one and three-fourths inches for all but exceptionally large horses, is adopted as the measure for the upper branch of the cheek piece. This measure is taken from a line passing through the center of the straight portions of the mouth-piece to the point of the upper ring, where the curb hook acts.

The lower branch of the cheek piece should be made exactly twice as long as the upper branch; that is, from the same line as before to a line passing through the center of the lower ring (Fig. 28).

If a curb bit is put into a horse's mouth without attaching a curb chain or strap to it, when the reins are pulled the bit turns round, and its cheek pieces come to lie in the same line as the reins. There is no lever action whatever, because there is no prop or fulcrum, and a snaffle would, on account of its center joint, be more efficient. The same thing will partially happen with a very loose curb chain or strap. The bit is then said to "fall through."

The opposite fault to this is when the bit "stands stiff," without any play, the slightest pull on the reins causing the horse pain externally, or just in the wrong place. This stiffness is often produced by a tight curb strap, and the horse, instead of following the rider's hand, pokes out his nose. Good bitting lies between these two extremes, equally removed from stiffness and falling through.

The length of the upper branch of the cheek piece will of itself cause this instrument either to stand stiff or fall through, according as it exceeds or falls short of the height of the bars of the mouth, as shown in Fig. 29, where de represents the height of the bars, db an upper branch equal to de, dc one of only half the same length, and da one double the length. When a pull of the rein acts at f on the lower branch, the curb will be drawn closer to the chin, and the mouth-piece back against the bars; and supposing the amount of this closing up in all three instances to be equal, the bit with a long upper branch da, will assume the position $a'df'$. It will be stiff, and the curb acting upwards in the direction ea', will press on the sensitive part of the jaw. There will be no lever action;

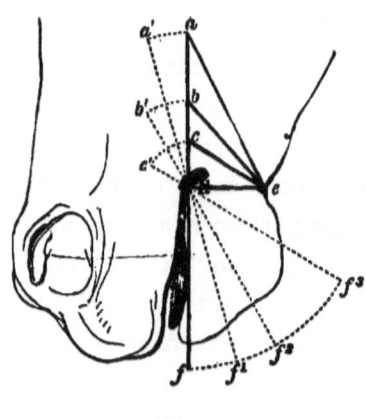

Fig. 29.

the two arms of the lever being equal, and the horse will bore in the rider's hand.

On the other hand, the bit with the short upper branch dc, equal half de, will assume the position $c'df^3$—that is, it will fall through. The curb chain or strap will remain in the chin groove, and act forward in the direction ec', but forming a very acute angle with the branches of the bit itself, will have scarcely any value as a fulcrum. The lever action, however, will be very great; in fact, it will be too great.

The intermediate upper branch db, equal de, will assume the position $b'df^2$; it will neither be stiff nor fall through; the curb will remain in the chin groove, acting obliquely forward in the line eb', and will afford a sufficient support; and the lower branch of the lever, fd, being in the proportion of two to one to the upper one, db, there will be sufficient lever action.

In order to prevent a bit with a very short upper branch

from falling through, riders are driven to using a very tight curb, the result of which is that the whole action is transplanted from the interior of the mouth to the chin; also, in order to prevent one with a very long upper branch standing stiff, they use a very loose curb, which has the effect of making the bit fall through.

The angle at which the reins act on the bit is a matter of importance. In the case of a lever, the action is most favorable when the power is applied at a right angle. If the bit (Fig. 28) were pulled in the direction of c it would have no other effect than to pull it downwards and out of the horse's mouth, unless prevented by the headstall. If the pull were made in the direction b, it would only lift the bit up till the angles of the mouth stopped it. In neither case would there be the slightest lever action. It is therefore evident that the direction a, which is equally remote from both, must be the most efficient, and this is precisely at a right angle to the lever.

Having adopted the height of the bars, or one and three-fourths inches, as the length of the upper branch of the bit, if the lower branch is made double that length, or three and a half inches, it will give lever power ample for all purposes of bitting the average horse. This gives a total length to the cheek pieces of five and one-fourth inches, measured from the point where the curb hook acts above to that where the lower ring acts below (Fig. 28).

Next to the dimensions of the cheek pieces of the bit, the most important to be considered is the curb chain, or rather the position of the bit in the horse's mouth, taken in conjunction with the curb chain. The curb chain must lie in the curb groove, without any tendency to mount up out of it on to the sharp bones of the lower jaw; otherwise it ceases to be a painless fulcrum, and renders the best constructed bit uncertain in its action.

The only way to attain painlessness of the curb, on which so much depends, is by placing the mouth-piece as nearly on that part of the bars opposite to the chin groove as possible. It is only in this position that the right angle triangle is secured, as shown in Fig. 29. There is also another reason, for that part of the bars which is best suited for the action of the mouth-piece is found here, just above the tusks.

It may be well to mention that there is considerable irregularity as to the position of the tusks in the mouth, and mares seldom have any at all. For this reason it is difficult to prescribe the position of the mouth-piece by any reference to them, except that the bit should not touch them.

The best fitting bit, even when placed in the correct position, will not act properly unless the curb chain be made correctly, and exactly of the right length. A double chain worked flat, without rough or sharp edges, is the best kind of curb for general use, although leather is used exclusively in the American service. The curb chains at one time issued were not properly made, and were abandoned for leather straps. The latter are subject to stretching and contraction, and are apt to be stiff and harsh after a few soakings in water, but they possess the one great advantage of being easily replaced or repaired, which is not the case with the chain.

It is not practicable to prescribe any fixed dimension for the width of the curb chain or strap. It should be made to lie in the curb groove without altogether filling it up. If very narrow it will cause pain, and if very broad it is liable to mount up and come in contact with the sharp cheek bones at every pull on the reins.

It is not practicable to prescribe the length of the curb chain or strap in inches. It will be found that the proper length for the curb is about one-fourth more than the width of the mouth, exclusive of curb hooks; or in case of a strap, the total length should be one and a half times the width of the mouth-piece. If, then, the mouth-piece have exactly the same width as the mouth, the curb strap will wrap close around the chin, pressing equally over a large surface. If, on the contrary, the mouth-piece is too wide, the chain or strap will bear more or less on a particular spot, and get up a sore in the curb groove.

The curb hooks for use with a chain must be flat, and shaped so as to hold the chain in place securely, and not cut the lips of the horse.

The mouth-piece, through which the immediate impression is made on the mouth, is of equal if not greater importance than any other part of the curb bit. It appeared advisable before discussing it to show that there are certain narrow limits to the size of the upper and lower branches of the cheek pieces, that the operation of the curb chain or strap should be confined wholly to the function of a painless fulcrum, and the entire action of the bit concentrated in the mouth-piece.

The form and proportions of the mouth-piece must be deduced wholly from the interior conformation of that part of the mouth on which it is intended to act, and these are the tongue and the bars. The fleshy tongue is much less sensitive to pressure than the bony bars, covered only with a very thin membrane. If a perfectly straight unjointed mouth-piece of moderate thickness is used, this resting wholly on the animal's tongue, would, notwithstanding the lever action, be the lightest form of curb bit that could be devised.

If by means of a "port," or upward curve in the mouth-piece, pressure is removed from the tongue and transferred entirely to the sensitive bars, with the same amount of lever action as before, the severest form of curb bit results.

Between these two extremes there is a wide range, and the whole art of bitting consists, so far as the mouth-piece is concerned, in determining how much of the pressure shall fall on the tongue and how much on the bars, and this is regulated in each particular case by the nature of the service required, and the temperament of the animal. The diameter of the mouth-piece may vary from a half to three-quarters of an inch in thickness.

It is necessary that the parts of the mouth-piece to act

on the tongue and bars respectively should keep their places. This requires that the mouth-piece fit exactly the width of the mouth, and the width of the port be not greater than the width of the tongue channel. If a mouth-piece with a port be too wide, a slight pull on one rein will suffice to displace it, so that the bar at that side gets either altogether under the port, in which case the pressure is thrown on the tongue, when the corner of the port will, by being pressed into it, cause great pain, and make the action of the bit very irregular and unsatisfactory. If the port is wider than the tongue channel, a similar thing occurs, and if narrower it fails to admit the tongue.

The height of the port is the most variable dimension of all, depending on the thickness of the tongue and sensitiveness of the bars, on the temperament and conformation of the animal, as well as the use to which he is to be put.

The most severe bit it can ever be necessary to use is one in which the height of the port is equal to its width, or about one and one-third inches. Any higher port would strike the palate, causing more or less pain, and induce the horse to bore with his head away from the rider's hand.

The plane of the port should coincide with the plane of the cheek pieces, if straight throughout; if curved below, then with the plane of the upper branches.

The upper branches are always straight, but while the lower branches of the cheek pieces are straight in the best class of civilian and many foreign military bits, they are usually curved in the American service. The point where the lower ring is attached, however, is in a straight line with the center of the top ring and center point of the mouth-piece rivet.

Some years ago the headstalls were attached to the upper branches of curb bits, in the American service, through a horizontal slit, but such bits are now generally made with a ring at the top, which prevents so much of the pull on the reins from being conveyed to the poll, as was the case with old style bits.

In some bridles the cheek pieces of the headstall are sewed directly to the bit, but in most military bridles, arranged to fit many different horses, buckles are used in order to admit of adjusting the bit, and also to permit of its being removed for cleaning (Fig. 30).

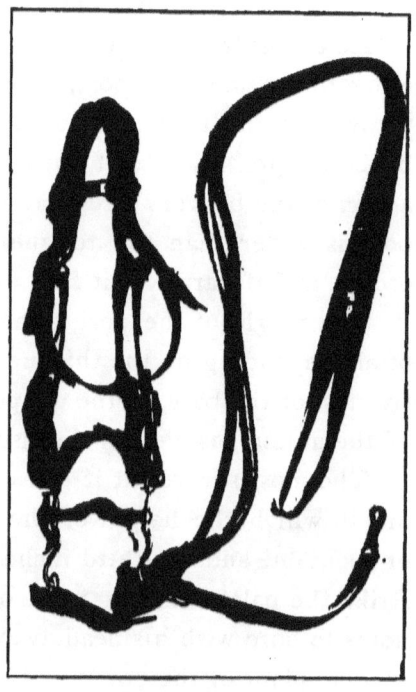

Fig. 30.

The subject of bits has received attention in the past, but has been much misunderstood, and as a consequence the government arsenals have been periodically filled with

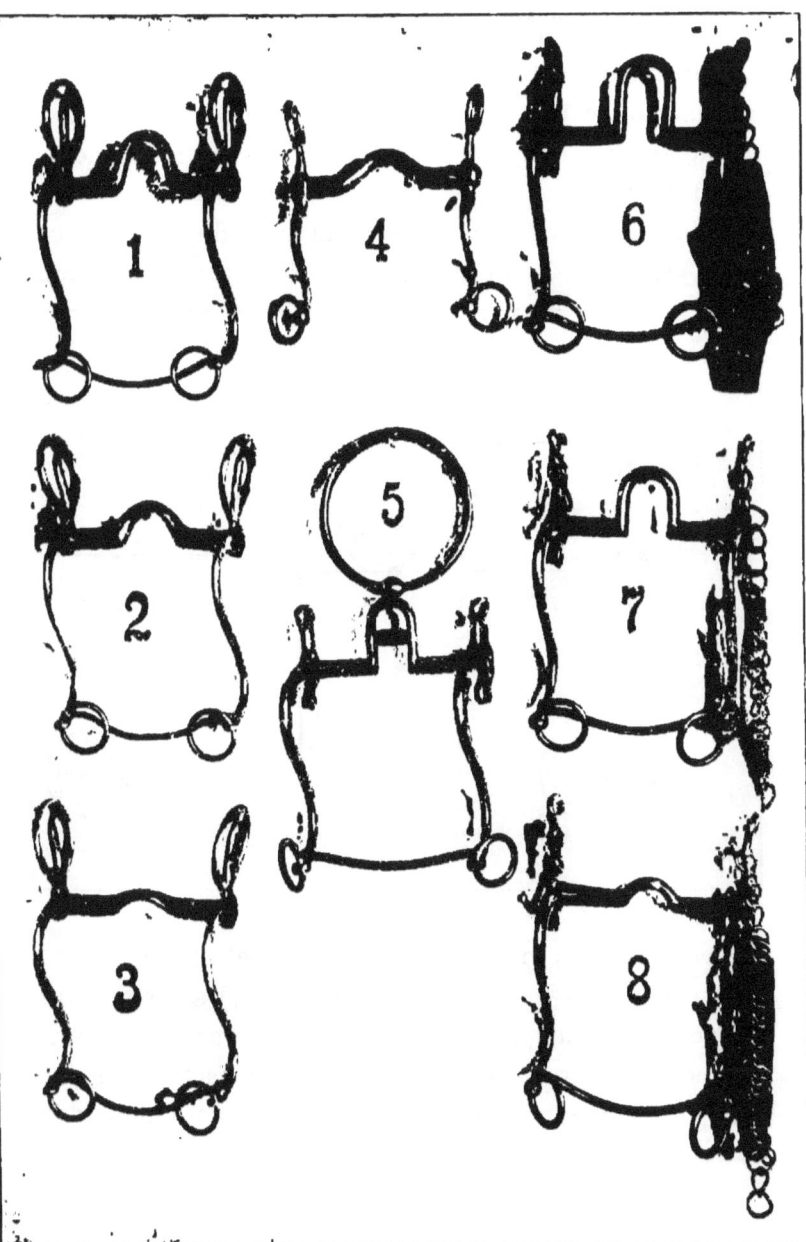

tons of discarded bits, and hundreds of horses have been condemned really because indifferent riders could not handle fresh young horses with the severe instruments issued as bits.

The bits in use in the American army during the past thirty years are shown in Plate IX. Nos. 5, 6, 7 and 8 are

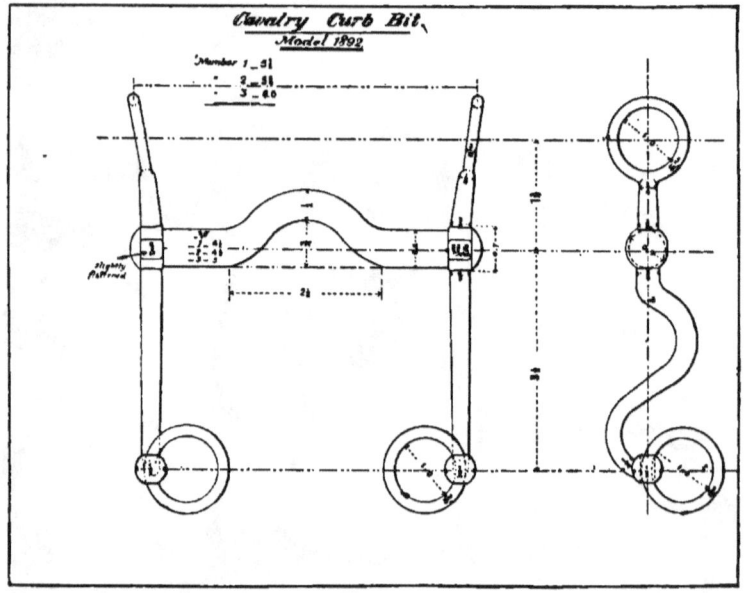

Fig. 31.

the various sizes and shapes of the model of 1863. The high port of No. 6 and the ring bit (No. 4) show that the troopers were taught that great severity was necessary to conquer their mounts, whereas the very fact of putting such instruments of torture in the average mouth will cause the horse to become frenzied under a rough hand.

Nos. 1, 2 and 3 show the "Shoemaker" bit, which has been in use for about twenty years, and which was recently abandoned for the model 1892 bit shown in the same plate as No. 4, and also with all its dimensions in Fig. 31.

This is a very mild bit, having but one height of port for all. The only variation is in the length of mouthpiece, which for the three sizes is four and one-half, four and three-fourths and five inches.*

A snaffle bit, with rings and toggles or snaps to attach to the halter, and known as a watering bridle, is issued for training purposes, riding to water and exercise, but is never used as a bridoon. The bridle with curb bit and only one pair of reins is used for all military riding. (See Fig. 30.)

Nearly all nations in Europe use the curb bit and bridoon for military purposes. In Plate X are shown the British bits (No. 1), the German (No. 2), the French (No. 3), the Russian (No. 4), and Austrian curb bit (No. 5).

The British curb bit is quite heavy, and as powerful as the one recently abandoned in the American service. The curb chain is too large, and altogether it is the most unsatisfactory combination throughout of any in the illustration. The bridoon is much larger than such secondary bits are usually made. It does not compare favorably

---

*The horses of the Fort Leavenworth school squadron, consisting of four troops, were recently measured with an Austrian mouth guage to determine the width of their mouths. One-third measured less than four inches. Nearly all were between three and three-fourths and four and one-fourth inches. Only two horses measured as much as five inches.

PLATE X.

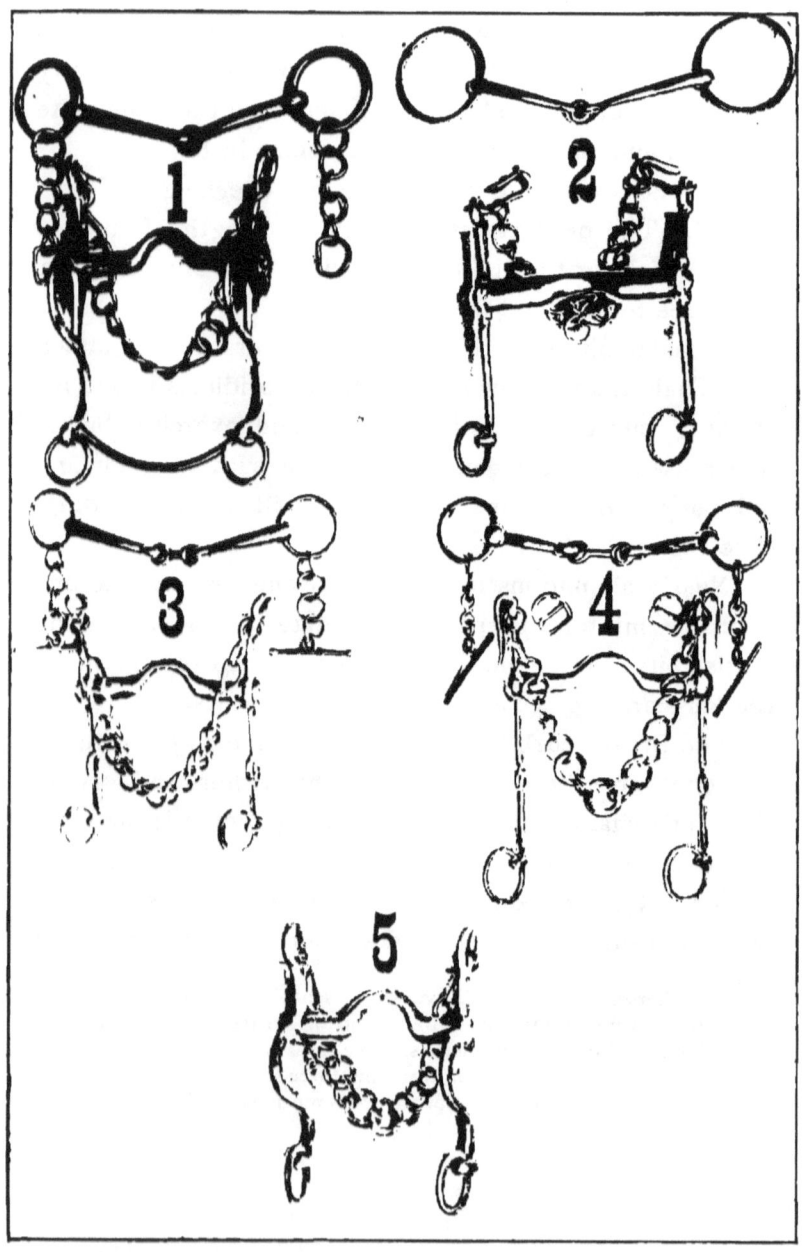

with the other equipment of the British cavalryman, which is second to none in Europe. The weight of the two bits is two and three-fourths pounds.

The French bit is well made and mild in its action. The curb is a flat steel mail chain, of good quality. The bridoon is a double-jointed snaffle. It is attached to the headstall by toggles. The cheek pieces of the curb bit are straight, and contain lip strap rings on the lower branch. The weight of the two bits is two pounds.

The German bit has a hollow mouth-piece of large dimensions, and is intended to be a very mild bit. The cheek pieces are straight, except at the bottom there is a slight curve to the rear where the ring is attached. The curb is a double mail chain, neatly and strongly made. The bridoon is the most perfect of any shown in the illustration. The quality of material and workmanship is of the highest class. The weight of the two bits is one and three-fourths pounds.

The Russians use the curb bit and bridoon, both being hooked to the double headstall. The headstall to which the snaffle is attached forms the essential part of the halter. The bridoon, which is a double-jointed snaffle, is attached by toggles. The curb bit is provided with hooks bent outward, instead of rings, for attaching it to the headstall. These hooks are broad and flat, and are passed through small steel rings in the lower end of the cheek pieces of the bridle. The rings are shown in the illustration with the bits. The bit is provided with lip strap rings. This curb bit has the longest lower branches, in proportion to the upper, of any of the other bits. The weight of the two bits is one and three-fourths pounds.

The Austrian bit is made upon the principles laid down in their cavalry regulations, and which are about as set forth in this chapter. The bit illustrated is very heavy, being made of steel, with solid mouth-piece. The flat mail chain curb is the best of its class, and is not apt to be broken or stretched by ordinary service wear. The snaffle used with this bit is a single-jointed bit with rings and half cheek guards. The Austrians make nine different sizes of bits in order to provide amply for fitting average horses. The weight of the curb bit alone is one and five-eighths pounds.

It is observed that the bit and bridoon are used generally by European, and also by the British cavalry. The accurate bitting and training of their horses is sufficient evidence to establish the great value of the combination for military purposes; but the single rein and curb bit alone will probably be more acceptable in America, because of those who would form the bulk of the recruits in time of war but very few would have ever seen or used a double-reined bridle.

In comparing these bits it is observed that there is no very material difference in those used in Europe. The German is the mildest, but it probably answers the purpose fully with their carefully trained horses.

The American bit is made of the best steel, and neatly

finished. It is intended to be very mild, and will, with slight alteration, answer its purpose for all but very exceptional cases, provided the horses are properly bitted and trained. It is much lighter than any ever before issued, and this is some compensation for such faults as may be developed in its future use.

Taking a pound out of the amount carried in the horse's mouth may not seem to be a very important matter at first glance, but when it is considered that a first-class handicapper may, by adding or taking off a pound here and there, entirely upset all calculations as to the result of a race between animals of equal form, it must be seen that a pound more or less at the end of his neck makes a great difference to the horse.

It will not do, however, to carry this reduction to an extreme, for cavalry horses are subject to exciting conditions, and bits of sufficient size and degree of lever power must be retained for the purpose of controlling animals at the charge and in the resulting meleé.

CHAPTER VIII.

BITTING AND TRAINING.

End and Aim of Bitting.—Principle Governing all Bitting.—Importance of Knowledge of Subject.—Effect of Head and Neck.—How Bit should be Regarded.—Rational Treatment.—Training.—Horse Made Familiar with New Surroundings.—Equipped with Snaffle Bit.—"Dumb Jockey."—Riding School and Track.—Establishing Gaits.—Jumping.—Use of Longe; Training Halter; Running Rein.—Saddle.—Use of Saber and Fire-Arms.—Selecting and Fitting Curb Bit.—Mouth Gauge.—Trial Bit.—Hard and Tender Mouth.—Effect of Seat of Rider.—Riding with One Hand.—Guiding by Pressure of Rein on Neck.

The end and aim of all bitting should be to bring about such confidential relations between rider and horse as to cause the slightest wish of the former, when indicated through the bit, in conjunction with pressure of the reins upon the neck or the legs upon the flanks, to be obeyed without constraint, resistance or exhibition of temper.

The various purposes to which horses are applied demand of course different details of handling. One principle applies to all, namely: to get the whole lever power of the animal to act in conjunction with its weight in the required direction, and with such a degree of leaning on the bit that all its motions may be controlled without interfering in too abrupt a manner with its action.

The knowledge of bitting is very essential, for it is only by means of it that perfect control of the horse can be obtained without the infliction of unnecessary pain. It is especially important to cavalrymen, for upon its application depends the steadiness of the horses in all maneuvers on the drill ground and the field of battle.

The head is the lever by means of which command over the neck is gained; its size, shape, weight, and the manner in which it is set on, all exercise more or less influence. A very large head makes it extremely difficult to get the horse into anything like equilibrium, but it does not follow that horses with such conformation are always heavy in hand, for more depends upon the way in which the head is set on the neck, and the facility thereby afforded for assuming a great variety of positions, than on the absolute size of the head itself.

In considering the lever action of the head and neck, it is proper to remember that the effect produced depends not only on the absolute power applied, but also on the direction in which it is applied. Considering the horse's head as a lever which is to act on the neck and bring it towards the rider's hand, it is evident that if the former be stretched out in continuation of the latter, as is done on the track by race horses, there is no lever action. In the same way if the horse's head is brought in until it touches his neck, there will be little if any lever action.

The lever action is greatest when the head is at a right angle to the neck; the more it departs from this position, in consequence of severe bitting or other causes, the less will be the useful lever action. With the great majority of horses the physical conformation of the jaws opposes no obstacle to the head assuming this desirable position.

The bit should be regarded as a means of communication between horse and rider, as well as an instrument which may check and master the animal. The impression it conveys may vary from the slightest sensation to the most intense pain.

If the intensity of its effect does not accord with the degree of sensibility and the intelligence of the subject, it produces effects opposite to those which are desired, and may provoke stubborn resistance which man cannot always easily master.

If, on the contrary, the mechanical effect of the bit be in proportion to the sensitiveness of the mouth, it becomes a rational and useful instrument, through which the wish of the rider may be indicated.

The theories of bits and bitting are given quite fully, because ignorance as to such matters is so common amongst bit makers that no reliance can be placed upon general representations as to bits and other implements necessary or useful in training the young horse.

Rational treatment produces better results than harsh means, and if the officer will himself direct the training of horses until he is assured that the troopers to whose care the animals are intrusted fully appreciate the value of the primary lessons, there will be less labor and disappointment when the remounts are placed in the ranks. A little patience and expenditure of time at first makes matters easier later on.

There are many books which prescribe in detail all the various steps in training, but these are seldom carried out for the reason that men are not available for the performance of this important work, which, to be valuable, must be not only progressive but continuous. It is not advisable to waste any time in teaching unusual gaits, but it is absolutely necessary that pains should be taken to establish every young horse in his gaits during the period he is being bitted.

The period of training will of course vary with the amount of instruction the horse has received before purchase. Horses frequently arrive at stations in such a forward state of training that all they require is to be familiarized with the sound of firing, trumpets, and other unusual noises and sights. In general, however, the new horses require considerable work before they are fit for the ranks, because curb bits are seldom used on ordinary horse farms.

Contracts all describe most perfect animals as to form, as well as that they shall be free from vice, gentle and broken to the saddle, but these requirements produce no such uniformity as is demanded in a well instructed squadron.

It is not enough that the horse can be ridden along with the others, but that he shall be under such perfect control that he will leave the ranks at any time and under any circumstances, without refusing or crowding towards the other horses.

Occasionally an animal will be found to resist all training. It is customary in the American service to apply the Rarey system to such animals until brought into subjection. This system is subsequently applied to all horses in order to finish their education, to make them recognize how completely they are in the power of man, and to give the troopers a knowledge of the means to conquer, as well as to render their horses gentle.

Practice varies in different organizations, but a brief description of only what is practicable in the average regiment will be given.

Upon arrival of new horses they should be examined, with a view to determining if they are suffering from any injury or disease which would prevent their being put to work. Those that are well should then be scattered amongst old and gentle horses at the picket line. While the hoof numbers are perfectly plain, the descriptive lists should be compared, and the horses entered in the troop records, and a name assigned to each.

A horse should be allowed to grow familiar with his surroundings, and made to understand that he is perfectly safe from any injury. He should be fed but little grain until all signs of the feverish condition incident to his change have passed away.

His feet should be handled, and he should be led into the blacksmith shop while other horses are being shod.

Horses are often severely injured when frightened at the noise and sights about the forge and anvil. It is not necessary to shoe the horse unless the ground where he is to be trained is rocky or hard, but his hoofs should be rasped down enough to prevent them from splitting.

Troopers mounted on old horses should lead the new animals about the post during ceremonies and drills, in order that they may not be frightened at the band, movements of troops, fluttering of flags, and many other things not to be seen in the vicinity of farms.

The horse is now ready to begin his training in the riding hall, or where there is none, on a ring prepared on ground selected for the purpose at some place where the attention of the animal will not be distracted from the work in hand.

As all animals are ridden before being accepted, it is usual to put on a snaffle bit at once. This is attached by toggles, or snaps, to the halter, but for training new horses it is much better to use a regular headstall with the snaffle bit buckled on, so that it can be adjusted properly on the bars at the same place the mouth-piece of the curb bit will rest when it is put on.

If the young horse frets and fails to feel or take the bit properly when mounted, he must be handled very gently, and allowed to follow the lead of an old horse quietly about the ring at a walk until he establishes himself in the new conditions of equilibrium sufficiently to move up to the bit without leaning upon it, refusing to feel it, or to allow it to exert pressure on his mouth. This must be continued from day to day, the bending lessons prescribed in the drill regulations being taken up gradually. The importance of the bending lessons is seldom appreciated and much neglected.

If the horse continues unable to take the bit he should be fitted with a "dumb jockey," which is a cross-tree of wood on a padded surcingle. The reins of the snaffle bit are attached to the cross-trees at about the height of the rider's hand, and straps in rear are carried back to a crupper, to prevent the cross-tree from falling forward. The straps should be so adjusted that the animal feels the pressure of the mouth-piece, and this may be gradually increased from day to day until he arches his neck or raises his head enough to lighten his forehand. This will be easily determined by the appearance of his step. The horse rigged in this manner should be turned loose by himself in a small enclosure, so that he may devote his brain to working out a solution of the problem before him. The instruction in this way should not be continued for more than half an hour at a time, for if left until very tired the horse loses his fear and leans so heavily on the bit as to destroy much of the sensitive feeling necessary to a good mouth.*

The rider mounted on a blanket should continue the

---

*Under the advice of a "practical horseman" of considerable local reputation, the author, some years ago, turned a colt loose for hours at a time with a dumb jockey, well tightened up, to give him a good mouth. The result was to reduce the animal's mouth to so insensitive a condition as to seriously impair his value for any purpose.

work on the track or in the school day by day, varying the gaits from a walk to a trot, and finally to the gallop. The horse should be taught from the very first to execute the turns by the pressure of the outer rein upon his neck, the mouth-piece being pulled, if necessary, by the inner rein. The rider must avail himself constantly of the use of his legs as aids.

It is never done, but would be a useful innovation, to have a track laid off at every post, so that at this period of the training the young horse could be established in his gaits of walk, trot and gallop at the regulation rate per mile.

It is presumed that good results have followed the lessons which have occupied such time as the intelligence and progress of the animal demanded. The animal should now be taught to leap the ditch and hurdle. For this purpose he is taken out with a good safe jumper, and led quietly at a walk across ditches and over such obstacles as present themselves, like logs, rails, piles of earth, brush, etc. He is next made to leap them at a slow gallop, care being taken to vary the course as much as possible. When the animal ceases to have any fear, or to make any resistance in the fields and pastures, he should be taught to jump the bar and hurdle in the riding school. In order that he may not be expected to be led over all the time, he should now be equipped with a longe, or rope lariat; he should be taken up to the obstacle by a dismounted man, giving him but little rope at first, and he should then be made to jump. If necessary, another man may go in rear of the horse with a whip, to touch him if he tries to come back. If he jumps without fear no snapping of the whip or shouting should be allowed, else he will connect these in his mind with jumping.

The longe may be ordinarily attached to the halter ring, but as some horses are what is not inaptly termed in the service "bull-headed," something else must be provided.

A useful training halter may be prepared by attaching a strong strap to the lower part of the cheek pieces of the bridle, to go around the nose above the nostrils, and which can be tightened under the chin by means of a buckle on one end of the strap in rear. This adjustable nose band may carry a ring in rear for the snap-hook of the longe, or an iron cavesson with a nose-ring may be padded and riveted on in front to the nose band.

This latter gives the longe holder a powerful instrument for controlling the horse, and should be used with great care.

Sometimes the horse will not hold his head in a proper position, and it becomes necessary to apply a running rein, which acts directly on the snaffle bit, independently of the reins. The action of the running rein may be increased or reduced without the necessity for any alteration of buckles or straps.

A running rein consists of a strap about eight or ten feet long, of the size of an ordinary bridle rein, with provision at one end for buckling it to the ring on the near side of the saddle. A chin strap, carrying a ring sewed on in rear, is buckled into the snaffle rings in the same manner as a curb strap. A single martingale, with a ring held at the height of the point of the shoulder by means of a strap around the neck, completes the parts necessary to operate the running rein, which passes from the ring on the left, side of the saddle through the martingale ring, thence through the curb strap ring, back through the martingale ring, and then to the right hand of the rider.

A pull on the running rein will act directly on the mouth-piece and draw the mouth backward and downwards towards the horse's chest. In connection with the snaffle reins, the horse's mouth may be pulled horizontally upwards or downwards.

The horse is now ready to be saddled, and the same course should be continued by the rider until the animal performs everything required of him in an intelligent manner in the school and outside. During this period, after he is saddled, he should be accustomed to the saber and to fire-arms until he permits both to be used by the trooper without fear or exhibition of nervousness. He should be ridden near the pistol targets until he goes equally well to the right and left and between the targets without fear.

The horse is now ready for the curb bit, which should be carefully fitted to him. Very little attention has ever been paid to this subject in the American cavalry. It is of much importance, as has already been shown. A bit with but slight height of port should be selected and placed in the horse's mouth over the tongue. By pressing it lightly against one side it will be seen if it is of the right width of mouth-piece. If it is too narrow it will pinch the lips, and another must be tried. If too wide, a measure of the amount which projects over must be taken, and a mouth-piece that much shorter be selected. The selection of a bit of proper width may be facilitated by slipping a smooth stick into the horse's mouth, placing it opposite the chin groove, and then bringing the thumbs lightly against the horse's lips. Hold the hands firmly in place on the stick while removing it from the horse's mouth, and have an assistant cut notches opposite the ends of the thumbs. This will give the length of the mouth-piece between the cheek pieces.

A proper width of bit having been determined upon, it should be attached to the headstall and adjusted as nearly opposite the chin groove as possible, having due regard to the position of the tusks.

If a horse has been accustomed to a curb bit buckled up against the corners of his mouth, he will fret a good deal when the bit is lowered to a place opposite the chin groove. If after trial during a period sufficiently long to determine whether the bit suits the mouth, it is found not to be severe enough, a bit of the same width, but with a higher port, must be selected.

Theoretically it is desirable to have several heights of port for each width of mouth-piece. In several European armies the number of sizes has been reduced recently to very few. In the American service three sizes are issued, but the only difference is in the length of mouth-piece. If two heights of port were made for each size, this would provide amply for all service requirements.

After having secured a bit of satisfactory dimensions, the curb strap or chain should be carefully adjusted. It should never be made quite tight; there should be room enough left for the first and second fingers of the right hand to pass flat between it and the chin. By gently pulling the reins with the left hand, whilst the two fingers of the right hand are in this position, it will be easy to ascertain whether any pinching action occurs, in which case something is wrong. The chain or curb strap should tighten in the chin groove before the end of the cheek piece has passed over an arc of $35°$.

After going over the adjustment of the bridle and bit sufficiently to insure its correctness, it is then necessary to mount and try the horse with it, to determine if the mouth-piece is adapted to the particular mouth under consideration as regards severity. If not, try different heights of port until a correct bit is found.

Horses seem able to adapt themselves after a time to many brutal forms of mouth-pieces, but it is well to remember that a total absence of stiffness, constraint, or painful action, are the characteristics of good bitting; if these be attained, ready obedience to the rider's hands and legs will follow.*

The dimensions and proportions prescribed for bits should be productive of satisfactory results in most cases. Some horses will of course be found which will appear to defy all rules. Some may need greater severity than is produced by the bit prescribed for average horses. If the lower branch be lengthened it will of course give greater power, and some horses seem to require this.

After the government has been put to the expense of providing horses which turn out utterly unsatisfactory as to bitting and saddle qualities, it appears at first thought wasteful to cast them out, but mature consideration should govern in such matters, and whenever an animal exhibits qualities which prevent his being ridden in ranks with the ordinary appliances furnished for the purpose, he should not receive any more consideration than a bent gun barrel or broken saber blade. It is more economical to condemn bolters and vicious horses than to supply an infinite variety of bits.

An Austrian, VON WEYROTHER, invented a mouth gauge for ascertaining all the necessary dimensions of the horse's mouth. It is made of steel, and consists of a bar,

---

*The U. S. cavalry bit, model of 1863, was used in all the successful cavalry raids and actions during the last two years of the war. The length of the lower branch is three times the distance from the center of the mouthpiece to the point of attachment of the curb chain hook. The width of port is 1.09 inches, and the height of port for the four sizes of bits issued is .5, 1.5, 2, and 2.25 inches, and one is a ring bit (Plate 9).

a b (Fig. 32 *A*), about six inches long, fitted on one side at right angles with a fixed cheek piece *c d*, and having on the other side a sliding cheek piece *e f*, fitted with a screw for fixing it where required. The bar *a b* is made oval in the transverse section, with the greater axis about one inch, in order to displace the lips nearly as the mouthpiece does, and is usually graduated throughout.

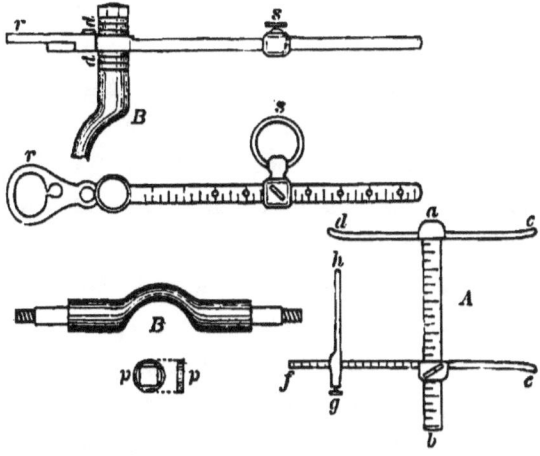

Figs. 32 A and 32 B.

If this gauge be placed in the horse's mouth like a bit, with the bar *a b* at exactly the proper place for the bit, opposite the chin groove, the fixed cheek piece *c d* being then held gently up to the off side of the mouth, the operator facing the horse's forehead, the sliding cheek piece *e f* may be shoved up close enough to the cheek, at the near side, not to displace the lips, and then fixed with the screw. Removing the gauge, the proper dimension for the width of the mouth-piece may be read off the scale on ab.

The instrument is also fitted with a rod gh, which slides up and down the movable cheek piece cf, which is graduated into inches, and eighths or tenths on its lower limb. This contrivance enables the measurement of the height of the bars to be taken. The instrument, adjusted to the proper width of the horse's mouth, is placed as before, with the bar ab exactly opposite the chin groove, but underneath the tongue, and is then wheeled around on its own axis until the upper limbs of the cheek pieces stand nearly perpendicular to the general line of the horse's face. This brings the lower limbs in the opposite direction towards the neck, and the rod gh is then shoved up until it presses lightly into the chin groove, taking care that the gauge stands square, and that the mouth-piece lies equally on both bars of the mouth. The rod gh is then screwed fast whilst the cheek piece cf is loosened altogether, so that the latter may be removed without disturbing the rod gh; the height of the bar may then be read off on the lower limb of cf.

A Prussian officer invented a trial bit some years ago (Fig. 32 B). This consists of two cheek pieces, into which may be fitted in succession spare mouth-pieces, the width being varied by the adjustment of a number of small plates pp one-tenth of an inch in thickness, removable at will from the inside to the outside of the cheek piece.

Having the width of the mouth, and obtaining the height of the bars by means of the mouth gauge, the sliding ring pieces rr may be shifted until the upper cheek piece has the required length. There only remains now to slide the rein rings ss up or down until the proper proportional length of the lower cheek has been obtained. The curb hooks and headstall may now be attached and the horse tried with the bit. If the adjustment is correct, and he takes to the bit readily, it is only necessary to read off the dimensions and have one constructed accordingly.

It should be borne in mind that the two common and grave defects of bits are "falling through" and "standing stiff;" that nothing is more certain than that every horse will go much better with a well-fitting bit, properly placed, than with the contrary, and that many otherwise fretful and dangerous horses become perfectly tractable if properly bitted.

Civilians need not use a curb bit, but cavalrymen have no option in the matter, and should by all means be taught the practical value of a properly fitted curb bit, and its advantages over one that does not fit.

It may be well to explain here why the fresh and sensitive mouth of the young horse conveys the sensation of hardness to the hand of the rider, and why the same mouth, after it has really been rendered more or less callous by the application of the mouth-piece to its delicate organization, comes to be called tender.

When a horse is mounted for the first time the equilibrium of the animal is disturbed; the young horse bores on his bit, trying to acquire a new point to lean on—a fifth leg, as it were; he is hard-mouthed. But when the animal has learned to carry itself and the rider, or acquired an artificial equilibrium suited to the altered circumstances, it no longer seeks this support, and the mouth is called tender.

If a horse be first ridden without a bit until brought into equilibrium with his rider, and a light snaffle bit be then put in his mouth, it will be found very sensitive, and it will be several days before he will take the bit.

From what has just been stated, it will be easy to understand how the seat of the rider comes to exercise so great an influence on the horse's mouth, that the same horse will go light with one and heavy with another rider. It is a question of equilibrium. One rider assumes a seat that favors; another, one that more or less impedes the efforts of the horse to get into balance—for horses always try to do this. Supposing the seat, so far as the distribution of weight is concerned, to be identical, the unsteady rider will seek a support in the reins, and the horse immediately bores on the bit; the rider with a steady seat has a light hand, and the horse is therefore tender-mouthed.

Lightness or heaviness of the rider's hand depends mainly upon the stability of his seat. If he has not a good seat, and relies mainly upon stirrups and reins, the only thing to be done is to put as light a bit as possible in the horse's mouth, to save it from pain.

If the horse is harassed by a very tight curb chain or strap pressing against his under jaw, or by a high port rasping the tender ridges of his palate, he cannot properly take the bit, even though he has already been trained to the action of a mouth-piece.

The high port bits used by cow-boys, some of which have tongue rings in addition, serve their purpose with the hardy little ponies on the range, but in recent years the tendency is to discard the harsh bits, and depend more upon the training of the pony.

As a matter of fact, cow-boys must have well trained ponies for all round-up work, and it is only during the period of probation that the animal's mouth suffers. After being properly trained the horse is never ridden on the bit. The cow-boy does not ride with a tight rein, and his seat must be so secure as to be entirely independent of the horse's mouth. His methods are of little value as models for any part of cavalry training, but on his own ground the cow-boy naturally holds the cavalryman in contempt.*

All horses should be trained with the snaffle bit until they understand thoroughly the use of the bit and reins.

---
*During the past year the author visited a large ranch in New Mexico, and witnessed the method now practiced in breaking range horses. It formerly was, and still is in many places, the custom to saddle and bridle young horses, and lead them into heavy sand. Here a rider mounted, or more often a bag of sand was tied on, and the animal encouraged to buck until exhausted. The range horses referred to were ridden by selected horse breakers; no bit was used, but reins were attached to rope halters. The horses were taken out across country, and encouraged to run rather than buck. They were taught to turn by the reins without that disturbance to equilibrium which comes from bitting in its early stages.

A horse that cannot bear the pressure of the bit in moderation is of no value for saddle purposes. If he cannot perform satisfactorily with a snaffle bit, a curb bit will produce that fidgety, uneasy motion characteristic of jibbers and prancing horses.

A trooper must ride with one hand, and have the other free to use his arms; therefore the horse must be trained to obey the pressure of the reins upon his neck, and the legs upon his flanks. This is the most essential, yet the most neglected part of training. The bit should be mainly used to prevent the horse from forging ahead of the line, from bolting, to moderate the gait, and to halt. All changes of direction should be accomplished by pressure of the outer rein upon the horse's neck. In this way the horse can be moved on the circumference of a large circle, or he may be turned to the right or left on his own ground.

Even with rational bits, good results can only be obtained through the exercise of judgment, patience and painstaking care. The difference between riding a properly bitted and trained saddle animal and the ordinary leather-mouthed horse, is about the same as that between riding in a carriage and a coal cart.

CHAPTER IX.

SADDLES.

Value of Knowledge of Construction and Adjustment.—Under Surface: Shape; Size Proportioned to Weight Carried.—Upper Surface: Size Proportioned to Bulk Carried.—Importance of Shape of Seat.—Where to Put the Weight in Saddle.—Position of Saddle on the Horse.—Materials for Construction.—Military Saddles.—Side Bars: Length; Shape; Adjustable.—Experiment to Show Proper Adjustment of Pack.—Padding: Pads; Blankets.—Cruppers.—Breast Straps.—Rules for Selection and Arrangement of Saddle and Pack.

It seems incredible that the mechanical arrangement of the saddle, and the manner in which it is adjusted to the horse's back, can have any effect upon success in war; yet so marked are the results of defective saddles, or ignorance as to their proper adjustment on service, that the evil effects are as much to be feared as an enterprising enemy.

It is a matter of importance that the mechanical principles applicable to saddles should be well understood, as it will enable the rider to ascertain exactly what is desired, and to attain the end with a minimum of injury to the horse's back. This protection of the back from injury is a matter for constant consideration in all cavalry commands, and the full accomplishment of that end demands knowledge, experience, and painstaking care on the part of officers.

In examining the saddle, beginning with the under surface or portion coming in contact with the horse's back, two principal points present themselves for consideration: its shape and its size. One general mechanical principle applies to both, namely: that the larger the surface over which a given amount of pressure is equally spread or divided, the less will be the action on any given point of the other surface in contact. In other words, the under surface of the saddle should bear as nearly as possible the same relation to that part of the horse's back it is intended to occupy, as a mould does to the cast that is taken from it, excepting that strip lying over the horse's backbone, which should remain altogether out of contact.

The idea of making one portion come into closer contact than another, "giving a gripe," with the intention of preventing the saddle slipping, is altogether erroneous, for the result of concentrating the pressure on one point or line is very apt to be a sore back.

As regards size or extent of the under surface, the greater this is with a given weight, the less will be the pressure on any given point, and consequently the less risk of sore back; provided always, that the pressure be equally distributed over the whole surface.

There must, however, be some limit to the size of a saddle, for its own absolute weight is a matter for serious consideration. The size should be proportioned to the weight to be carried. The jockey's saddle may be reduced to a mere contrivance upon which to hang a pair of stirrups, but the average individual requires something with more substance.

There are two ways in which the weight of the saddle may be decreased without its useful under surface being made too small. The first is to avoid extending the frame beyond the surfaces where it really has to support pressure. This being exercised chiefly in a perpendicular direction, it is useless to extend the side bars far down over the ribs. The second way is to use for the saddle-tree materials combining great strength and moderate elasticity, with the least possible weight.

As the under surface of the saddle is large in proportion to the weight to be carried, so the upper surface, or seat, should be proportioned to the bulk of the rider. There is positive disadvantage in having the seat larger than is necessary, but it is the form or shape which is of greatest importance.

If the ridge of the saddle be horizontal, imperfect contact results; it is therefore best to dip this ridge and spread it into a more or less concave surface where the weight of the rider is applied. As the form of seat used by the rider will depend considerably on the location of the lowest point of this concave surface, it must be arranged with accuracy; then the rider can bring the greatest amount of surface possible of himself and saddle into permanent contact without undue constraint on his part.

Supposing the saddle to have the proper form and size, the next point to be determined is where to put the weight. As man cannot be distributed over the whole upper part of the saddle like inert matter, it is necessary to place the rider's center of gravity over the center of the bearing surface of the saddle, for this is the point which, being loaded, transmits the pressure equally to the rest of the surface.*

The saddle only covers a portion of the back, and is calculated to fit approximately in one particular location. It should be so placed as to interfere the least with the action of the muscles of the horse, and this condition will be best met when the saddle is located on the broad flat tendon covering the center of the horse's back. (See Plate II.) This will also locate the weight near the perpendiculars passing through the centers of motion and

---

*For a simple and practical illustration of this fact, take a small rectangular table and place it exactly level on sand or smooth, soft ground; put a weight precisely in the center of the table and measure the depth to which the feet have been forced into the soil; it will be found, if the soil is homogeneous, that all of the legs have penetrated to an equal depth. Shift the table to a new location, place the weight near one end, measure the penetration again, and it will be found that the two legs nearest the weight have sunk deeper than the others. The effect of the weight at one end of the table is similar to what happens when a rider sits at one end of the saddle, generally the hinder one; the pressure on the hind end of the saddle tilts up the front end, and the tendency of every movement of the horse and rider is to shove the saddle forward until stopped by the withers. The immediate result is to slip the saddle blanket back, and expose the withers to a bruising more or less severe.

gravity, and therefore cause an equable distribution of the weight of both horse and rider on all four legs, both in a state of rest and motion. There will be less tendency to disturbance of the saddle or the seat of the rider when the horse is in motion than at any other point.

The point where the center of the saddle should rest may be found practically by locating the fourth and fifth short ribs from the rear, and following up the space between them to the back. This will be the point on the spine near the center of motion, but the shape of the horse will have much to do with the saddle remaining in this position. The American, or McClellan saddle, will not so remain on many horses unless a double cincha is used.

Wood, iron or steel plates, and leather, constitute the principal materials of which saddles are constructed.

Military saddles are best made wholly of wood, or with only such simple plates of metal added as are necessary to secure wooden parts in place. The necessity of attaching a pack makes the question of neat appearance altogether secondary, and the weight to be carried renders it imperative to economize every ounce that is possible.

There is much variation in military saddles, both as to shape and capacity for carrying packs. They are nearly all provided with large side bars, some of which are much longer than others. Nearly all are made with arches sufficiently high to clear the horse's withers and back.

The object of long side bars is to enable the pack to be attached so that it will not rest on the back, but they are a disadvantage when made so long that they receive any of the muscular action of the fore and hind quarters. The short and broad side bars answer the purpose when the pack is secured, as in American saddles.

The shape of the side bars is a most important item, and the angle which they make with each other must be fixed to suit the average horse of the class purchased for cavalry service.

Saddles with adjustable side bars have been tried with some success, but they have not been deemed worthy of adoption for military use in America, although the Austrians have introduced the principle in a portion of their cavalry saddles. The advantage claimed for saddles constructed on this principle is, that in campaigns where hard marching and scanty forage prevail, the horses fall away rapidly, and the loss of flesh under the saddle is not always uniform; hence, the ordinary saddle ceases to fit and the horse's back becomes sore, whereas the saddle with adjustable side bars may be altered to suit the varying condition of the horse.

If a wooden horse be placed with the legs upon two platform scales, and the packed saddle be placed upon it as nearly as possible as it would be upon a live horse, it will be found that the cantle end is almost twice as heavy as the pommel end. Let a rider now seat himself in the saddle with his feet in the stirrups, and the proportions become materially changed, being about five pounds weight at the pommel end to every six pounds at the cantle end. By standing in the stirrups, or pressing them slightly to the front, the preponderance of the cantle is further decreased.*

To cause the pressure of the saddle to be equable it is necessary to remove the preponderance of weight from the rear of the saddle. This may be done by putting more of the pack on the pommel, or by placing the stirrups in front of the center of the saddle, where they theoretically belong.

Owing to the muscular action which takes place near the withers, it is found in practice a dangerous expedient to overload the pommel, and the usual plan adopted is to attach the stirrups slightly in front of the center. This enables the horse to carry the load to better advantage, and the rider to occupy the seat with his legs in some one of the positions customary amongst civilized nations, particularly that prescribed for American soldiers.

---

* The following practical experiment is of interest in directing attention to the arrangement of the saddle and some of its attachments:

If the point on each side bar be found, which is equi-distant from the saddle nails placed at the junctions of the pommel and cantle with the side bars, and a line be made to connect the two points thus found, it will cross the seat at its lowest point. If now the saddle tree be suspended by a wire attached at the middle of this line, it will balance quite accurately. This may then be taken as the center of the saddle. The centers of the cincha rings should be on the prolongation of the line connecting the points found, thus assuring equable pressure when the cincha is tightened.

While the saddle is still suspended by the wire attach the stirrups, cincha, equipments, arms and pack. It will be found that the balance has been destroyed to such an extent that from twenty-three to twenty-five pounds will be required on the pommel before it is regained. If rations, horseshoes and ammunition are added to the load in the saddle-bags, the preponderance of the weight at the cantle will be still greater.

Aside from equalizing the weight at the two ends of the saddle, the question of distribution of pack presents itself in another way.

While the rider sits with his legs hanging down, the heaviest part of his body is above the horse's back. When the pack is added, if piled upon his back, as is the custom in some armies, it will make the horse with his load top-heavy.

As the center of gravity lies below the middle of the horse, the adjustment of the pack must be such as to prevent elevating this center too much. For this reason the saddle-bags, lariat, canteen, carbine and saber should be hung well down on the side of the horse, and the pommel and cantle packs strapped down near the ends to keep them close to the saddle.

The inability of an animal to recover itself with a top-heavy pack has been frequently demonstrated in service, when sure-footed pack mules have rolled down mountain sides, or fallen over cañon trails, while following scouting detachments of cavalry.

It is necessary to place a yielding substance between the horse's back and the saddle bars. This may be done by padding the under surface of the bars, or by the use of a detachable pad or a blanket.

Padding is usually confined to civilian saddles, but there are several nations which still use it on military saddles. The objection to the use of padding in saddles designed to carry heavy loads is that it dries in lumps, draws out of shape, and it is a matter of much difficulty, usually requiring an expert saddler to rearrange the stuffing to meet the varying conditions of the horse's back on service. Upon arriving in camp at night accumulations of dust and sweat are apt to be neglected, resulting the following day in abrasions of the skin.

The only semblance to padding on heavy American saddles, such as are used by cow-boys, consists in a layer of sheep skin on the under surface, and this is more to prevent the saddle blanket from slipping than for use as a cushion.

Saddle pads made of hair, felt and wool have all been tried very thoroughly in the American cavalry. There can be no variation from day to day in the position of the pad on the back, and in case of a bruise or sore, it is frequently necessary to cut a hole in the pad. None of the pads are of use to cover the animal. The hair pad is the most expensive when properly made, and is probably the best. The felt pad while useful for pleasure riding is not adapted to military service. It works up into the opening between the bars, producing much discomfort to the rider. It also wears out rapidly in particular spots where pressure is permanent.

The saddle blanket was adopted for American cavalry because it has stood the severe trials of service better than any proposed substitute. It can be used to cover the horse in bad weather, and when not needed by the animal is used by the trooper to make his bed on the earth a trifle less hard. The claim that a trooper will cover himself and let his horse suffer in bad weather, does not pertain to properly disciplined commands. The blanket does not change position with every movement of the saddle, and therefore does not wear off the hair of the horse's back. The blanket can be shaken out and refolded, so as to present a fresh, dry and soft surface, which is much appreciated by the horse, for he is made more comfortable, just as the trooper is by shaking out and rearranging his bed blankets in a permanent camp.

The only disadvantage possessed by the blanket is its tendency to work out behind, caused by the hair of the horse pointing to the rear, opposed to the smooth under surface of the saddle. This could be corrected by putting an under surface of sheep skin, felt or hair on the saddle, but it has not been regarded as sufficiently serious to demand the change.

After severe competitive trials the American cavalry pronounced in favor of the blanket's superiority over all pads.

A properly folded wool blanket will seldom cause any trouble in winter. Sore backs are then very rare, and when they do occur may nearly always be traced to some minor injury received in rolling, or from being bitten by another horse, and which subsequently becomes aggravated by the saddle.

In summer, however, the heat arising from the use of heavy wool blankets is a prolific source of puffed backs, which, if not properly and promptly attended to, soon result seriously. In warm weather men are much more apt to lounge in their saddles, particularly during night marches, when overcome by fatigue.

Expert packers recognize this, and as the large leather bags, called aparejos, are used with both blanket and corona of wool, they avoid some of the danger from heating by using a piece of cotton canvas, which is placed directly on the back, and upon which the blanket and corona are then laid. They take the additional precaution to leave the blanket and aparejo or pack saddle on the animal for some time after the load has been removed, to enable the back to cool gradually.

Cruppers no longer form a part of the saddle equipment for general use, but are issued in isolated cases where the shape of the horse causes the saddle to have a tendency to slip forward and bruise the withers. Their use for military saddles is to be avoided when possible, as the great weight of the rider and packed saddle is apt to cause the crupper to lacerate the tail, particularly in leaping over obstacles.

Breast straps are only used upon a few ill-shaped horses saved from condemnation by the possession of some good qualities, counterbalancing their defective girth.

The following rules should guide in the selection and arrangement of saddles:

First. Each horse should have a saddle fitted to his

back when in medium condition, the upper surface being of a size to accommodate the rider.

Second. The cincha should be attached opposite the center of the bearing surface of the saddle.

Third. The stirrups should be attached slightly in front of the center, so as to be under the seat of the rider, and maintain such equilibrium as will prevent one part of the saddle pressing more than another on the horse's back.

Fourth. The pack should be reduced to the lowest limit consistent with efficient service, and be so adjusted as to preserve as far as possible the equilibrium of horse and rider, and to prevent one part of the back from being saved up at the expense of other parts.

Fifth. The center of the saddle should be placed on the back over the center of motion of the horse.

CHAPTER X.

CAVALRY SADDLES AND PACKS.

Designed to Carry Heavy Loads.—Weights of Saddles and Packs.—Disadvantages of Heavy and Bulky Packs.—American Cavalry: The Saddle; Field Equipment; Pack; Field Uniforms.—British Cavalry: Service Orders; Saddle; Field Equipment; Pack; Remarks.—German Cavalry: Arms; The Saddle; Pack; Remarks.—Russian Cavalry: Arms; Saddle; Pack.—Belgian Cavalry: Arms; Saddle Equipments; Pack.—Austrian Cavalry: The Saddle; Pack.—Observations.

Cavalry saddles are all designed with reference to carrying heavy weights, for no nation has as yet discovered any method of sending cavalry out on extended operations without requiring individual troopers to pack a large amount of necessary equipment and personal kit.

The weight of saddles and packs varies in different armies slightly, but is large in all regular cavalry unaccompanied by extensive baggage trains, as will be seen by the accompanying tables of weights of equipments and kits.

The serious disadvantages of heavy and cumbersome packs is fully recognized by the authorities in every army, and the problem of devising means whereby the weight may be reduced without decreasing the efficiency of the trooper, is one always open for consideration and experiment.

Efforts to reduce the weights of saddles and packs have not always resulted favorably to efficiency. There are certain things necessary to enable the trooper to keep himself and his horse in serviceable condition, and the only possible method of reduction in some of these is by substitution of lighter material where practicable.

However, some things which are very necessary for one kind of field service are not only not required on other service, but may then be an absolute detriment to efficiency.

There are two opposite extremes to be avoided in experimenting with equipments as with anything else, and these are fulsome praise for every innovation on the one hand, or uniform condemnation of every proposed change on the other. A fair, honest trial under service conditions is justly due every modern improvement which does not contain elementary principles of construction already condemned.

As horses get used to almost any kind of a bit, so troopers grow accustomed to monstrosities in equipments, and cease to complain. There is no better illustration of this than a recruit's struggles during his first year of service to hang his carbine around his neck on the sling-belt, regulation fashion, while he lifts his leg over the bulky cantle pack.

In the American service there are only ten regiments of cavalry, all armed with carbine, saber and pistol, and equipped in the same manner. There is no distinction as to heavy and light cavalry, and the horses are purchased as nearly as possible of an average size. For the year 1893 the average weight of horses in service in the ten regiments was 1,052 pounds.

The troopers are enlisted only up to a weight of 165 pounds, and he must be a particularly good man at that weight or he will not be accepted. Men whose weight runs from 130 to 150 pounds are by far the best adapted for the requirements of American cavalry, the traditions of the service demanding a degree of activity in dismounting to fight on foot, in skirmishing, and in remounting quickly, which is incompatible with heaviness.

In the American service the cavalry, when turned out in full dress, uses the bridle without a halter, the saddle without any pack, and carry only the saber, which is attached to the saddle.

For purposes of drill and instruction the undress uniform, with forage cap or campaign hat, is worn, with such arms as may be ordered carried. These, however, are merely garrison functions, which are but preparatory for the real work of soldiers, and, therefore, the field equipment only will be considered.

Service against Indians has circumscribed the selection of all equipments to such limits as promised success in that field of action to which the savages confined the bulk of the army to within a few years.

At the present time it is only probable that the cavalry

will be called upon in isolated outbreaks, and a comparison of the American equipments with others may be candidly made with a view to determine whether the details of service in civilized war demand any change.

It is presumed that in the excitement attendant upon an outbreak of war, ample provision would be made for continuing the same careful inspection in the manufacture of the saddles and other parts of the equipment that takes place in peace, and thus give evidence that the expensive lessons of the early days of the Civil War have not been forgotten.

The details insisted upon in the manufacture of the saddles relate not only to perfection of shape and size, but also to the quality of all materials which is, and always should be, of the very best obtainable. The construction will be explained in full, because the present saddle, both as to shape and material, is the result of long continued experiments, based on actual service experience from British America to Mexico.

In order to understand the construction of the saddle it is necessary to learn the nomenclature of the various parts as understood in the United States. (Fig. 33.)

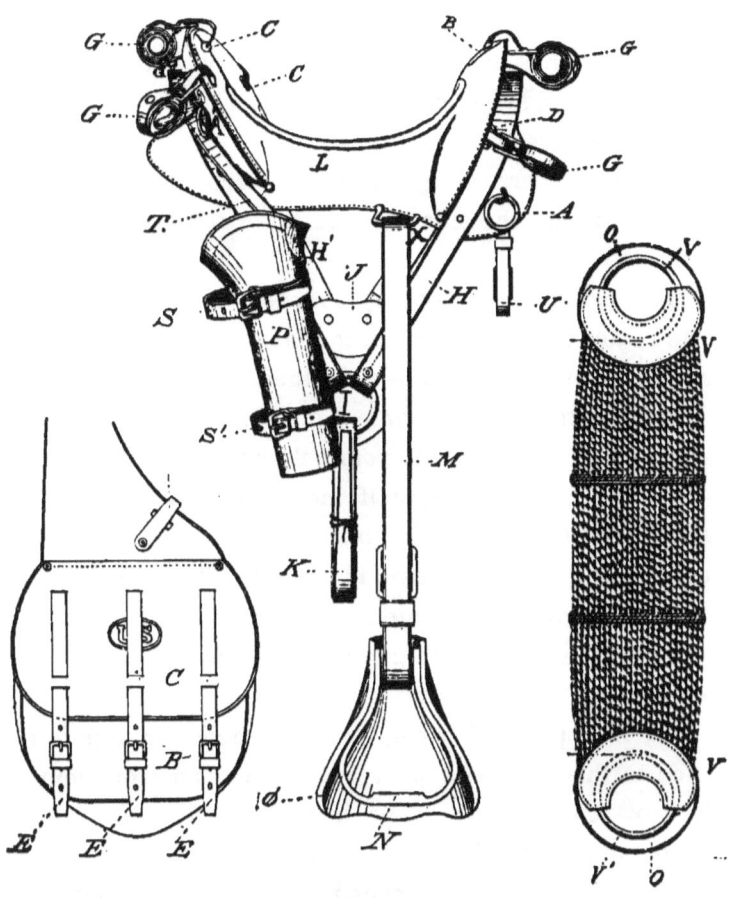

Fig. 33.

B. Pommel.
C. Cantle.
L. Side bar.
H. Front quarter strap.
H'. Rear quarter strap.
I. Quarter strap ring.
X. Stirrup loop.

J. Quarter strap ring safe.
M. Stirrup strap.
N. Stirrup tread.
O'. Stirrup hood.
Q. Saddle-bag stud.
G. Coat Straps.

AA'. Rings.
K. Cincha strap.
V. Cincha.
V'. Cincha rings.
O. Cincha ring safe.
P. Carbine boot.
SS'. Carbine boot straps.

The saddle-bags used with this saddle consist of two leather pouches connected together by a leather seat. B is the off side pouch, C the flap, and EEE, the straps for securing the flap.

In foreign armies generally the carbine boot is called the bucket, and the side bars are often referred to as sideboards.

The saddle-tree (Fig. 34) is made of wood, the pommel a and cantle b being of beech, each made of two pieces framed together at the top and glued. The two side bars c of poplar are each made of two pieces, and glued together; they are then glued to the pommel and cantle, and secured with eight two and one-half inch No. 12 screws. Holes are bored through the side bars along the junction of the pommel and cantle, front and rear, and the side bars are grooved underneath in line with the holes for fastening on the rawhide cover. The pommel has one mortise, and the cantle three, for coat straps.

An iron pommel arc d, with two holes on top, is fastened to the side bars with four rivets; an iron pommel plate of semi-circular shape is fastened to the front of the pommel with five rivets; an iron cantle arc f, with three holes on top, is fastened to the side bars with four rivets; an iron cantle plate g is fastened to the front of the cantle with four rivets. Arcs and plates are one-tenth of an inch thick, and let in flush with the wood; rivets are one and one-fourth inches No. 8.

Two stirrup strap hooks h, made of one-fourth inch

wrought iron, with the lower edges inclined from the horizontal upward and to the front, are made to swing loosely in iron straps *i*, which are let in and fastened to the side bars with three rivets.

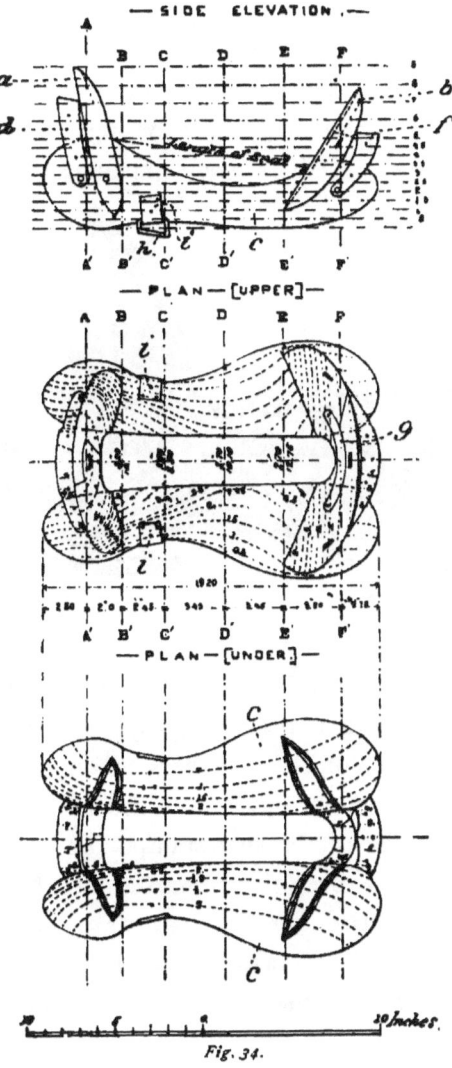

Fig. 34.

The tree is smooth, and painted with white lead before the rawhide cover is put on to strengthen it (Fig. 35). The top covering is secured in place with rawhide thongs passing through holes in front and rear of the pommel and cantle, and over the covering. The top and bottom covers are then sewed together with light thongs of the same material. (Fig. 36.) The tree is then covered with black collar leather, six to seven ounces per square foot, and the seams around the pommel and cantle are reënforced with welts of leather, and those on the side bars are placed so as not to chafe the horse or rider. Four wrought iron saddle nails, one inch long, with half heads japanned, are

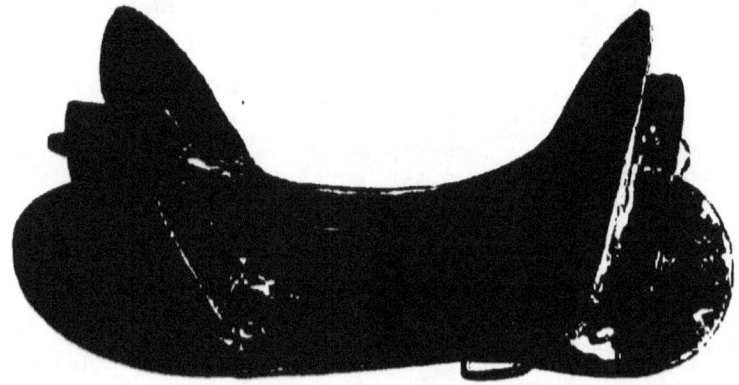

Fig. 35.

placed in the side bars at the points of junction with pommel and cantle. There are no leather skirts to the saddle.

Two one and one-fourth inch brass rings A (Fig. 33) are attached in the front ends of the side bars by one and five-eighths inch staples driven through and clinched. A brass shield B, with the size of the seat stamped on it, is fastened on the pommel with three three-quarter inch No. 2 screw pins above the mortise, for the coat strap. Six brass guard plates or ovals C are fastened on the cantle, three on each side over the mortises, for the coat straps, and one in front of the pommel, each with two three-quarter inch No. 2 screw pins. Four foot staples D one-fourth inch by thirteen-sixteenths of an inch, for coat straps, are placed two on the front of the pommel and two carrying one and one-fourth inch brass rings on the rear of the cantle under the ovals, each staple being fastened with two seven-eighths No. 6 screws. Two foot staples seven-sixteenths of an inch by three-fourths of an inch, are fastened to the side bars

Fig. 36.

through the rear girth straps with two seven-eighths inch No. 6 screws, for attaching the saddle-bags. The saddle-bag stud is fastened to the rear of the girth strap with a three-eighths inch No. 10 rivet, and to the saddle through the girth strap and cantle arc with a one inch No. 8 oval-head rivet.

The service saddles are issued in three sizes: Nos. 1, 2 and 3, the length of the seat being respectively eleven, eleven and one-half and twelve inches. The length of the bars correspond with the length of seat, but all the other dimensions are the same for all trees. The measure is taken as shown in Fig. 34.

To form a cincha attachment, two quarter straps H and H', made of harness leather, are passed over the pommel and cantle arcs, to which they are riveted. The ends of the front and rear straps are brought together on each side and sewed into wrought iron rings I two and one-half inches in diameter. Safes of leather J are fastened under the rings to prevent sores from tight girthing. Two cincha straps K are sewed in these rings, one for each side.

The cincha V is made of twenty-four strands of hair rope knotted at the ends into four-inch iron rings V' with leather safes O underneath. The cincha is seven inches wide at the center. The knots are covered with leather and sewed on to the safes.

The stirrups N are of hard wood, five and one-half inches wide and four and one-half inches deep, with a hood O' of thick harness leather riveted on. Stirrup straps M, without sweat leathers, are used with the stirrup.

The six coat straps G are passed through the mortises and foot staples. Leather stops are riveted on to limit the play of the straps.

The carbine boot P is hung over the saddle-bag stud by a strap T, and also secured by two straps S and S'.

The saber is attached at U to a small strap hung from the ring A, and to another passed through I.

The American cavalry saddle compares most favorably with those in use by the more prominent military nations as regards strength, durability, packing capacity, and comfort for man and horse. It has been in use for more than thirty years, and has stood the severest tests of active field use that the varied climate and service of the country demanded.

It must be placed to the credit of this saddle that when properly fitted and adjusted fewer sore backs occur than with any other saddle ever issued, and when through accident or carelessness a back is injured, it may be cured while continuing the horse in service by removing or rearranging the pack and so folding the blanket as to guard the bruised or wounded part. The under surface of the saddle being perfectly smooth, necessitates watchfulness to prevent the saddle blanket from slipping, and hence it is customary on the march to examine blankets at every halt.

The American saddle now in use is of the same general form as that used during the Civil War, but the saddle was then issued with only the rawhide cover, which was seriously affected by the alternate wetting and drying to which it was constantly exposed. The effect of this was to tear out the seams, the result being that the rawhide curled up on the edges, and compelled the troopers to cut off the covers to prevent chafing of the inner thighs.

The leather covered saddle, the details of which have

already been described, has made a good record for itself, if frontier marches of from 500 to 1,500 miles, interspersed with innumerable short marches of a few days' duration, are of any value in determining the adaptability of horse equipments for service.

In much of the wild country where the cavalry has been on duty the troopers were required to carry all they needed for a scout of thirty or sixty days, except rations, on their horses. The weight of the packs varied somewhat on different campaigns, according to the amount of ammunition, horseshoes, etc., ordered carried on the horse. The pack mules were usually reserved to carry rations.

The weight of the arms and equipments is practically the same for all troopers, no matter what their own weight may be, therefore the strong horses are selected for the heavy men, in order that all the animals may have the same chance of pulling through the fatigues incident to field service.

The weight carried by the horse depends upon the character of the campaigning. The summer work is done frequently with a much reduced load, but in the severe weather of the northern plains in midwinter both weight and bulk are much increased. The following table will show the articles carried ordinarily on the trooper's horse:

WEIGHTS OF ARMS, EQUIPMENTS AND CLOTHING OF U. S. CAVALRY.

Saddle with hair cincha, stirrups, stirrup straps, saber straps and coat straps	17.3	lbs.
Saddle bags	4.2	"
Carbine boot	1.1	"
Bridle and bit, mod. '92	2.6	"
Halter and strap	2.6	"
Nose bag	1.05	"
Lariat and picket pin, {picket pin, 1.5 lbs. / lariat, 1.8 "}	3.3	"
Canteen and strap, empty	1.1	"
Meat can	.95	"
Knife, fork and spoon	.38	"
Cup	.525	"
Surcingle	.75	"
Horse brush	.625	"
Currycomb	.65	"
Watering bridle	1.1	"
Saddle blanket	4.3	"
Spurs and straps, pairs	.35	"
Pistol holster	.5	"
Cartridge belt	.90	"
Side lines	1.72	"
Carbine	7.95	"
Pistol, cal. 38	2.06	"
Saber and scabbard	3.75	"
Saber knot	.2	"
Carbine sling and swivel	.80	"
Saber belt and plate and attachment	.90	"
Overcoat and cape	6.25	"
Blouse	2.00	"
Trousers	2.37	"
Blue overshirt, woolen	1.12	"
Undershirt, woolen	1.06	"
Drawers	.87	"
Socks, woolen, pair	.25	"
Campaign hat	.31	"
Gauntlets, leather	.43	"
Blanket, woolen	5.00	"
Shelter tent, half	2.00	"
Boots	5.00	"
Cavalry leggins, warm climate	.81	"
Two horseshoes, fore and hind	1.5	"

HORSES, SADDLES AND BRIDLES.

Shoes, warm climate .... 2.06 lbs.
Toilet articles and gun cleaning materials.............. .... "

Special issue for winter campaigns:

Canvas overcoat, blanket lined........ .... 10.5 "
Fur cap,... .31 "
Fur gauntlets,... .56 "
Felt or wool oversocks .... 1.00 "
Arctic overshoes .... 3.57 "
Horse cover and surcingle........ .... 6.00 "

Toe calks and ice nails issued in winter.

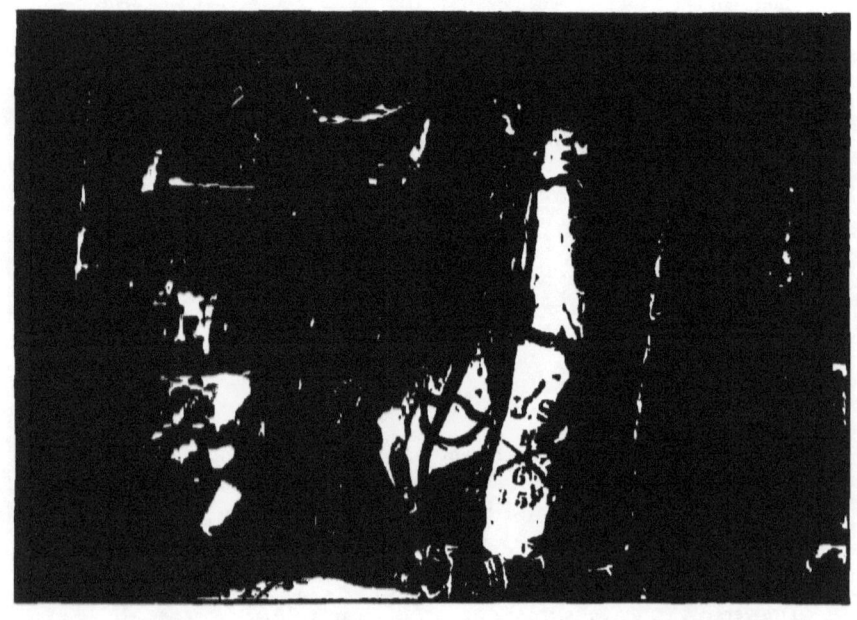

Fig. 37.

Grain sacks are not usually carried on frontier service, but a very serviceable canvas bag is issued for this purpose when required. The weight of the average kit and equipments complete is about ninety pounds.

198   HORSES, SADDLES AND BRIDLES.

The total weight carried by the horse may be, and frequently is, increased by the addition of rations for the

PLATE XI.

trooper and grain for the horse. It can be easily seen that the manner in which this load is secured is of the greatest importance.

Fig. 37 shows the saddle with saddle-bags and carbine boot attached. The saddle-bags are shown so that the stud which holds them in place over the arc may be seen. The foot staples project through on each side, and a keeper of leather is inserted in each to hold the leather piece connecting the two bags down on to the bars of the saddle. The overcoat and cape are tightly rolled, preparatory to being strapped on with the three pommel straps. The bed blanket and a suit of underclothes are tightly rolled inside of the shelter tent and the nose bag slipped over one end, the head strap being buckled over the other; this constitutes the cantle pack. When side lines are carried they are laid on top of this pack, the whole being secured to the saddle by three cantle straps. The lariat and picket pin, canteen, meat can, tin cup, and bridle with link strap and snap, are also shown.

Plate XI shows the trooper mounted and equipped for ordinary field service. The overcoat is attached to the pommel, and the blanket roll to the cantle, the leather end of the nose bag showing in the plate. The saber is attached by two straps, one in the brass ring in the forward part of the bars, and the other passing through the cincha ring. The end of the halter strap is tied in the same ring on the bars that holds the saber strap. The rolled lariat is hung to the cantle ring by the snap, which is used to attach it to the halter ring when the horse is picketed, or by a small strap specially issued for the purpose. The link strap is shown running from the lower ring of the bit to the buckle in the cheek piece of the bridle. This is used to link the horse to the halter ring of the next horse on his left when dismounting to fight on foot. (Plate XII.)

PLATE XII.

Plate XIII shows the same trooper on the other side. The carbine is carried in the boot, which does not cover the muzzle. When crossing streams it is withdrawn from the boot, and carried at an advance with the butt resting on the thigh. The long carbine boot, made to entirely cover the gun, is heavy, and retains moisture when much

PLATE XII.

rain falls, but it protects the barrel and sights better than the short boot. The canteen, with its strap passed through the handle of the tin cup, is attached by a snap to the off cantle ring. Cartridges and the pistol are carried on the belt around the trooper's waist. Extra ammunition, horseshoes and nails, rations, watering bridle, currycomb and horse brush are carried in the saddle-bags.

The carbine is attached to the swivel of the sling-belt, and passed over the right shoulder and let fall behind the back in mounting and dismounting.

The saber remains attached to the saddle, but the carbine and pistol are always carried when dismounting to fight.

The equipment was devised for frontier service, and has well served its purpose. The side lines and lariat with iron picket pins might be discarded in civilized warfare, although use for lariats is constantly found for temporary ground picket lines, crossing streams, tying loads on wagons, and various other purposes.

PLATE XIV

The ends of the pommel and cantle packs are always bent downward, the heavy articles put in the bottom of the saddle-bags, and the carbine and saber hung well down on the sides of the horse. The result of this combination is to keep the horse's center of gravity nearly as low as in nature, so that the saddle seldom has any tendency to turn, as would be the case when everything is piled upon the horse's back.

Plate XIV shows the dismounted trooper uniformed in a dark blue flannel shirt, trousers and canvas leggins, for service on the Mexican border and other warm stations.

Plate XV shows the dismounted trooper uniformed in winter costume for service on the northern plains, where extremely cold weather prevails. The overcoat is of heavy canvas, with blanket lining; fur cap and gauntlets, heavy wool or felt oversocks or leggins, and

PLATE XV.

wool-lined overshoes complete the costume. On service requiring this dress the horses are also provided with

PLATE XVI.

blanket-lined canvas covers. It was only with such protection that American troops were enabled to inaugurate and carry to a successful termination a series of winter campaigns against Indians, unparalleled in severity and unexcelled in successful results.

Plate XVI shows the Whitman saddle and bridle, which was recommended some years ago by a board of officers for adoption in the American service. This saddle is intended for the use of officers, those for the troopers being equipped with packing straps. One model is provided with a large horn pommel for the purpose of carrying the carbine slung across the saddle. Many of the Whitman saddles are used by officers, but the cavalry saddle previously described is the only one used by the American trooper.

THE BRITISH CAVALRY.

The British cavalry is composed of dragoon guards, dragoons, hussars and lancers. All are armed with the carbine and saber, and the lancers, in addition, carry the lance. The equipment and accessories composing the pack vary according to the service, which for this body of troops includes a wide range, because of the extent of the colonial system.

The recognized orders include those for "review and field day," "drill," "service marching," "home marching," and "light service." The "service" and "light service" marching orders are the only ones which will be discussed in detail.

The British cavalry saddle (Fig. 38 and Fig. 39) is made with long wooden side bars of beech, and narrowed towards the rear ends, where they are covered with leather to prevent chipping. The front arch is of channeled steel, having slots for the wallet straps; the rear arch is of beveled steel, with curved spoon cantle, both arches being

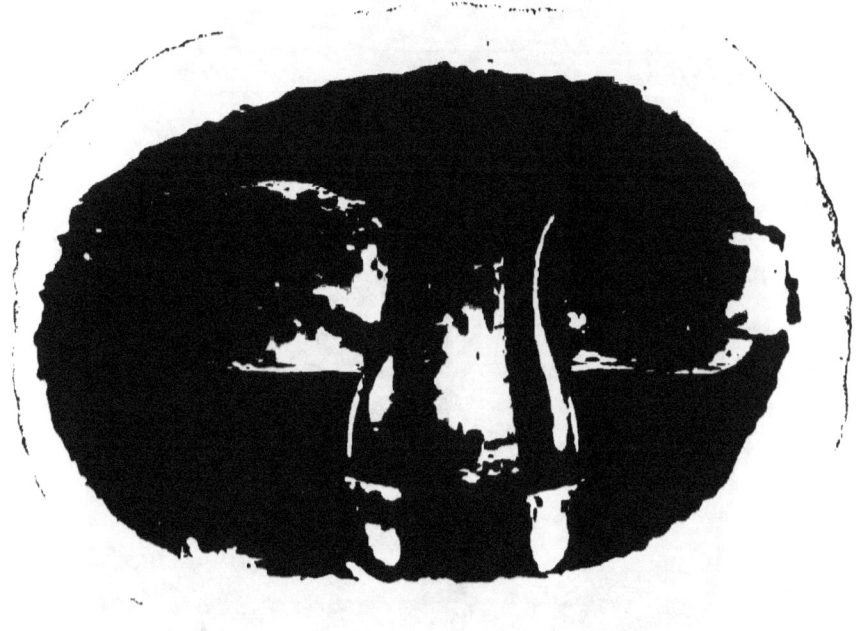

Fig. 38.

riveted on to the side bars. The links or plates for attaching the stirrup leathers are placed on the side bars about three inches from the front arch.

The leather seat is laced to the arches, and supported underneath by broad webbing, crossed. Leather flaps, or saddle skirts, are secured to the side bars with screws.

Fig. 39.

The girth is made of leather, as is also the carbine boot, which is hung on the off side and attached to the girth by a strong piece of leather. Fair leather is used for both saddle and bridle.

The substitution of the metal for the wooden arch of the Nolan saddle, in use some years ago, has not been entirely satisfactory to the British cavalry, and the cost of the saddles has been somewhat increased. It is believed that with broader side bars, and pommel and cantle made of well seasoned beech, secured with light metal plates, as in the American tree, the British cavalry would have a more serviceable saddle for carrying the packs necessary in colonial service.

The following table shows the articles carried by the dragoon guards and dragoons on "service marching order." The articles carried by the hussars and lancers are practically the same:

	Lbs.	Ozs.
Flannel shirt	1	1
Drawers	1	0½
Socks		5
Braces		4¾
Head dress	1	14¼
Tunic (or frock)	3	1
Pantaloons	2	14½
Flannel belt		6¼
Boots, knee	4	6¼
Spurs, jack		15
Gauntlets		12½
Field dressing		2
Sword and scabbard	4	6
Sword belt	1	3½
Pouch belt		11

	Lbs.	Ozs.
Haversack, full	1	8
Pocket knife, etc.		6
Pouches, (2)		11½
Ammunition, 30 rounds	3	0
Carb	7	9½
Saddle and bridle, complete	26	5
Breastplate	1	3
Wallets, packed	9	14¾
One pair ankle boots	3	13
Shoe case, fitted	2	3
Frog for carrying sword		
Numnah	2	5
Blanket	4	6
Hoof picker		2½
Nose bag, full	8	3
Head-rope		10
Built-up-rope	1	15½
Peg		3
Carbine bucket	2	2
Water bottle, empty	1	0
Cloak	7	13
Forage cap, active service		4¾
One pair spare pantaloons, One pair putties,	3	0
Waterproof sheet	2	5
Cape	2	0
Forage net	2	2½
Corn sack	1	13
Mess tin and ration	1	9
	121	15¼

The articles carried on light service order are the same as the foregoing, omitting the following:

	Lbs.	Ozs.
Forage cap, active service		4¾
One pair ankle boots	3	13
One pair spare laces		2
One pair drawers	1	0½
One flannel shirt	1	1

	lbs.	*Ozs.*
Hold-all (except spoon)		9
Housewife		3¾
One pair spare pantaloons	2	8
One pair putties		8
Corn sack	1	13
	11	15
Service M. O.	121	15¼
Less	11	15
	110	0¼

PLATE XVII.

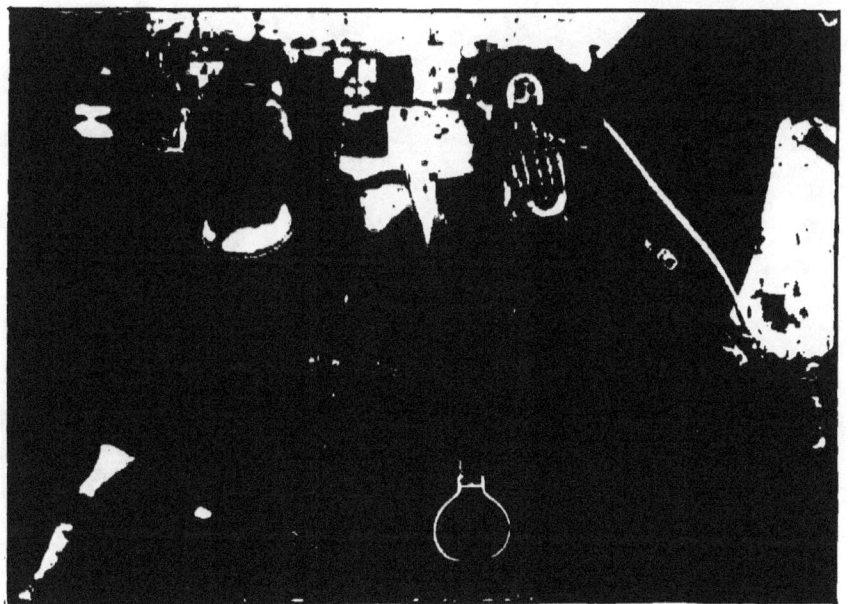

The manner of packing the kit and carrying the arms is shown in the plates. Plate XVII shows the carbine in the bucket suspended from the right side of the cantle and attached to the girth by a stiffened leather pad. Wallets are attached to the pommel, over which is strapped the cloak and a pair of ankle boots, one on each side. In the wallets are carried the horse brush, currycomb, drawers, shirts, socks, pipe clay, brushes, blacking, hold-all, etc.

PLATE XVIII.

The sheep skin in rear contains the stable jacket, trousers, gloves and picketing gear. The water bottle hangs under the right end of the sheep skin.

The same animal and kit are shown in Plate XVIII, on the reverse side. The method of attaching the saber is of

more interest than anything else in this view. It is attached opposite the carbine, undoubtedly with a view to balancing it, which is an excellent plan, provided that the saber can be quickly drawn, and that in marching it does not injure the leg.

A front view is shown in Plate XIX and a rear view in Plate XX. The pack appears to be snugly and tightly adjusted in all the views of it, and in the new "light service order" it is reduced to a very moderate limit.

The double-reined bridle for bit and bridoon is used, and a pipe-clayed halter rope takes the place of a leather strap.

Some things are carried by the trooper which would only be taken in America when pack mules or wagons are available.

There are too many "marching orders" in the British cavalry, judged from an American standpoint, but on the whole there is nothing for them to learn from Continental nations as to packing and arms.

British officers have had but little opportunity to test the value of dismounted fire action of cavalry armed with repeating carbines, but it is safe to say that when such experience does come to them, they will recognize as clearly as Americans, that horsemen do not cease to be cavalry because they can dismount and fight on foot. On the contrary, they will find their men more willing to push forward, knowing they cannot be stopped by ordinary

home guards, raw levies, or any but as good troops as themselves in equal or greater numbers.

The target and skirmish records in the American service show that the cavalrymen shoot equally as well as the infantrymen, and they have never failed to charge mounted when circumstances demanded it.

The work of the British cavalry on duty in the colonies is much like that of the American cavalry on the frontier, and their equipment and kit is carried in a somewhat similar way. The carbine in the American service is never allowed to remain on the horse without the trooper. Before dismounting all carbines are attached to the swivels of the sling-belt and hung over the back. In this way a command is not apt to be disconcerted by a sudden attack, as would be the case if the carbines were on the horses after the men had dismounted.

From the kit carried it appears that the horses are attached to the picket line in front and to the ground in rear by heel ropes. Whether this is better than the American plan is not known, but in either case constant watchfulness is necessary to prevent horses from burning themselves below the fetlocks.

It takes a long time for most horses to learn how to stand quietly at a ground picket rope, or when grazing attached to a lariat. By winding a rope about the heel a fine horse may in a few minutes reduce himself to an utterly unserviceable condition, requiring weeks for recuperation. Such heel galls are almost invariably followed by a rough, unsightly cicatrix. The difficulties arising from such accidents in the field, in addition to the wider range for grazing, induced American officers many years ago to teach all cavalry horses to herd whenever the proximity of the enemy did not prevent it.

There is no such article in the American equipment as a forage net, the shelter tent being usually called into use whenever it is necessary to pack hay. There are many occasions in war when forage nets, weighing but a few ounces, would be of great value.

THE GERMAN CAVALRY.

The German cavalry still retains the distinctive titles of cuirassiers, uhlans, dragoons and hussars, but the only difference between them is in the weight of men and horses. The cuirass is only worn on occasions of ceremony, and will not be used in the next war.

In heavy cavalry, cuirassiers and uhlans, the average weight of the horses is 1,083 pounds, and the troopers 187 pounds. In the light cavalry the horses average 866 pounds, and the troopers 143 pounds.

All German cavalry regiments are armed with lance, saber and carbine. The pistol is carried in the field by officers, first and vice first sergeants and trumpeters. There is some variation in the saber issued to different regiments, but the lance is the same for all. It consists of a hollow steel tube with a four-edged point of forged steel and a shaft of cast steel. The length of the lance is ten feet six inches, and its weight is 4.36 pounds. The carbine is the same in all regiments.

Four patterns of saddles were formerly in use, but at the present time all the cavalry is equipped with the army saddle, model of 1890, which is made in four sizes to suit horses of different conformation.

This saddle consists of a wooden tree with wooden arches, strengthened by iron plates and supported by angle irons. Between the arches is laced a leather seat, after the method in use in the old Hungarian saddle, over which is the felt lined saddle cushion, which is also laced to the arches.

To the bars are attached panels stuffed with wool, and secured by pockets laced over the fans or ends of the bar.

The girths and stirrup leathers are attached by means of D's on the bars. The stirrups are made of steel.

The leather saddle-flaps, with knee pads stuffed with hair, are attached to the arches and also to the wallets, which are strapped on the front or pommel arch.

The shabraque has holes cut in it in rear to let the cantle of the saddle and D's fixed on the bars pass through it; also in front on the off side to let the carbine muzzle pass into its socket, which is fixed on the off wallet. A breast strap is used. All the horse equipments are of fair leather.

The saddle-blanket is of white wool, and folded from nine to twelve times.

The following articles constitute the dragoon equipments for field service:

Army saddle	17.60 lbs.
Girth	1.45 "
Surcingle	0.66 "
Breast strap	0.74 "
Saddle-blanket, white wool	7.38 "
Saddle-bags	4.84 "
Carbine	6.83 "
Carbine boot and strap	1.98 "
Saber	3.87 "
Lance	4.36 "
Grain sack, with one-third of a ration	5.53 "
Stirrup strap	0.99 "
Stirrups, with lance socket	2.53 "
Forage line	1.02 "
Cooking vessel, leather case and strap	2.86 "
Headstall, halter and halter rope	2.20 "
Curb bit and reins	1.54 "
Snaffle bit and reins	0.88 "

The following articles of clothing and kit are carried:

Overcoat,	Field dressing,	Horse brush,
Tunic,	Sword knot,	Tin of grease,
Linen stable jacket,	Currycomb,	Haversack,
Neck cloth,	Three brushes,	Spoon,
Forage cap,	Tin of pipe clay,	Two pairs socks or foot
Pantaloons,	Button brass,	cloths,
Two pairs drawers,	Pay book,	Shoulder belt and box,
Two shirts,	Mess tin and case,	Hymn book,
Gloves,	Waist belt,	Two double lance buck-
Riding boots,	Three bags, with rice,	ets,
Wellington boots,	salt and coffee,	Fore shoe,
Spurs,	Shoe case,	Hind shoe,
Helmet,	Sixteen nails,	Sail cloth bucket.
Linen trousers,	Nose bag,	
Mark of identity,	Carbine sling.	

The weight of arms and saddle equipments is 57.36 pounds, and the clothing and other articles of the trooper's kit will average more than forty pounds. The total weight

Fig. 40.

carried by the horse, exclusive of rider, will seldom be less than one hundred pounds.

Fig. 40 shows the saddle and bridle removed from the horse. The method of attaching the carbine indicates that it is secured in place before the trooper mounts. The

PLATE XXI.

wallets are carried on the pommel, and the overcoat in rear of the cantle.

Plate XXI shows a trooper of the First Dragoons of the Guard. The saber is attached to the saber belt, and the cartridge box seen behind the back is hung from the shoulder belt, and contains thirty cartridges.

The left wallet has a small pocket in the front, in which are carried fifteen cartridges. The horseshoes are strapped on the outside of the wallet. The white end of the grain sack and the overcoat are seen just above the leather case containing the cooking vessel, which is hung from the cantle on the left side.

Plate XXII shows the same trooper on the right side. The lance rests in the boot or socket attached to the stirrup. The grain sack and overcoat are seen as from the other side. The leg is enclosed between the carbine and the saddle as if wedged there. The whole presents an appearance of top-heaviness, conducive to turning over the saddle, and interfering with the stability of the horse at speed over rough ground. The weight upon the withers appears to be greater than a fair proportion of the total, which would interfere with locomotion, and cause fistulous withers.

It is apparent at a glance that it would be impossible to mount any but perfectly trained and steady horses with a carbine strapped alongside of a saddle in the manner adopted by the Germans. In time of peace they have such horses, for none are bought unless thoroughly broken and gentle, and then they are given two years careful training before being put in ranks. They become accustomed by constant use to all the sights and sounds incident to service, and so well established in their gaits that a horse seldom breaks the indicated gait, and never bolts, even in large bodies of horsemen moving rapidly.

The method of attaching the carbine is not suited to untrained horses, such as would be sure to come into the ranks in large numbers in a prolonged campaign, or a brief one involving much fighting.

The saber should be attached to the saddle, so that when the troopers are dismounted to fight on foot no time will be lost in looking for a place to hang it. It is presumed some arrangement has been made for securing the lance to the horse when the trooper dismounts, for it is well recognized in the American service that the horse holders must follow up an advancing line, or take the horses back to cover when a defensive line is to be held.

Much care is devoted to this training, for the morale of a fighting line of dismounted cavalrymen is much enhanced by the knowledge that their comrades will find cover for their horses and yet have them on hand promptly in case there is need for them to secure victory by a rapid advance, or to escape capture by a mounted retreat.

It is a question whether the German equipment does not show that they are divided as to the lessons of the American Civil War, and that they have attempted to satisfy both the admirers of the lance and those who recognize

PLATE XXII.

that fire action is a necessary accompaniment to successful raiding columns of cavalry. The result may not be disaster, but it will fall far short of the success attained by cavalry commands during the last two years of the Civil War in the United States.

It would not be practicable in America to campaign without baggage wagons unless some blankets or shelter tents are carried on the horses. The system of billeting may do away with this necessity in Europe, but it would never work in America.*

No blanket, shelter-tent or cover appears to be included in the German cavalryman's equipment. This makes it absolutely necessary to billet the men, which involves scattering them about villages in a way which is not conducive to cavalry success, although it may be entirely applicable to infantry.

---

*During the Civil War several general and many subordinate officers learned by bitter experience that they were not safe billeted in houses, even in the midst of troops. A notable occurrence was the capture of General STOUGHTON while asleep in bed at the house of Dr. GUNNEL in Fairfax Court House, Va., several miles within the Federal lines. This was accomplished by MOSBY, who, with his men, passed through the picket line in some heavy pine timber during a dark and rainy night. The guards on the streets were approached under the guise of patrols, and all were captured without firing a shot. A captain and a number of men were captured, and also nearly sixty animals, many of them being officers' horses. A number of individuals were captured in this way during the progress of the war, among them being the late Major-General CROOK.

THE RUSSIAN CAVALRY.

The Russian cavalry is composed of cuirassier, uhlan, hussar and dragoon regiments, the greater portion having the last named designation.

The non-commissioned officers and privates are armed with the saber and rifle with bayonet. Trumpeters carry the saber and revolver. The rifle is carried slung over the

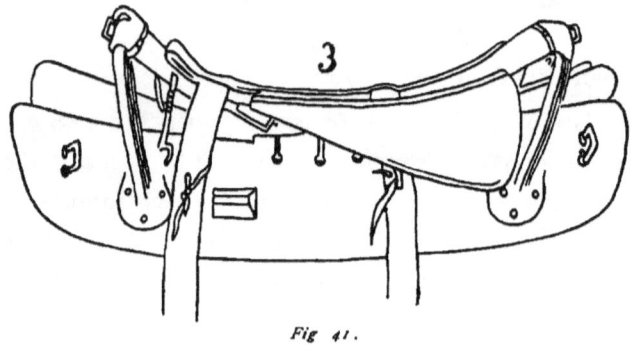

Fig 41.

back, muzzle in rear of the left shoulder, and the saber is also attached to the person of the trooper.

The Russian cavalry saddle is made with somewhat larger side bars than the usual military saddle, but the arches appear very light. The arches forming the pommel and cantle are riveted to the side bars, and are connected together by a strap which supports the cushion or seat. Fig. 41 shows the tree; the staples seen near the ends of the side bars are for attaching the straps to secure the front and rear packs.

Felt pads are placed under the side bars, being held in

place by a pocket over the front and a strap around the rear end of the bars behind the cantle arch.

Fig. 42 shows the saddle packed for service. No. 1 is

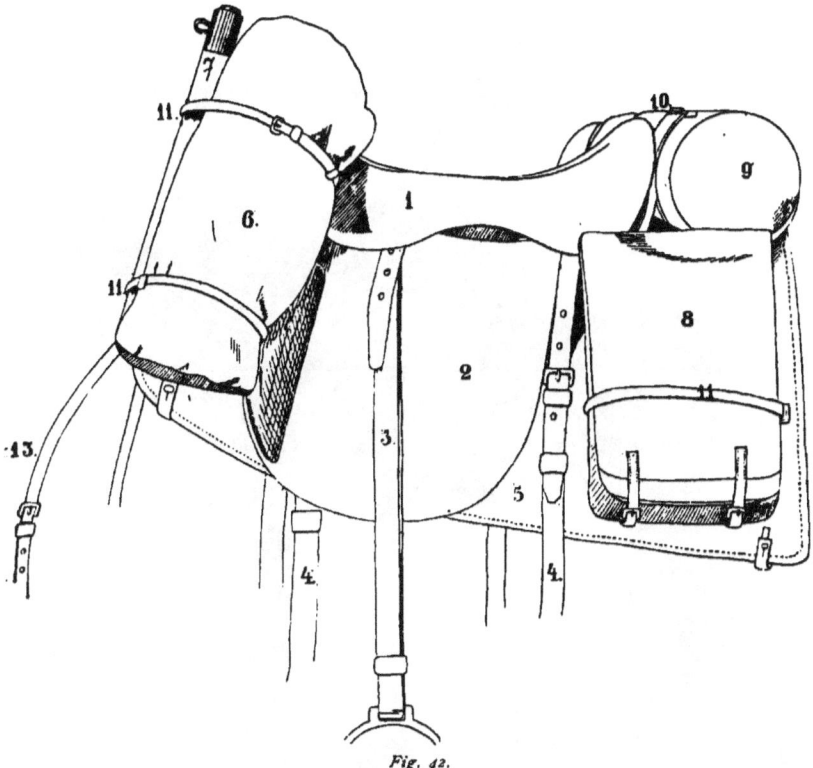

Fig. 42.

the cushion or seat; 2, the skirt; 3, the stirrup strap; 4, 4, the saddle girths; 5, the saddle cloth; 6, the overcoat; 7, the picket-pin; 8, the saddle-bags; 9, the kettle; 10, the horse blanket; 11, 11, the pack straps; 13, the breast strap.

The front pack consists of the overcoat, grain bag, with

one day's forage, picket-pin, and two leather holsters into which the ends of the grain bag are firmly tied.

PLATE XXIII.

The saddle-bags, carried in rear of the cantle, contain such of the following articles as are not strapped to the cantle:

228 HORSES, SADDLES AND BRIDLES.

Right side—Brush, shirt, pair drawers, pair short top boots, linen pieces for socks, hay net, halter, two horse-

PLATE XXIV.

shoes, sixteen nails and a currycomb, in a leather bag.

Left side—Bread in bag, three pounds; bandages for wounded; bags with groats, salt, sugar and tea, wrapped in a piece of cloth to be used for mending; soap, towels, etc., wrapped in a piece of linen; hopples, with leather straps; nose bag and horse brush.

The total weight of the Russian cavalry equipment, including the rifle or carbine and thirty-six rounds of ammunition, is about 120 pounds, and the estimated weight of the soldier, as given in their latest hand-book, is 167.4 pounds. This makes the total weight carried by the horse about 288 pounds.

Plate XXIII—copied from a photograph taken at the Officers' Cavalry School—shows a Russian dragoon equipped for field service, and Plate XXIV shows the same trooper on the reverse side.

THE BELGIAN CAVALRY.

Although Belgium is a comparatively small country, its proximity to powerful and warlike nations offers the opportunity for keeping in touch with modern and progressive ideas.

The Belgian cavalry consists of chasseurs, lancers and guides, the first and last named being armed with carbine and saber.

All cavalry non-commissioned officers above the grade of corporal carry the revolver, and do not carry the carbine.

The Belgian cavalry saddle (Fig. 43) is composed of beech side bars, to which are riveted arches of hammered steel, forming the pommel and the cantle. The side bars are covered with felt pads, which are attached by means of leather pockets. There is a broad strip of fair leather on the under side covering the space between the bars, and which is attached to the pommel and cantle.

Fig. 43

The side bars are pierced with mortises for the stirrup straps. The left bar has two screw staples, with rings for the saber boot, and a plaited rawhide loop for the forage cord.

There is a seat piece of fair leather attached to the arches, between which and the tree is a pad stuffed with hair. Two skirts or flaps of fair leather are riveted to the seat piece. The stirrups are narrow, and made of steel; the stirrup straps are of fair leather.

Two leather pouches, joined by a broad band, are hung over the pommel, and brown canvas saddle-bags are carried in rear of the cantle.

PLATE XXV.

The equipments vary slightly for the different classes of cavalry, those of the guides being nearest like the

HORSES, SADDLES AND BRIDLES.

American. The following is a list of clothing, kit and equipment carried by them:

	Lbs.	Ozs.
Overcoat	8	12.
Cloth blouse	3	11.
Pair trousers with leather bottoms	4	5.
Fatigue cap		4.
Flannel jacket	1	6.6
Busby	1	11.
Cord for same		1.5
Two collars		2.9
Two pairs half boots or high shoes	5	4.7
Pair leather gloves		2.4
Two pairs socks		13.4
Two shirts	4	1.
Pair linen trousers	3	3.5
Two pairs drawers	1	11.5
Towel		8.6
Comb		.5
Pair scissors		2.8
Bag for needles, thread, etc.		.9
Set of brushes, (three—clothes, gun, grease)		11.
Two pairs of spurs		4.2
Pair of spur covers		1.
Saber knot		1.7
Water bottle (canteen) with sling	1	1.7
Surcingle		6.8
Horse brush		11.
Currycomb		14.5
Forage cord		7.
Sponge		.5
Grease box		1.2
Grain sack		15.8
Nose bag		10.
Pair of saddle-bags of brown canvas	2	5.
Two bags for small articles, (brushes, etc.)		.4
Bidon, (serves the purpose of our meat can and tin cup)	1	4.
Saber belt		10.
Saddle with girth, straps, felt pads and stirrups, complete	34	6.
Saddle blanket of brown wool	8	6.

HORSES, SADDLES AND BRIDLES. 233

	Lbs.	Ozs.
Bridle, complete, with halter	4	15.
Carbine with sling	8	13.
Saber with scabbard	4	8.

Add to the above one knife, one fork and one spoon; also one screw ring for hitching horses to trees, posts, etc., and weighing about 8.8 ozs.

PLATE XXVI.

The manner of packing the saddle and carrying the arms in the guides is shown in Plate XXV, and the same trooper on the reverse side in Plate XXVI.

THE AUSTRIAN CAVALRY.

The Austrian cavalry, like the German, is divided into dragoons, hussars and lancers, but all are similarly armed and equipped, the only difference being in designation and uniform.

The troopers are armed with the saber and a magazine carbine of small caliber, which they are taught to use on foot.

The Austrian cavalry enjoys the reputation of being as good, if not better, than any in Europe. It is mounted upon a good class of saddle horses with great powers of endurance. The Hungarians, Poles and Gallicians have always been celebrated in Europe as horsemen, and they furnish a considerable portion of men for the cavalry.

Men and horses are both comparatively light; there is no distinction as to light and heavy cavalry.

The interests of the arm are constantly studied and cared for by the Inspector-General of Cavalry and the Cavalry Bureau, which is specially charged with all matters pertaining to the personnel and material of the cavalry branch. This is a matter worthy of consideration in the American service, even in times of profound peace.

The saddle-tree and cover are shown in Fig. 44.

The saddle-tree is composed of two wooden side bars, to which are riveted a wooden pommel and cantle. The

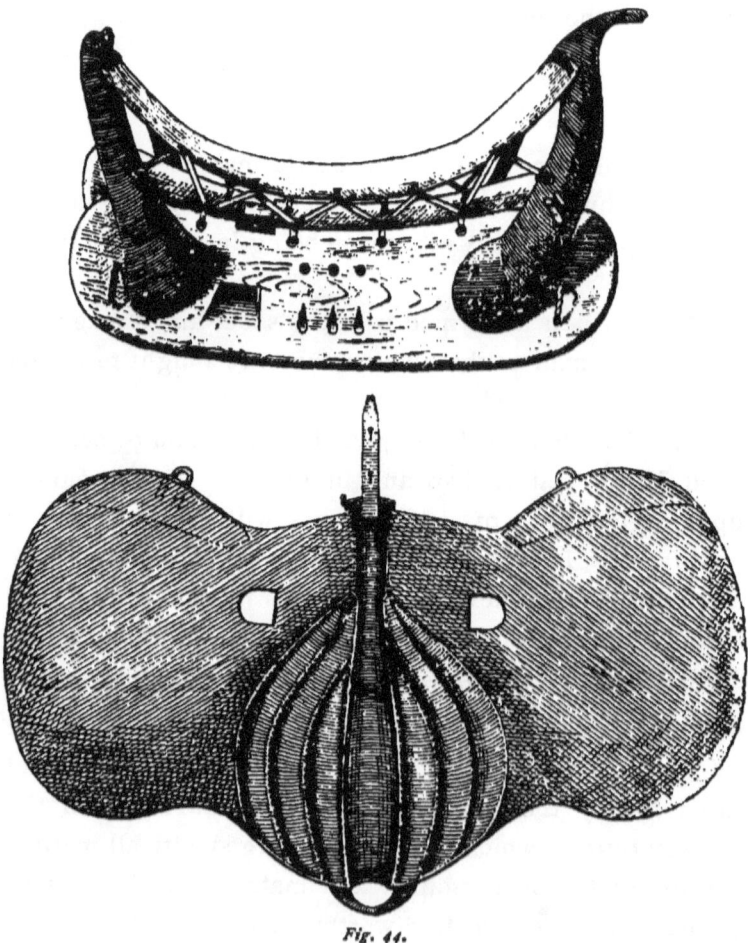

Fig. 44.

slope of the pommel and cantle is about forty-five degrees, the cantle being somewhat longer than the pommel.

The side bars contain holes for the stirrup straps, and also small orifices through which the ties pass for fastening the girth to the saddle-tree. The bars are encased in felt covers with leather corners. The pommel and cantle are connected by a piece of leather, upon which the leather seat rests; the seat and flaps or skirts form one piece, which is fastened to the pommel and cantle by thongs. The flaps have holes through which the stirrup straps pass. The girth is of two pieces of leather fastened to the side bars and with a buckle on the longer piece. The surcingle, also of leather, is fastened over the saddle. Heavy steel stirrups with a broad tread are used.

The saddle is comparatively light, and the seat is high enough above the horse's back to admit of a good circulation of air. Careful attention is paid to fitting saddles, and fifty with adjustable side bars are allowed each regiment for special cases. The simplicity, dimensions and general shape of the saddle-tree commend it for military purposes.

A black leather breast strap is used, but no crupper.

The saddle blanket is about five feet square, folded in six folds. The saddle is prevented from slipping by the felt pads on the side bars.

When the trooper is equipped for field service (Plate XXVII) the saddle is packed as follows: in the right wallet, reserve rations for three days, two shirts, two pairs of drawers, foot-cloths used as socks, forage cap, housewife and toilet articles; in the left wallet, the nose bag, currycomb, horse brush, one day's ordinary ration exclusive of bread, knife, fork and spoon, oil, grease, blacking, brushes, and other minor articles for cleaning arms.

PLATE XXVII.

A horseshoe pouch of black leather with flap is fastened to the left side of the saddle near the cantle, and contains two fore shoes, nails, a hoof-pick, and in winter twelve sharp and four dull screw ice-calks, the latter being carried in a small pocket with a nipple wrench.

A wooden picket-pin, with an iron point and ring, is strapped on the left wallet with the rope hopples for the fore feet.

A forage sack, containing two grain bags, each packed with half of the grain carried, is fastened at the middle of the cantle. The bread ration, in two parts, is carried under the grain bags. When a feed is taken from one side the balance of the grain is equally distributed between the two bags. When the grain bags are empty they are folded up and laid on the sack with the bread.

The mess pot, in a canvas case, is strapped on the great coat. When hay is carried it is twisted in a long circular whisp, and fastened over the wallets on the pommel.

A telescopic canvas water bucket is strapped to the near wallet.

A felt-covered water bottle is carried over the right shoulder, strung on a cord. The cooking utensils and eating tin are carried on the saddle.

The carbine is carried slung on the trooper's back (Fig. 45), butt down, and muzzle opposite the left shoulder. Each trooper carries fifty rounds of carbine ammunition, distributed as follows: twenty rounds on the waist belt, in two boxes, each containing ten; twenty rounds in a special pocket on the front edge of the left saddle-bag, and ten rounds in the left pocket of the latter. Thirty rounds of pistol cartridges are carried in two pouches by the officers and those of the men who are armed with the pistol.

Fig. 45.

The average load carried by the horse, including trooper, equipments, rations, forage, and a share of the tools, weighs more than 297 pounds. This load must be reduced, or the Austrians will have to abandon the idea that they possess the typical light cavalrymen of Europe.

A set of fours of hussars is shown in Plate XXVIII, which illustrates the method of attaching the horses together when dismounted action occurs. This illustration does not accord with American ideas on the subject.

No other nation has ever fought its cavalry on foot to such an extent as was done in America during the Civil War and since. This experience taught, that in order to follow up a line fighting dismounted in rough country,

PLATE XXVIII.

through and over obstacles, it is necessary to link the heads of the horses firmly and *close together*. They lead much better and do not become tangled up in each other's bridles. Even when properly and carefully linked together, horses require much drill before they can be conducted rapidly from place to place. Horses in column of fours should be linked so that their heads will not be more than eighteen inches apart.

It is observed that not only the Austrians, but Continental nations generally, with the exception of the Germans, carry the carbine on the trooper's back instead of attaching it to the saddle.

Theoretically, the slinging of the carbine over the left shoulder and strapping it snugly to the back is the best way for the gun, as well as for the horse. In this position the carbine is not liable to injury, and is always with the trooper when he dismounts, no time being lost in detaching it from the saddle. It is very much harder on the trooper, the fatigue being doubly severe whenever the trot is taken. The horse has to carry the weight whether it is on the man or the saddle. Everything being considered, Americans prefer not to put the weight on the trooper, for the fatigue occasioned by carrying a gun across the back all day is apt to produce lounging in the saddle, which, in the end, is more disastrous to the horse than if the gun is hung in some manner from the saddle.

Sabers are carried on the person in some armies and attached to the saddle in others. A saber suitable for a mounted man is an encumbrance to him on foot, and should always be attached to the saddle. In this position it makes but little noise compared to that produced when hanging from the trooper's waist.

There is not much difference between the equipments

and kits in various armies as to weight, but there are many opinions and customs regarding the distribution and adjustment of the packs. Many little things which appear trifling may have great bearing upon the comfort and endurance of both men and horses.

Saddles and bridles for military purposes abroad are very generally made of fair leather. The use of felt pads laced on to the side bars is so general, that it might be profitable to try the experiment with American saddles, to determine whether the saddle blanket can be prevented from slipping by such means.

CHAPTER XI.

SEATS.

Variety of Seats.—Value of a Well Balanced Seat.—Safest and Best Seat.—Balance, Friction and Stirrups.—Seat Depends upon Purpose in Riding.—Long or Chair Seat; "Tongs-across-a-wall" Seat; Fork Seat; Military Seat.

In observing riders from day to day it is surprising to note what a variety of attitudes are assumed by them in the saddle. The conformation of the rider of course has some influence, for a short, heavy-built man must not be expected to present the same appearance as a man with very long legs projecting down below the body of the horse.

Those who have absorbed a practical knowledge of riding early in life constitute a class almost distinct and apart from those who have deferred mounting horses until full-grown men, although many of the latter become accomplished horsemen. Boys who learn to ride, and have no fear of horses, almost invariably sit well down in their saddles ever afterwards, whereas a large proportion of those who have never mounted a horse until their muscles and bones are "set," are very apt to lean forward instead of sitting down closely and maintaining continuous contact with the saddle.

This latter style of riding is nearly always accompanied by a heavy hand on the bit, instead of that easy "give and take" feeling on the horse's mouth, which is so necessary in order to derive any pleasure or comfort in the saddle. This light and changeable feeling of the horse's mouth is incompatible with any but a secure and well-balanced seat.

The necessity for relaxing the pressure of the mouthpiece on the bars, except when it is desired to gather the horse in hand, ought to be apparent to any thoughtful person, yet more horses are ruined for saddle purposes by a neglect of this than from any other cause. A rider with little confidence in his seat is almost certain to depend upon a good steady pull on the reins for assistance. Hence it arises that when such a person mounts a well trained saddle horse with a delicate mouth, accustomed to regard the lightest pressure of the reins as an indication or signal from the rider, he at once confuses the animal, which being unable to understand what the pulling means, begins to fret and prance, thus making the already insecure seat more so.

It has already been stated that lightness or heaviness of the rider's hand depends mainly upon the stability of his seat, and this cannot be too often impressed upon the minds of those learning to ride.

Aside from the great value to the rider himself of a well-balanced seat, the stability of the saddle and the safety of the horse's back are also involved. It is treading on dangerous ground to prescribe one seat as applicable and the only correct seat for all riding. So long as whole nations ride certain seats entirely different from those used by other nations, it will be seen that habit has much to do with riding. By early training and long practice one may be able to accomplish the ends for which he mounts a horse while riding a seat apparently at variance with all orthodox ideas upon the subject.

The safest and best seat is that which permits a proper use of the stirrups in combination with balance and friction. If proof of this were required, it would only be necessary to point out the fact that Indians and other uncivilized nations accustomed to bareback riding, which is the perfection of balance and friction riding, uniformly adopt saddles and stirrups as soon as contact with other riders teaches them the value of these articles.

The varieties of seat all depend primarily upon balance, friction, and the aid of stirrups. Of these balance is by far the most important, otherwise a broken stirrup strap or loose cincha might produce a fall from the horse. The combination of all three, without exclusive dependence upon any one, will give the most satisfactory results.

The purpose for which the rider mounts his horse determines to a great extent the kind of seat he will ride. The jockey, in the merest apology for a saddle, his feet shoved home in light steel stirrups, and whose sole duty is to ride to orders and land his mount first under the wire, presents few points of resemblance to the cow-boy, who, in his fifty-pound saddle, fearlessly ropes half-wild cattle, and holds them down by wrapping his rope around the horn of his saddle and "stretching them out."

Military riding cannot be properly classed with any other kind of riding, because its object is entirely different. Park and road riding present no resemblance to it, because in these the individual taste of the rider dictates all his appointments and the gait of his horse. It is here that the trained and many-gaited saddle horse finds his proper field of action. A light leather saddle is all that is required, whereas in military riding a heavy wooden frame, capable of having a hundred-pound weight of pack attached, is an absolute necessity according to the ideas which have generally prevailed on the subject. This military saddle must also have a high pommel and cantle, which detract much from its appearance, but are indispensable because of the pack.

Hunting involves rough riding across country, but the seat is not limited by any such necessities as apply in the case of military riding. In following the hounds the rider has usually a trained jumper, and his riding is practically over a straight-away course involving no sudden turns or halts except in event of accident. Even though the huntsman keeps well up with the hounds, and may at times find himself bunched with many others, it is vastly different from the rushing, thundering noise of a boot-to-boot charge over unknown ground, perhaps in a cloud of dust or smoke, where a secure seat, entirely independent of the reins, is an absolute necessity.

HORSES, SADDLES AND BRIDLES. 247

In any particular form of seat all men do not appear exactly the same. Aside from lack of uniformity in

PLATE XXIX.

instruction there must be some reason for minor variations of seat, and the most probable one is that certain forms of

248   HORSES, SADDLES AND BRIDLES.

legs are adapted to grasping the horse correctly without undue constraint, whereas it is quite impossible for men

PLATE XXX.

with legs of other shapes to sustain the proper grip when necessary for prolonged periods.

There are several well recognized varieties of seats besides the military seat, which, however, contains the essential elements of all good seats. These various seats may be fairly classed under three general forms: The long seat, in which the rider sits well back and raises his thighs almost to a horizontal position; the "tongs-across-a wall" seat, in which the legs are held straight, with the toes stuck out and to the front; and, finally, the fork seat, in which the legs are held straight down beside the horse, perpendicularly to the ground.

The long seat is not adapted to military saddles, particularly the American. The position of the legs is shown in Plate XXIX, but of course in order to ride this seat the stirrups must be shortened.

The long seat with short stirrups is used very generally for hunting and cross-country riding, where difficult jumps may be expected. It is claimed, and generally conceded, that the horse held between the legs from the calf up, with the knees far forward, gives greater security when landing after a big jump. In jumping, the difficulty of remaining in the saddle increases rapidly as the obstacle is higher. For this reason hunting saddles are quite often provided with rolls against which to brace the legs.*

---

*At a high jumping contest which took place at a horse show in Madison Square Garden, New York, between FRED. GEBHARDT'S "Leo" and a Canadian horse, it seemed impossible for the rider on "Leo" to come down elsewhere than on the animal's neck. "Leo" approached the bars slowly and bucked over, while the Canadian horse took them at a flying leap, the rider of the latter appearing but little disturbed in the saddle.

The "tongs-across-a-wall" seat (Plate XXX) is not adapted to difficult riding of any kind, for a lost stirrup or broken strap will compel the rider to change his form of seat or fall off. It may do at a walk or canter on a very easy gaited animal, so far as the rider is concerned, but the weight is transmitted to the fore legs in such a way as to have not only a retarding effect on the movements of the horse, but also to create permanent injury to the fore legs. This is a serious matter in active service, because a very large proportion of horses break down in the fore legs, while the hind legs remain uninjured.*

Keeping the knee straight produces much weariness. When the trot is taken the rider instinctively leans back, curving the lower part of his spine, and sitting well up on the cantle, more on the back part than on the bottom of his buttocks. To maintain this position the feet are stuck forward and outward. The seat, viewed from behind (Plate XXXI), shows it to be not only awkward but very insecure in every way. With the feet stuck forward the saber cannot be properly used to make effective points, nor can the trooper lean out of his saddle to make cuts to the right and left. It is emphatically a parade and not a service seat, and should be avoided by those who desire to attain perfection in horsemanship.

---

*After General SHERIDAN's raid with the Cavalry Corps to Richmond, an expedition of about thirty days' duration, the unserviceable and broken-down horses were gathered together in a park at City Point, to the number of about 6,000. A careful inspection of these animals showed that while they were remarkably free from bruised withers and sore backs, they were all thin, and mostly broken-down in front.

HORSES, SADDLES AND BRIDLES. 251
PLATE XXXI.

In the fork seat (Plate XXXII) the legs are carried down perpendicularly to the ground, and the rider does

PLATE XXXII.

not remain seated on his buttocks, but rests on his crotch and the inside of his thighs. In this position the rider is very solid, for his legs embrace the horse very firmly from the calf up to the crotch.

The fork seat is a very common one in various parts of America, as well as other parts of the world. While by no means the seat for all-around purposes, it is ridden exclusively by whole tribes and nations of natural riders, some with the stirrup short enough to hold the sole of the foot parallel to the ground, while with others the stirrup is so long that the toe is bent down to gain contact with the tread. It is condemned for military purposes as unsuited to long marches at a trot, although it is frequently used for long distance rides made on the frontier with small native horses, whose habitual gait is an easy canter.

The mechanical disadvantage of this seat arises from the fact that when the leg is straight the thigh is round instead of flat as required for gripping the horse.

It is very commonly assumed during the excitement of the charge by a majority of troopers, who, in order to use the saber effectively, stand in their stirrups.

In the military seat (Plates XXXIII and XXXIV) the rider should sit in the middle of the saddle, taking his weight upon his buttocks equally; the body and head erect and square to the front, with shoulders well back and the chest pushed slightly forward; the forearm of the bridle hand horizontal, and the elbow close to the body without pressing against it; the right arm hanging naturally, with the hand behind the thigh; the inner surface of the thighs in close contact with the horse and saddle from the knees

254 HORSES, SADDLES AND BRIDLES.

to the buttocks, the direction of the thighs being about parallel to the horse's shoulders; the lower part of the legs,

PLATE XXXIII.

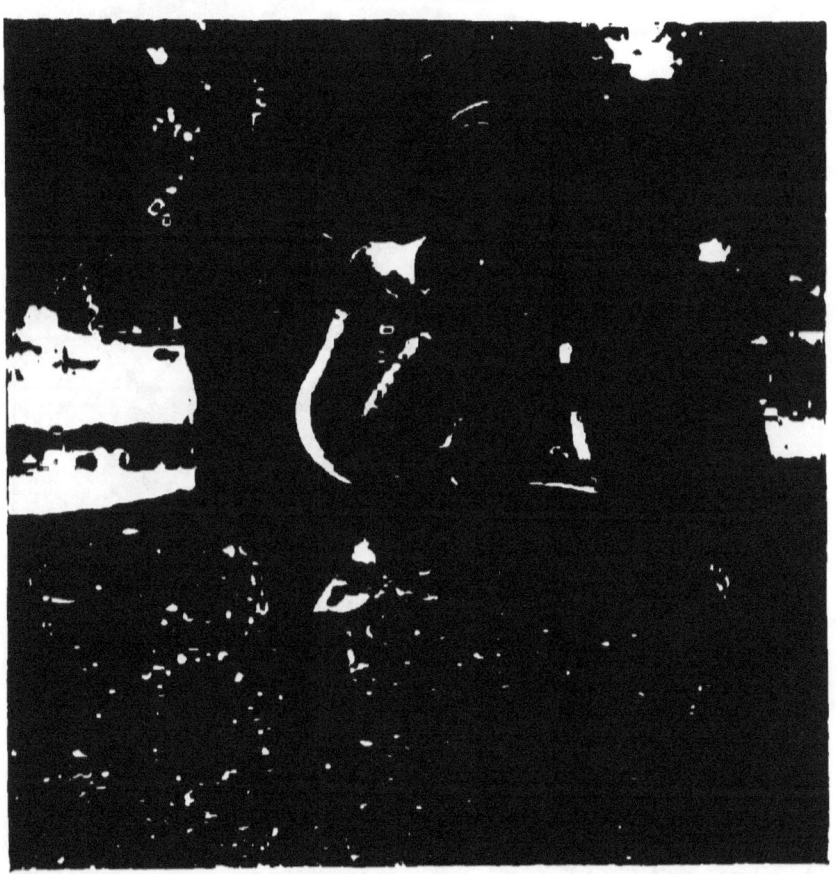

from the knees down, should fall naturally, and be completely under the control of the rider for use as aids in directing the horse. The stirrups should be adapted to

PLATE XXXIV.

the seat, and the stirrup leathers should be of such length that when the ball of the foot rests on the tread of the stirrup the heel will be slightly lower than the toes, and both leathers of exactly the same length.

Stirrups should not be worn so long as to render the tread on them insecure, nor so short as to cramp up the legs. In either case the rider is to some extent deprived of the proper use of his legs as aids, and is not able to maintain a correct seat.

The position of the foot giving the greatest satisfaction is that which requires no muscular effort to prevent the toe from turning out, and in which the sole remains firmly upon the tread of the stirrup when the horse trots.

With a military seat as described, the rider should be able to bend the body forward, backward, or to either side without disturbing the grasp of the thighs or moving the feet. He should also be able to move the legs below the knee with entire freedom without altering his seat or disturbing the carriage of the body. The toes should not be turned out, as it causes the calves of the legs to grip the horse, and involves unintentional spurring every time the horses crowd in ranks. By keeping the feet nearly or quite parallel to the side of the horse the rider is enabled to move the lower part of his legs so as to indicate through them, in conjunction with his hands, what movement the horse is desired to execute. The rider also avoids contracting the very bad habit of continually pounding the horse with his heels, as is done often by the rider who turns out his toes, and always by Indians and Oriental nations.

While the rider should sit erect, all appearance of stiffness should be avoided, for rigidity of the rider is incompatible with the supple action of the trained saddle horse in motion.

When mounted bareback, or with the blanket and surcingle, the trooper sits in the middle of the horse's back with the same seat practically except as to the feet. While these are kept parallel to the sides of the horse, the toes are lower than the heels, and point in a natural way forwards and downwards.

It will be apparent at a glance that to keep the heel lower than the toes without a stirrup would involve much unnatural constraint, which, instead of adding security to the seat, would seriously impair its stability.

In long continued trotting exercises on the ring or in the riding hall, without saddles, the tendency of most horses is to gradually work the rider forward to the withers. In such cases the rider should place his hand or hands on the withers and move the body back to its proper place, for the rider feels less of the roughness of the trotting gait at the middle of the animal's back than when seated against his withers.

For military riding much uniformity is demanded at all times, and this circumscribes the variations of seat allowed to very narrow limits. The best way to secure this uniformity, which is desired not for the sake of appearances but for the cavalryman's legitimate performance of duty, is to arrange the saddle and stirrups so that the average recruit, when fairly instructed, will find it easier to sit properly than any other way.

The cavalry soldier is often compelled to stand in his stirrups in order to make effective use of his arms. It is therefore necessary to place the stirrups so that when the trooper rises he can do so without constraint to himself or disturbance to the equilibrium of the horse. This condition is best secured when the stirrups are placed only a short distance in front of the center of the saddle, for then the rider in rising does not have to move forward and can resume his seat with ease. Furthermore, no muscular action is required to keep the stirrups in position, since they support the legs in their natural fall.

It has always been the custom in the American army to teach recruits to ride bareback, or with a blanket and surcingle, before allowing the use of a saddle. Inasmuch as the most difficult thing to attain is balance, and the stirrup was devised for the purpose of assisting in acquiring and maintaining it, it would seem reasonable to first teach the correct seat in the saddle and afterwards perfect it by riding without a saddle. For teaching a firm, close seat, nothing is as good as the trot without stirrups.

When this seat is once acquired the rider has better control of the horse than through any other seat which can be devised. If through fear or temper the horse swerves, the rider instinctively grasps with his thighs, and the stirrups being directly below the seat, balance is not lost. If the horse stops suddenly there is no tendency to shoot over his head, as when the feet are stuck forward and the legs straight. If the horse rears, no time is lost in bringing back the feet and counteracting the tendency to slip off over the cantle. In fact, every sudden or unexpected movement of the horse is better provided for in the correct military seat than any other, and the rider, appreciating the security afforded by it, is less likely to degenerate into dependence upon reins and stirrups.

The military seat described contains all the elements essential to successful riding, either for pleasure or service. It varies but little in the regular cavalry of all military nations, and the trooper marching upon active service, fully equipped, with a sure prospect of hard work and scanty provender, cannot vary this seat with the same impunity as the casual rider seeking recreation and exercise.

The European seat is not adapted to the American saddle, because in bringing back the feet and elevating the toes the leg is brought against the cincha strap knot. The position of the leg is shown approximately (Plate XXXV), but with steel stirrups, such as are used by British and European troopers, the stirrup leathers must be worn much shorter, so that the sole of the foot will not lose contact with the tread.

Confidence in the saddle depends much upon the first lessons. As soon as the stirrups are crossed, or the recruit mounted on the blanket and surcingle for the very prosaic operation of being shaken into a good seat, everything

260   HORSES, SADDLES AND BRIDLES.

possible should be done to eliminate faults. Small, gentle horses, with easy gaits should be selected at first, but when

PLATE XXXV.

sufficient confidence has been acquired to perform the mounted exercises prescribed for recruits, horses should be changed daily. Care should always be taken to avoid having beginners hurt or frightened by horses that fall over backwards, bolt or kick; such things are not easily forgotten. Many a good jockey has been ruined by the mental impression left after witnessing a bad accident.

After acquiring a good seat recruits will be ready to take their chances in the ranks; however, timid men should not be forced too fast or made to mount vicious horses, but left for time and their own ambition to overcome their fears.

If necessary to put men in the ranks for active service before preliminary instruction is completed, special attention must be paid to them, else they will become confirmed in their faults and resent later instruction because of having participated in a campaign.

The herding of the troop horses in the field is of great assistance in making bold cross-country riders of many otherwise timid men. If a recruit can be given enough confidence in his seat and horse to enable him to stay with a stampeded herd until the horses have recovered their senses sufficiently to be rounded up, there need be no fear of his not learning to ride.

A trooper whose seat is insecure almost invariably makes it manifest in the horse, which becomes nervous and uneasy in ranks. The insecure seat causes the rider to constantly jerk or pull on the reins. When this fault continues it is often necessary to put the rider on his horse with folded arms, and have another trooper, mounted, to lead the horse at a trot around the hall or riding-ring for prolonged periods. This will compel the offender to learn to ride without depending upon the horse's mouth for support.

There is a vast difference between good riders and accomplished horsemen. Many of the former possess such secure seats that the meanest of brutes cannot dislodge them from the saddle, and yet they may be unable to train or to appreciate a well trained saddle horse.

It is not merely the ability to stick on which should characterize the cavalryman. He should by all means be a horseman, and the more accomplished he becomes in that line the more valuable he will be as an example to others; increase of pride and self-respect will urge him on to perfection when he discovers his ability is recognized.

The average trooper requires a great deal of individual instruction to prevent him from contracting habits which spoil horses. It is a most noticeable fact that when a beginner gets tired and irritable he almost invariably jerks his horse to punish him for his roughness. If the horse stumbles he is given a vicious jerk long after any possibility of sustaining him has passed. If the squad be at a trot the horse is jerked to make him change his gait while the instructor's back is turned.

If the troop is ordered to trot, there will always be one or two men who will purposely keep their horses so excited that they will not trot. The only remedy is to put such men on steady old horses, that are well established in all the gaits, and punish them for any repetition of the offense.

A most effective way to do this is to put such men on the ring to ride, bareback, the roughest trotters to be found.

There is a very common and unsightly fault which requires constant attention. This is the habit of curving the back and sitting on the lower part of the spine. This is usually accompanied by a drawing in of the chest and rounding of the shoulders. This position is utterly incompatible with correct military riding, and no effort should be spared to correct it. If it becomes apparent that ordinary admonition has no effect, it may be corrected by causing the trooper to hold a flat stick passed behind his shoulders, the ends being held by the hands opposite the shoulders, backs to the rear. This of course necessitates the horse being led by another trooper.

It must be kept in mind that a few hump-backed, badly seated riders will not only detract from the appearance of an otherwise fine organization, but will be an actual detriment on the drill ground and the battlefield.

The military seat is prescribed with minuteness of detail in the drill regulations, and while it may be impossible for all men to conform exactly thereto, it should be insisted upon in the cavalry as closely as possible. Many men after acquiring bad habits in riding, through ignorance or stubbornness, are quite apt to imagine that they cannot do what is desired of them.

It is not possible, under the conditions surrounding American cavalry, to perfect the drill of all horses, as is done in some European armies, and therefore the necessity for making good riders of the men becomes paramount. After a single raid or battle many raw remounts must be obtained, and if a trooper has to depend upon being supplied with a gentle, well-trained animal, he may prove a detriment rather than a valuable factor in his squad and troop. A good, firm seat should be demanded, and any trooper who cannot acquire it should be transferred to a dismounted arm of the service.

On the other hand, any horse which persistently refuses to perform his work in a gentle and reasonable way under the guidance of careful and selected troopers should be cast out just as if he were hopelessly diseased.

A horse with many blemishes and defects which will do his work honestly in ranks will render more efficient service under careful treatment than a sound and well-bred horse which keeps a trooper always engaged in trying to keep him quiet, and to preserve his own seat. In addition to worrying his rider, a nervous horse will annoy all the men and horses in his vicinity, and distract their attention from the performance of their legitimate duties. A horse should not be condemned, however, until it is assured that this nervousness is not caused by the insecure seat of the rider.

Men who cannot ride, and horses which cannot be ridden, are useless and expensive members of any cavalry organization.

CHAPTER XII.

FORAGE.

Allowance to Public Animals.—Standard Weights.—Hay: Upland; Lowland; Wet Meadow; Good; Inferior; Mow-Burnt.—Dust in Hay.—Haystacks.—Grasses in General: Timothy; Red Top; Bermuda Grass; Orchard Grass; Kentucky Blue Grass; Clover; Alfalfa; Buffalo Grass; Gramma Grass; Gietta Grass; Blue Stem; Blue Joint; Fodder or Roughness.—Weight and Measurement of Hay.—Oats.—Corn.—Barley.—Bran.

The forage supplied animals in the public service varies somewhat with locality. Hay, oats, corn, bran, and sometimes barley, are the usual components of the forage ration.

The allowance is ample for all ordinary purposes, and where grazing is abundant and opportunity is afforded the animals to avail themselves of it, a portion of the allowance can be saved.

The amount allowed is fourteen pounds of hay per day for each horse and mule, and one hundred pounds of straw for bedding for each animal per month. Grain is issued at the rate of nine pounds a day for mules and twelve for horses. In special cases of exposure, when the necessities of the service demand an increase, three pounds additional grain may be authorized for each animal daily.

Fig. 46. (Timothy)

When from any cause it becomes impracticable to supply full forage to public animals, a reduction is made by order, to affect all alike.

There is no government standard weight of grain per bushel. Grain is usually contracted for by the hundred-weight, and hay by the ton of 2,240 pounds, or by the hundred-weight.

In a majority of States the weights per bushel are as follows: Shelled corn, fifty-six; on the cob, seventy; barley, thirty-eight, and oats, thirty-two pounds; bran not less than twenty pounds.

Hay is the natural food of the horse, and upon it alone he can not only sustain life but can at the same time do a fair amount of work. It is rich in materials for repairing waste of the animal tissues, and aids digestion of the more concentrated foods. It loses in value the more it is handled, because of the breaking off of the tender flowers and leaves, and for this reason, when it is necessary to transport it to any distance, it should always be baled. It may be classed as upland, bottom, or wet meadow hay.

Upland hay, which is the best for horses, is known generally by the fineness and firmness of the stalks and the narrowness of the leaves.

Lowland hay is known by the coarseness of the stalks and by the broad leaves of its grasses. The hay, though coarser, is softer, less firm and crisp than upland hay. The color is also darker.

Wet meadow hay is recognized by its very coarse, often

Fig. 47. (Redtop.)

reed-like stalks, and by the broad, flag-like leaves, and also by the admixture of water-rushes and sedge.

Good hay should be moderately fine, sweet-smelling, well cured, and have a good, fresh color. The flowering heads of the grasses should be present. A proportion of herbage other than grass is desirable, but no weeds. Hay is not improved by keeping over one season. It should be cut as soon as it matures and before the seeds are fully ripe. Much judgment is necessary in harvesting and storing or stacking hay. Musty hay is not fit for horses, and great care must be taken to properly cure it before it is put in the stack or barn, in order that there should be no danger from heating.

Hay may be composed of the very best varieties of grasses and yet be inferior because cut too late or badly saved. Hay is usually cut late for one of two reasons: the farmer either delays in a dry season, in hopes of securing a heavier yield, or the season may be so wet that the cutting is deferred for fine weather. As the seeds ripen much of the nutritive value of the plant passes into the seeds, which usually fall off as they ripen, and are only valuable for reproduction of their kind; it is for these reasons that hay should be cut while the plants are flowered and before seeds form.

Any considerable amount of rain falling on hay causes it to lose its characteristic odor and to have a lusterless, washed-out color, according to the amount of exposure to which it has been subjected.

Fig. 48. (Bermuda Grass.)

Mow burnt hay is a term applied to hay which has heated in the stack, either from being stacked before thoroughly cured or whilst wet with dew or rain.

Dust in hay commonly arises from the hay having become slightly damp, and afterwards quickly dried without passing into the stage of mouldiness. The apparent dust is the débris of the outer coats of the stems and leaves, which decay and fall off in the process of heating which has taken place as the result of damp. Dust may also arise from hay having been overdried before being stored, or from having been much exposed to bad weather. In any case and from whatever cause it arises, it must be regarded as an unfavorable feature in hay.

Hay for the army is usually delivered baled, or in stacks. Hay baled when wet will rot just the same as loose hay. A sufficient number of bales should always be opened to determine its condition, unless a government agent witnessed the baling.

Haystacks must be built solidly, neatly topped, and raked from the peak down, to facilitate the shedding of water, otherwise the rain may penetrate, and not only turn the hay black and rot it in places, but may cause the entire stack to become musty and worthless.

In the United States there are many climates, varieties of soil, geological formations, and variations in degree of moisture and dryness; it is apparent, therefore, that no one species of grass can be equally well adapted to growth in all parts of this extensive territory.

Fig. 49. (Orchard Grass.)

Cultivated grasses were once wild, and are still so in their native homes.

The grasses in general are of greater economic importance as furnishing food for man and animals than all other plants. The truth of this will be recognized when it is considered that all the staple cereals, as wheat, rye, barley, rice, oats, etc., are grasses. They have been cultivated for a long time, but there can be no doubt that they were originally selected from wild forms on account of the size, quantity and nutritive value of their grains.

This was the beginning of agriculture, and agriculture made possible the numerical increase and diffusion of the horse, as well as the human population.

The selection and cultivation of particular kinds of grasses with reference to their grazing qualities, and for the production of hay, is, however, a comparatively modern practice. In the early history of this country, while the settlements were sparse, the natural pasturage was abundant, but in the course of time the farms began to crowd each other, and the open range for feeding was restricted.

Perennial rye grass began to be cultivated early in the seventeenth century, and was about the only grass so cultivated for nearly one hundred years. Timothy, or Herd's grass, named after one TIMOTHY HERD, its discoverer, was cultivated in America about 1720, and was not introduced into England for more than forty years after. This has continued to be a popular grass for hay down to the present time, and divides in favor with blue grass, orchard grass

Fig. 50 (Kentucky Blue Grass.)

and red top, according to locality, and is frequently found in combination with clover. The number of species of grass now catalogued is over 3,000.

The variety of plants and grasses used for forage is very large, and consists of both wild and cultivated species.

The plains lying west of the one hundreth meridian, together with much mountainous and broken interior country, are unreliable for the ordinary purposes of agriculture, but are very valuable for the pasturage afforded by the native grasses, which are celebrated for their rich, nutritious properties, ability to withstand dry seasons, and for the quality of self-drying or curing on the stalk. This quality is not possessed ordinarily by grasses at lower altitudes than 3,000 feet above the level of the sea. Many of these are called "bunch grass," from their habits of growth.

It would require a separate volume to describe all the grasses and plants useful for feeding to domestic animals. A very brief reference only is made to those in common use for animals in the public service, and which officers are called upon constantly to inspect before purchase under contracts.

Timothy.—(Fig. 46.) This is extensively cultivated as a hay crop in all the older agricultural sections of the country; the height of the grass varies according to soil, from one to three feet; it has a fine seed top; thrives best on moist, loamy soil, of medium tenacity; is not suited to light, sandy or gravelly soils; is perennial, and yields as

Fig. 51. (Alfalfa.)

high as four tons to the acre. It is often sowed with clover, and makes the best hay for horses of all known grasses.

Redtop.—(Fig. 47.) This is extensively cultivated as a hay crop; the height of the grass varies from two to three feet; it makes a firm sod; is a perennial grass; it thrives in swampy meadows and is much valued by dairymen. It should be fed close if pastured. It makes hay in large quantities.

Bermuda Grass.—(Fig. 48.) This is the most valuable grass in the South; it spreads rapidly by means of its roots, and is difficult to eradicate when once located; its chief value is for summer pasture; it is much used as a lawn grass, and for terraces and embankments; it is affected but little by droughts, and it yields from a ton and a half to two tons per acre; is perennial.

Orchard Grass.—(Fig. 49.) This is a very popular grass in the Eastern and Northern States; it grows to a height of three feet; is perennial; is adapted to a wide range of soils, climates and treatments, making good winter pasturage; when cut for hay it affords a heavy aftermath; it yields on medium land from one to three tons of excellent hay, and is easily cured and handled.

Kentucky Blue Grass.—(Fig. 50.) There are several well marked varieties of this grass. It is extensively used for pasturage; it does not afford so heavy and profitable a hay crop as some other grasses; it attains its highest luxuriance and perfection as a pasture grass over the limestone formation of middle Tennessee and Kentucky; it accommo-

Fig. 52. (Buffalo Grass.)

dates itself to a great variety of soils and climates, and does not run out on good land; no reasonable amount of grazing can destroy it; it is a perennial.

Clover.—This family embraces a large number of plants, varying greatly in size and quality. It is not deemed necessary to illustrate a plant so familiar in Europe, Asia and America. The most common varieties are the red and the small white or Dutch clover.

Clover is one of the most important of cultivated grasses, not only for feed, but as an improver of the soil. It is usually sowed in conjunction with some other grass. It lasts several years, but is frequently plowed under as a fertilizer before it runs out.

It is not suited alone for grazing, except for a few minutes at a time, as it is apt to bloat both horses and cattle. It yields about two tons or more to the acre, and will grow best on clay loam, although it thrives even on sandy soil.

Alfalfa.—(Fig. 51.) This plant is known in Europe as Lucerne, and has been cultivated for hay since ancient times. It is not so hardy as red clover, and not adapted to cold climates. It thrives best in a permeable soil, and is well adapted to, and reaches its highest development in the warm and dry climate of the Southwest, where irrigation is used. Its roots penetrate fifteen to twenty feet in the soil; it is best used as a soiling plant, but is much used as hay in the Rocky Mountain region, New Mexico, Arizona, and the far West generally; it affords two or three

Fig. 53. (Gramma Grass.)

cuttings a year, yielding two or three tons per acre at each cutting, and lasts without replanting for some years; it is not well adapted to transportation owing to brittleness.

Buffalo Grass.—(Fig. 52). This grass is extensively spread over all the region known as the Plains; it is very low, the bulk of leaves seldom rising more than three or four inches above the ground; it grows in extensive tufts, or patches, and spreads largely by means of offshoots similar to those of the Bermuda grass; it formed the main supply of food for immense herds of buffalo, antelope, and other game which formerly existed in the West; next to gramma grass, it is perhaps the most valuable plant of the region in which it thrives.

Gramma Grass.—(Fig. 53.) This is the commonest and best grass in the far West; it grows in small, roundish patches, the foliage being in a dense cushion, like moss; the flowering stalks seldom rise over a foot in height, and bear near the top one or two spikes each about an inch long, standing out at right angles; when much grazed these spikes are eaten off and only the mats of leaves are observable; it is highly nutritious, and stock of all kinds prefer it to any grass growing with it; it dries and cures on the ground so as to retain its nutritive properties in the winter. For many years after troops occupied Arizona and New Mexico this grass was cut with hoes and used as hay, with roots and dirt hanging to it; the horses kept strong and fat on it.

Fig. 54. (*Gietta Grass.*)

Gietta Grass.—(Fig. 54.) This is one of the characteristic grasses of the arid districts of Texas, New Mexico and Arizona, where it is sometimes erroneously called black gramma. It is found sparingly in Colorado and Utah. It is relished by cattle and horses, and is next to the gramma in value in those regions. Like the gramma grass, it can only be cut with hoes, knives or scythes.

Blue Stem, or Western Blue Joint.—(Fig. 55.) This species prevails on the plains from Texas to Montana, and is well known to stockmen. It is generally of a light, bluish-green color. It is the most prized of the native grasses, and wherever it occupies a large area exclusively, as it frequently does, it is cut for hay. It does not yield a great bulk, but its quality is unsurpassed. In the valleys and along the streams it frequently forms large patches, and grows thickly and abundantly. This grass extends into the mountain region, and is common in Colorado and New Mexico.

Blue Joint.—(Fig. 56.) This is a stout, tall grass, growing chiefly in wet, boggy ground or moist meadows; its favorite situation is in cool, elevated regions. It prevails in all the northern portions of the United States and in British America; in these districts it is one of the best and most productive of the indigenous grasses. It varies much in luxuriance of foliage, according to location; it grows from three to five feet high, with leaves a foot long. While not equal to some upland grasses, it gives a larger

Fig. 55. (Blue Stem, or Western Blue Joint.)

yield, makes very good hay, and is much relished by horses and cattle; is perennial.

In addition to those mentioned, the entire area of the United States, particularly the Western plains and Rocky Mountain regions, is more or less covered with various kinds of bunch grass, all very good for pasturage, and many for hay, except the annuals, which, as a rule, do not seem to have sufficient nutritive qualities for horses engaged in marching or heavy work. This refers particularly to grasses which spring up after rains, and grow rapidly to great height in a few weeks.

It would require a volume to properly describe and discuss the various native grasses and their relative merits. Where there is any choice of grasses the best should be insisted upon for hay. What is considered good in one locality is regarded with contempt in others. The government is frequently compelled to accept inferior hay or nothing. Wild mesquite beans were at one time received as forage in the absence of other available food in Arizona, and the horses got along very well, and continued to do their regular work.

Among the common grasses used for hay may be mentioned white or tall gramma, crow-foot, various reed grasses, wild oats, and several kinds of bunch grass.

During the Civil War the animals were frequently dependent upon the broad leaves of the cornstalk, called "fodder" or "roughness" in the South. When pulled off

Fig. 56. (Blue Joint.)

at the right time and properly cared for it makes a palatable forage, but is not to be compared with good timothy or other hay.

Cured hay from the grasses herein described varies greatly in weight per cubic foot. Officers are continually required to approximate the amount of hay in stacks at various military stations, and the only correct method of determining this with any approach to accuracy, is to cut from the stack a sufficiently large cubic section to obtain a fair average of the stack, and weigh it so as to get the weight of a cubic foot; the measured cubical contents of the stack multiplied by the actual weight of a cubic foot, will give the weight of the stack.

It must be remembered that the top is lighter per cubic foot than the lower portion of the stack, which has been well packed as the stack was built up. Allowance must also be made for the ends.

It will usually be found more satisfactory to estimate the volume of the solid stack separately from the volume of the lighter and peaked top. Obtain the weight of a cubic foot of each and multiply by the volume, adding the two results together for the total weight. This does not require much time or labor, and is infinitely preferable to guess work.

Oats are the best of all grains for giving animals muscular tissue, and are easily digested. They should be clean, plump and full of flour, and have a metallic luster.

It is not material whether they are white or black varieties, but they should be free from all appearance or odor of mustiness, mouldiness or sprouting, for these defects are productive of serious digestive disorders. In a sample of oats the grains should be about the same size, and there should be no admixture of small seeds of grass and weeds. Oats containing small pebbles, grit and dirt, even if otherwise good, should be rejected until cleaned.

New oats have almost a glazed appearance, which is lost in old oats, and the former have a fresh, earthy odor, which disappears in the latter. The taste of the new oat is fresh and somewhat milky. The beards are well defined in new oats, but in old oats they are knocked off by the friction of handling, being very brittle.

Corn is one of the best of foods for producing fat, but that is seldom desirable in saddle horses. It is good in cold climates on account of its heat producing qualities. In warm weather it readily undergoes fermentation, causing derangements of digestion, which is a prolific source of disease and death in horses. This is particularly the case in early spring. It is fed whole or crushed, the latter being preferable, particularly for old horses. It should not be fed mixed with other grains.

Barley is seldom received by the government, except in the Southwest, where it grows to perfection under irrigation. The animals there thrive upon it and keep in good, hard flesh under heavy work. It is frequently threshed with horses or sheep, and consequently very poorly cleaned.

Bran is a very valuable component of the forage ration. It is rich in muscle-making constituents, prevents constipation when given as a mash, is slow to ferment, easy to digest, makes good poultices, and is easy to transport, though bulky. It supplements, but does not take the place of grain.

CHAPTER XIII.

STABLE MANAGEMENT.

Herding.—Stables.—Ventilation.—Water.—Feeding.—Stable Routine.—
Grooming.—Shoeing.—Nursing Sick Horses: Discharges; Hand
Rubbing; Sponging; Hot and Cold Applications; Steaming; Poultices;
Bandages; Pulse; Temperature; Blankets; Removing Shoes; Balls;
Drenches; Injections.—Supply Table of Medicines.—Instruments.—
Explanation of Medicines.—Prescriptions.

In American cavalry garrisons the horses are usually housed at night, and herded when not in use during the day, not only for grazing but also in order to keep up the habit of coming quietly to the picket line, which is so essential for frontier service. The stables are frame buildings at the northern, and open sheds at the extreme southern stations. A few of the new and more permanent stations are provided with brick stables of modern design.

Doubtless the thorough ventilation of the frame stables and sheds is the cause of the general good health of the horses. Pure air in abundance is the one thing insisted upon for animals which may be called for at any moment to make a ride for life. To carry this idea out completely, open corrals or yards are usually attached to stables, and when not otherwise provided for the horses are turned loose, except on very stormy days. There is none of that senseless hardening of horses, so-called, by exposing them unnecessarily to extremes of weather, nor on the other hand any hot-house coddling.

To accomplish good results constant personal supervision is necessary; in no instance is the attention to duty or neglect of it so quickly reflected as in the condition of cavalry horses. In the field advantage must be taken of every circumstance which redounds to their benefit. None but those who have had experience in such matters can appreciate the difficulty encountered in keeping up the condition of horses subjected to irregular hours, short rations, and carrying heavy weights.

In garrison the stable should be kept as even in temperature as possible by opening or closing doors and windows. During violent storms or "blizzards" in cold climates it may be necessary to close everything but the top ventilators to prevent suffering. As soon as the storm has ceased thorough ventilation should be resumed. The best time to test the ventilation or purity of air is at morning stables when the doors are first opened. The stables are seldom closed in summer, the doors being replaced by bars.

While ample ventilation is very necessary, draughts should be avoided. Provision should be made to let in a gradual and constant supply of fresh air, and also for the egress of the foul air which rises.

Ventilating shafts should be constructed in the roof,

and the number of these should correspond with the size of the stable and number of animals assigned to it. In addition to these ventilators, the space between the wall plate and the roof is often left uncovered in mild climates. There should be openings of from twenty to thirty square inches, covered with grating, left at frequent intervals along the wall, a few inches from the floor.

All ventilators should be arranged so that the stable men can close them on either side, according to the state of the wind and weather; it should seldom be necessary to close them on both sides at the same time. When hollow walls are used the small openings, with gratings, may be arranged so that the one on the outside will be above the one on the inside, which will prevent all direct draughts.

Although not so important as ventilation, the lighting of the stable should receive careful attention. As far as possible the light supplied by windows should be admitted so as not to produce a glare directly in front of the horses. If the arrangements are such that it is necessary to have the horses face the windows the window frames should be put in lengthwise of the wall and up above the heads of the horses.

Ventilation should never be dependent upon the opening and closing of windows, but they should all be arranged so that this can be easily done.

The watering of the horses requires careful supervision to insure that they are watered at the proper times and are never hurried while drinking. Horses should be watered three times a day in warm weather. When turned loose, free access to water should be had at all times. In winter twice a day is as often as a horse will drink, as a rule. The first watering should be several hours after sunrise and the last just before being tied in for the night. The proper time to water a horse is before and not immediately after feeding.

In civil communities horses are usually fed three times a day, but in the army feeding in the morning and evening is the general rule. Hay and grain are fed in the evening and grain in the morning. When the animals are not in use the regular ration is supplemented by as much grazing as season and locality permit. When bran is fed it is given as a mash and never mixed with whole grain.

The stomach of the horse is comparatively small, and should not be distended by large feeds at long intervals; however, twice a day is all that it is practicable to feed in campaign.

The inclination to eat depends upon climate, work, and the nature and quality of the horse's food. In many cases of sickness, health is restored by a change of diet, but as a sign of health, the horse's appetite is not to be entirely relied upon. When horses are sick they should receive their food in small quantities, and if not completely eaten, what remains should be removed before the next feed is given.

After the horses have finished their morning feed of grain they should be tied on the picket line, where they are to be groomed. The stable men at once go to work removing the manure and shaking up the bedding. Such of the bedding as is too much soiled for further use is put with the manure; the balance is forked over and lightly piled in the front end of the stalls. This gives the earth floors a chance to dry out, for cavalry stables on the frontier are seldom provided with drains; in any event the stall will be more or less damp from the urination of the horse over night.

As soon as the stalls have all been cleaned out the manure is loaded on the troop wagon and hauled to the place designated as the dumping ground. The hay is next hauled and distributed in the stable at places convenient for putting it in the mangers. The straw for bedding is then distributed, and the stable men begin at one end, and working on both sides proceed to arrange the beds.

The morning feed of grain is usually put in the feed boxes at the first call for reveille, the feed cart being taken down the center of the stable while the stable orderlies dip out the grain in ration boxes made to hold one feed. The grain for the evening feed is put in the boxes at afternoon stables.

The officer attending stables inspects the hay, grain and bedding of the horses. If the forage is musty, dirty, or otherwise unfit for the animals, he takes the proper steps for obtaining a fresh supply without unnecessary delay. Should the bedding be too much soiled he directs its removal, and causes fresh straw or hay to be littered down. The stalls should be inspected occasionally to see that they are kept level, and that holes pawed out are refilled.

Above all other considerations next to pure air, dryness should be insisted upon about the stables. Horses prefer warmth and dryness, and putting them in damp stables is apt to cause debility and disease.

Grooming is essential to the general health and condition of the domesticated horse, and is not altogether for appearances. With hard work and high feeding the excretion of worn-out materials through the skin is very great; hence artificial means are necessary to remove the refuse.

Grooming removes from the skin those particles of perspiration, dust and dirt which would otherwise impede and clog the free action of the sweat and oil glands. It also removes the scurf or worn-out cells which are no longer required on the surface of the skin, and which would, when cemented together by particles of sweat, add to the obstruction of the glands. The grooming should take place outside of the stable when the weather permits, to avoid filling the mangers with dust.

The thorough cleaning of the skin of the horse is an operation requiring both skill and hard labor. To produce the greatest effect with the least expenditure of power and in the shortest time, the trooper should aid his muscular strength with his weight. He should stand well away from the horse and lean his weight on the brush, which will thus do its work more effectually than if operated by muscular strength alone. The working of the brush should follow the natural direction of the hair. The currycomb should be used as little as possible, and principally to loosen accumulations of mud.

When a horse is worked, and grooming is neglected, he soon loses flesh and deteriorates in health; actual disease of the skin may follow, for the presence of parasitical insects is induced by filth, and when not disturbed by grooming they breed rapidly.

Horses should not be washed, even on the legs, except in warm weather, to remove caked mud; they should be at once dried and groomed thoroughly. Horses should, under no circumstances, be allowed to dry by evaporation.

Each morning as soon as the horses are tied on the picket line the blacksmith selects those which require shoeing, and separates them from the others so that they may not be turned out on herd.

At many posts where the ground is free from stones horses are not shod continuously, but a proportion are left without shoes in order to let their feet spread out and assume a natural shape. This practice saves many horses from suffering with contracted feet.

Shoes are kept fitted for each horse at all times, for tests made on service show conclusively that horses cannot stand hard field service with unshod hoofs.

In cold climates ice nails are kept on hand, or shoes are fitted with calks for such horses as are likely to go on service. After horses are shod for winter with sharp calks it is dangerous to turn them loose, and even at the picket line they must be watched constantly to prevent serious injuries from kicking.

Shoeing is regulated in the army by the following order, which cannot be too closely followed:

"In preparing the horse's foot for the shoe do not touch with the knife the frog, sole or bars. In removing surplus growth of that part of the foot which is the 'seat of the shoe,' use the cutting pinchers and rasp, and not the knife. The shoeing knife may be used, if necessary, in fitting the toe clip.

"'Opening the heels,' or making a cut into the angle of the wall at the heel, must not be allowed. The rasp may be used upon this part of the foot when necessary, and the same applies to the pegs. No cutting with a knife is permitted; the rasp alone when necessary.

"Flat-footed horses should be treated as the necessity of each case may require.

"In forging the shoe to fit the foot, be careful that the shoe is fitted to and follows the circumference of the foot clear round to the heels. The heels of the shoe should not be extended back straight and outside of the walls at the heels of the horse's foot, as is frequently done. Care must be used that the shoe is not fitted too small, the outer surface of the walls being then rasped down to make the foot short to suit the shoe, as often happens.

"Heat may be used in preparing and shaping the shoe, but the hot shoe must not be applied to the horse's foot under any circumstances. Make the upper or foot surface of the shoe perfectly flat, so as to give a level bearing. A shoe with a concave ground surface should be used."

All officers cannot be expected to become veterinarians, but each one should familiarize himself with such injuries and diseases as occur with frequency in cavalry stables, and acquire a knowledge of such simple remedies as can be administered by the stablemen in the absence of a veterinary surgeon.

It should at all times be kept in mind that prevention of disease is more creditable than a successful cure, and that when disease or injury does come, good nursing will in most cases avail as much, if not more, than medicine.

As a rule the attachment which exists between the troopers and favorite horses will insure the latter good treatment, but there are always a few rough, vicious or unappreciative animals whose condemnation or death would not cast any gloom over the command; these latter will require the attention of officers to prevent their being neglected.

There are many minor ailments to which cavalry horses are subject which may be treated in the stalls or at the picket line, but for an animal whose sickness affects the nerves or lungs, rest and quiet are essential. To this end, if in garrison, a box stall about twelve feet square should be provided for each troop; this will remove the sick horse from all the excitement which is bound to exist about a large stable, and give him room to turn around and assume whatever position may seem restful to him. The box stall should be separated from the main building if practicable; if not, it can be partitioned off in the stable, so that it can be darkened if necessary. The walls should be whitewashed and the floor covered with clean straw.

Fresh water should be provided in a bucket, for a feverish horse will frequently help himself if left alone. In this way some medicines can be administered, but the sense of smell is so acute in horses that they may refuse water if there is any strong odor of medicine attaching to it.

The appetite of a sick horse is often very capricious, and during fever he may refuse food altogether. Place before him, in small quantities at a time, as great a variety of food fit for his consumption as can be obtained. Uneaten food should be removed before it becomes sour.

When not prevented by swollen head or neck, a horse discharging at the nostrils should, as a rule, be fed from a bucket placed near the ground, as the depending position of the head will be more comfortable to an animal in such a condition. The bucket should be used for no other purpose, and should be cleaned carefully after use. All wood work should be particularly cleaned where any particles of a suspicious discharge have been thrown or lodged.

Hand rubbing of the legs is very useful in restoring circulation, as well as for the purpose of removing any swelling arising from want of exercise.

Sponging the nostrils and dock are refreshing to the animal, and the sheath should be frequently and well cleaned when the weather permits. Care is necessary to prevent injury by the finger nails, a slight scratch often producing much swelling.

Hot fomentations in cases of sprains, and to allay

inflammation, are very beneficial. To obtain good results they must be continued for a long time, say for two hours. The water should not be too hot; it should be at such a temperature that the hand can bear it comfortably. Allow the water to trickle over the inflamed parts. Flannel or woolen bandages may be wrapped around the parts, and kept wet with warm water; they will retain the heat for some time. Fomentations should be repeated three times within twenty-four hours, and between these operations the parts should be warmly covered to keep out the cold.

Cold applications harden and brace up the parts to which they are applied; they also reduce heat. They are very useful in cases of bruises, swellings and sprains, particularly after the inflammation has been reduced by hot fomentations. In some cases a rubber tube arranged to allow cold water to trickle over a specific part or surface is of great assistance in hastening recovery. Cold water bandages are the most common applications, owing to the difficulty of getting stable men to properly apply hot fomentations.

Steaming may be done with a nose bag, or a sack arranged for the purpose. Place clean hay in the bottom, and pour boiling water over it, and then hang the bag on the horse's head so that the steam will go up his nostrils. Chloroform, carbolic acid, etc., are sometimes added by veterinary surgeons to afford immediate relief in certain affections.

Poultices are often of great service, but they are difficult to apply. They should be inclosed in some strong but thin material in order to prevent the substances from which they are made becoming entangled with hair. They should not be left on long enough to dry, as they then irritate instead of soothe.

Bandages of cotton or wool are very useful for holding poultices in position, closing wounds, compressing specific parts, and for giving warmth to the legs. Roller bandages are used on the legs, but the size and shape of others depend on their use. It is at times not an easy matter to keep a bandage in position by ordinary means. The difficulty may be overcome by preparing some form of harness to which bandage strings may be attached, varying it according to the part of the body or limbs to be covered.

The pulse in the horse is an important guide in determining his state of health. It indicates the number, force and regularity, or irregularity, of the heart's action, and the quantity of blood sent forth at each beat. As a rule, the number of pulsations corresponds with the heart's contractions.

The pulse of a healthy horse varies from thirty-four to thirty-eight. It is generally quicker in young horses than aged ones, and also quicker in well-bred than in heavy, cold-blooded animals.

The most convenient places for taking the pulse are the arteries under the jaw and inside the fore leg above the fetlock joint. It may be taken by placing the ear at the left side of the chest. The slightest excitement when a horse is sick will cause an alteration in the pulse. The animal should therefore be approached very quietly, and soothed for a minute or two before applying the finger to the artery. The fore and middle finger should be placed on the artery in a transverse direction, and not obliquely.

A strong and full pulse characterizes health, and is seldom found when the animal is in any morbid state.

A weak and small pulse is indicative of great debility, especially if the pulse is easily extinguished by pressure.

A very slow pulse indicates probable disease or injury of the brain or spinal cord.

The number of pulsations per minute under different circumstances in disease varies from twenty to one hundred, or even more.

Temperature in the case of a horse is ascertained by use of a small clinical thermometer, which is inserted in the rectum and allowed to remain about five minutes. The ordinary temperature in good health is about 99° F. It should be taken without exciting the horse by removing blankets or moving him about. In continued illness, where the temperature is an important consideration, it should be taken at the same hours every day.

During the prevalence of influenza or other epizootic disease in stables, it pays to take the temperature of all horses daily; a rise of a few degrees, which indicates the approaching disease, is sufficient to cause the horse to be withdrawn from work, for this prompt action will often cause the disease to run a milder course. Work in the incipient stages of these diseases often causes them to assume a fatal form.

When the condition of the horse requires artificial covering the blankets should be fastened on loosely. They should be removed, shaken, and aired during the day, the horse being covered with others temporarily if necessary.

In cases of serious or prolonged sickness the shoes should be removed from the horse.

Artificial inflammation is often resorted to as a stimulant to parts deficient in vitality, or for the relief of inflammation in internal organs. This artificial inflammation is often needed to rouse to new and healthier action parts which have become, through disease, deficient in vital energy. The healing process in many ulcerative diseases is very sluggish and languid, and the effect of induced inflammation is often to rouse not only the part affected, but all the neighboring structures to new and healthy action.

This treatment may vary from the light, stimulating friction produced by hand rubbing the parts or a mild mustard plaster, to a strong cantharides blister or a seton.

By seton is meant the introduction of a tape or string, intended to act on the deep seated tissues and induce suppuration. The management of a seton requires a good deal of attention. It must be pulled up and down in the wound every day, the pus carefully pressed out, and the orifices washed with warm water. The two ends of the tape may be tied together, or small pieces of wood attached to the ends, to prevent the tape being accidentally drawn into the wound. The tape should be renewed about once a week, if intended to be kept in for some time.

Firing is the most rapid way of producing inflammation. Much of the firing done is of no value, and it nearly always leaves a blemish. It is not recommended for use by any but veterinary surgeons, since much irreparable injury may be done by useless or improper firing.

Medicine may be introduced through the following channels: by the mouth; by inhalation into the lungs and air passages; by the skin through absorption; under the skin by hypodermic methods, and by injections into the rectum.

Medicine may be given by the mouth in the forms of powders, balls or capsules, drenches and electuaries.

Powders should be as finely pulverized as possible in order to secure rapid solution and absorption. They should be free from any irritating or caustic action on the mouth. If dry the powders may shake down to the bottom of the manger; the practice is, therefore, to dissolve or suspend them in water and sprinkle on the feed. Those without disagreeable taste or odor are readily taken in the feed or drinking water.

Balls should be cylindrical in shape, about two inches long and half or three-quarters of an inch in diameter. They should be fresh, and wrapped in tissue paper when given; gelatine capsules may also be used. Balls are preferred to drenches when the medicine is disagreeable;

when the dose is not large, and when the medicine is intended to act slowly. Balls may be made up by the addition of honey, syrup or soap.

When medicine is given as a drench enough water or oil must be used to thoroughly dissolve or dilute it. Insoluble medicines may be given suspended in water, the bottle being shaken before administering it. If a drenching horn is not available, use a long-necked bottle without a shoulder, of suitable size to contain the dose. The head should be elevated enough to prevent the horse from throwing the liquid out of his mouth. The halter strap should be passed over a limb or beam, but if none are available a pitchfork or pronged stick inserted in the halter will answer to raise the head until the line of the face is horizontal, which is all that is needed in any case. The horn or bottle should be introduced at the side of the mouth and slowly emptied. If the horse does not swallow, remove the bottle and rub the throat gently. If coughing or any accident occurs, lower the head immediately. In no case should drenches be given through the nose.

Electuaries are medicines mixed with licorice root powder, molasses or syrup, to such a consistency that the mass will stick to the tongue and teeth. They are given with a wooden paddle or long-handled spoon.

Medicines are administered to the lungs and upper air passages by insufflation, which consists in blowing an impalpable powder directly into the nose, and by inhalation in the case of gaseous or volatile medicines. The first named method is rarely resorted to. It is a common and well recommended practice to add carbolic acid, iodine, or other prescribed medicine, when preparing a bag for steaming the horse.

Medicines are only applied to the skins of horses for absorption in local diseases, usually as liniments or blisters.

Medicine is frequently given under the skin with the hypodermic syringe. It should be done only by the veterinary surgeon.

Injections are usually thrown into the rectum with a large syringe, but a straight tube about twelve inches long, of a size easily inserted, and which carries an upright funnel at the end, is believed to be the best, for the liquid is carried in by gravity. This answers the purpose fully without the danger arising from using too much force. Medicine is injected in the rectum when local action is desired, or when it cannot be retained by the mouth.

The supply table of veterinary medicines does not contain, by any means, all those used by the professional veterinarian, but is quite sufficient for the average troop farrier. In fact, the rule should be, much nursing and little medicine, unless prescribed by the veterinary surgeon. Inasmuch as he cannot be with all detachments, it is wise to provide a few simple remedies for immediate use in easily diagnosed cases. The accompanying supply table and prescriptions composed of medicines contained therein, were adopted upon the recommendation of a board of cavalry officers:

TABLE OF SUPPLY OF MEDICINES FOR THREE MONTHS.

MEDICINES.	For 100 animals	For 200 animals	For 300 animals
	or multiple of same.		
Acid, carbolic, crystallized . . . . ozs.	16	18	24
Aconite, tincture of the root . . . . ozs.	4	4	8
Alcohol . . . . gals.	1	2	3
Aloes, Barbadoes . . . . ozs.	20	20	30
Ammonia, aromatic, spirits of . . . . lbs.	2	3	4
Ammonia, carbonate of . . . . lbs.	1	1½	2
Ammonia, solution of . . . . gals.	1	2	3
Belladonna, fluid extract of . . . . ozs	4	6	8
Camphor . . . . lbs.	1	1½	2
Cantharides (Spanish flies), powdered . . . . ozs.	2	3	4
Charcoal (powdered) . . . . lbs.	1	1½	2
Cosmoline, veterinary . . . . lbs.	4	8	12
Ether, spirits of nitrous (sweet spirits of niter) . . . . . . lbs.	3	6	8
Ether, sulphuric . . . . lbs.	2	2	4
Flaxseed meal . . . . lbs.	25	30	40
Ginger, powdered . . . . lbs.	2	3	4
Gentian, powdered . . . . lbs.	2	3	4
Glycerine . . . . ozs.	8	12	16
Iron, sulphate of, desiccated . . . . ozs.	8	10	12
Lime, chloride of . . . . lbs.	25	50	75
Lunar caustic . . . . ozs.	1	1	2
Oil, linseed . . . . gals.	2	3	4
Opium, tincture of . . . . lbs.	3	4	6
Oil, olive . . . . gals	1	2	3
Pepper, Cayenne, ground . . . . lbs	1	1½	2
Potassa, nitrate of (saltpeter) . . . . lbs.	3	4	6
Soap, Castile . . . . lbs	10	15	20
Soda, bicarbonate of . . . . lbs.	4	8	12
Sulphur, washed . . . . lbs.	2	3	4
Turpentine, oil of . . . . gals.	2	3	4
Zinc, sulphate of . . . . ozs.	8	10	12

DRESSINGS FOR SIX MONTHS' SUPPLY.

MEDICINES.	For 100 animals	For 200 animals	For 300 animals
	\multicolumn{3}{c}{or multiple of same.}		
Bandages, 2½ in. wide, 4 yards long, of heavy bed ticking . doz.	2	3	4
Bandages, 4 in. wide, 4 yards long, of heavy red flannel . . doz.	2	3	4
Oakum .... lbs.	10	15	20
Silk for ligature .... ozs.	½	¾	1
Sponges, coarse .... lbs.	1	1½	2

INSTRUMENTS FOR EACH POST.

Ball-forceps, (Fig. 7, Plate XXXVI) .... No.	1	2	3
Bistoury, (Fig. 4, Plate XXXVI) .... No.	1	2	3
Catheter, gum with stylet, (Fig. 1, Plate XXXVI) . . . No.	1	2	2
Cork-screw .... No.	1	2	2
Drenching-horn, tin .... No.	2	2	4
Fleam, 3 blades, (Fig. 2, Plate XXXVI) .... No.	2	4	6
Funnel, tin .... No.	1	2	3
Graduate-glass, 6 ounces .... No	1	2	3
Hobbles, casting .... No.	1	2	3
Hone .... No.	1	2	3
Lancet .... No.	3	6	8
Measures, tin sets .... No	1	2	3
Mortar and pestle, wedgewood, large .... No.	1	2	3
Needles, surgeon's .... No.	8	10	12
Needles, seton .... No.	8	10	12
Probang, celluloid, in two pieces, (Fig. 5, Plate XXXVI) No.	1	2	3
Scales and weights, shop .... No.	1	2	2
Scissors, curved .... No.	2	4	6
Slings, suspending .... No.	1	2	3
Spatulas .... No	1	2	3
Speculum, mouth, (Fig. 6, Plate XXXVI) .... No.	1	2	3
Syringe, rubber, 2-ounce .... No.	1	2	2
Syringe, rubber, 24-ounce .... No.	1	2	2
Thermometer, clinical .... No.	1	2	2
Tooth rasps .... No.	1	2	3
Trocar and canula, (Fig. 3, Plate XXXVI)	....	....	....

The medicines are not regarded as an expendable allowance beyond what is actually used, and such amounts only as will probably be needed are issued. The following explanation of their uses may prove of service.

Acid, Carbolic, Crystallized.— A dangerous poison, and a

PLATE XXXVI.

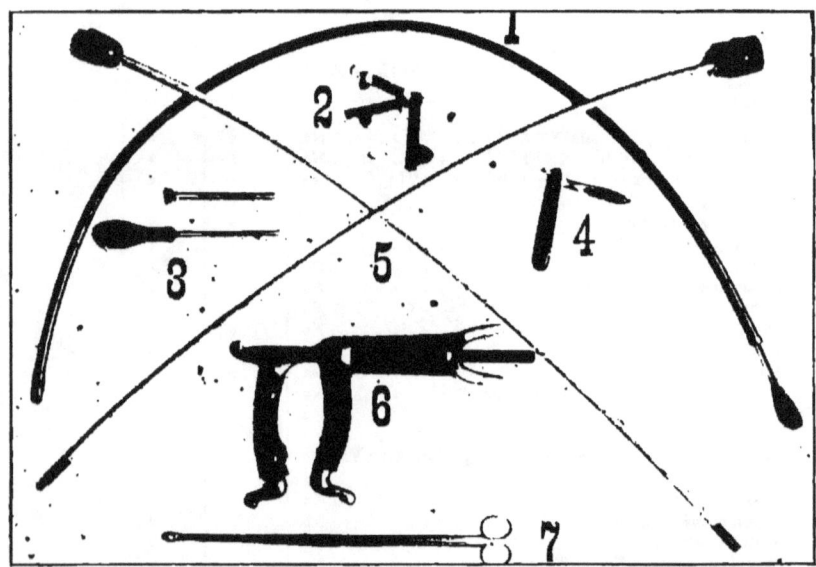

valuable medicine, used externally for destruction of parasites; internally for strangles, putrid sore throat, diarrhea, dysentery, and chronic indigestion accompanied by the passage of much wind or foul-smelling manure. Full dose, one or two drams diluted with twenty times the quantity of glycerine, linseed oil or gruel, and repeated once or twice a day. For application to sores make a solution of one part of acid to twenty or forty of water, soak some oakum, and apply with bandage. Poisoning by carbolic acid may be induced by too large doses internally, or by external application to a large surface; hence great care is needed in its use.

Aconite, Tincture of the Root.—A dangerous poison, used in fevers and inflammation of the bowels during the first two or three days. In pneumonia, not to be used except when heart beat is strong. Dose, ten drops; repeated every hour or two till six or eight doses have been given.

Commencing of sore throat, five drops, given every hour for a short time, will often cut the disease short. Medicine is dropped on the tongue, or added to a little water, and injected into the mouth.

Pain of colic, indigestion and constipation is sometimes relieved by aconite, in connection with other remedies. Aconite may be added to liniments.

Alcohol is one of the most important medicines used in making tinctures and some of the liniments.

For congestion of the lungs, colic, indigestion and diarrhea, give one to two ounces, diluted with three times the quantity of gruel, and repeated not oftener than every two hours.

Tincture of camphor . . . . 1 oz.
Tincture of gentian . . . . 1 oz.
Aromatic spirits of ammonia . . . . 1 oz.

The above tinctures are composed in great part of alcohol; hence their virtue, to a large extent, as in the treatment of disease alcohol is probably unequaled by any other medicine. Externally applied, is cooling; when confined, irritating, and may blister. Good when mixed with equal parts of water to harden tender skins subject to saddle galls. If skin is broken mix equal parts of white of egg and alcohol, and paint the parts over with the paste till a thick film is formed. As it is a volatile it should be kept closely corked.

Aloes, Barbadoes.—Used as a physic in spasmodic or flatulent colic, indigestion, constipation, etc. Give on empty stomach, the previous meal having been bran mash. As a rule aloes do not purge within eighteen hours; if it does not operate in thirty hours repeat dose, or give linseed oil.

Ball of {powdered aloes ....5 drams.
powdered ginger ....1 dram.

Soft soap, as much as needed to make the ball. Use with caution in colds, influenza and inflammation of the bowels.

Ammonia, Aromatic Spirits of.—Good for flatulent colic; in dose of—

Aromatic spirits of ammonia ....1 oz.
Opium, tincture of ....1 oz.

diluted with a half pint of gruel. Double above for first dose if necessary. Give at intervals of one hour.

Ammonia, Carbonate of.—Valuable stimulant for debility or loss of appetite. Keep the drug or dose from the air. Give a ball of—

Ammonia, carbonate of ....2 drams.
Gentian ....2 drams.
Camphor ....1 dram.

three times a day. Powder the camphor first, then the

ammonia, then mix the three ingredients into a ball. Dissolved with alcohol or water, may be used as a drench. An ointment of one dram, finely powdered, and an ounce of cosmoline, mixed together, is used to relieve rheumatic and other local pains.

Ammonia, Solution of.—A strong preparation, not to be used if the others are to be had. Can be used in from ½ to 2 drams, diluted with 8 ounces of gruel, and repeated every two or three hours. For liniment—

    Ammonia, solution of .... 1 part.
    Oil, olive................................... 2 parts.

It should be well shaken and applied with friction to sore throat, sprained joints, tendons and muscles, and for all temporary lameness. If stronger liniment is needed, take of—

    Ammonia, solution of .... 1 part.
    Turpentine, oil of .... 1 part.
    Oil, olive................................... 3 parts.

These liniments irritate the skin, and generally cause the hair to fall out, but unless the parts are bandaged after it has been used, the hair grows again. Undiluted ammonia blisters the skin, and may cause sloughing, which is followed by a permanent blemish.

Belladonna, Fluid Extract of.—For sore throat, give twenty to sixty drops, made into a tincture, with one to seven drams of diluted alcohol every three to four hours. In influenza, bronchitis, pneumonia, or other exhausting diseases, give a drench made of—

Extract of belladonna . . . . ½ dram.
Aromatic spirits of ammonia . . . . 1 oz.
Tincture of camphor . . . . 1 oz.

Dilute with half a pint of gruel, and repeat every four or six hours.

For a tonic, give a ball two or three times a day of—

Belladonna . . . . ½ dram.
Gentian . . . . 3 drams.
Ginger . . . . 1 dram.

For animals that sweat profusely, give—

Belladonna . . . . 1 dram.
Gentian . . . . 3 drams.
Nitrate of potassa (saltpeter) . . . . 2 drams.

Make into a ball and repeat twice a day.

Externally, belladonna is used in the form of an ointment, to dress painful wounds, frostbites, burns, scalds, cracked heels, scratches, saddle-galls, etc. The ointment is made up with cosmoline, and applied once or twice a day. The backs of some saddle horses have a great tendency to sweat, and gall. It may often be prevented by bathing the parts on which the greatest pressure comes with equal parts of the tincture and water. The tincture or ointment is used on rheumatic joints.

Camphor.—As a sedative, given in chronic cough, colic, diarrhea and influenza; dose, one to two drams, made into a ball with gentian, or given in gruel. Externally, spirits of camphor are used for sprains, bruises and wounds, and enter into many liniments.

Cantharides.—Used for making blistering ointments. The powdered drug may be sprinkled in small quantities over wounds, to keep them discharging.

Charcoal, Powdered.—Good for wind colic, chronic indigestion, diarrhea and fermentation of food. Make into a ball, and give two or three times a day—

Cayenne pepper	1 dram.
Gentian	2 drams.
Charcoal	4 drams.

Externally, powdered charcoal is used to sprinkle over sores having a tendency to become foul. In scratches where the discharge is profuse, sprinkle the surface with charcoal before applying the other dressing. When drinking water contains organic matter, thoroughly stir in some charcoal, and after it has settled, the water is ready for use.

Cosmoline, Carbolized.—Used for making ointments, application to sores, etc.

Ether, spirit of nitrous (sweet spirits of niter), used internally, for both wind and spasmodic colic. Dilute with half pint of cold gruel, and repeat every half hour.

Sweet spirits of niter	1 oz.
Tincture of opium	1 oz.
Tincture of ginger	½ oz.

Ether, Sulphuric.—Good colic remedy. Dilute with half pint of cold gruel or water, and repeat every half hour the following:

Ether	1 to 2 ozs.
Opium, tincture	1 to 2 ozs.

Externally it is used to produce loss of sensation in the skin when surface operations are to be performed, as firing, opening abscesses, fistula, etc. Being volatile, ether must be kept closely corked.

Flaxseed Meal.—Principally used in making poultices and balls; about one quart of the meal wet with water makes a good sized poultice, or it may be mixed with an equal quantity of bran. It should not be used longer than from twelve to twenty-four hours before being removed. Internally, flaxseed meal is a food of great value, and at the same time has certain remedial properties. Where the coat is rough and staring, the appetite poor or condition thin; or when shedding of the old coat is long delayed in the spring time, flaxseed meal can be fed with advantage. The dose should be half a pound twice a day, mixed dry with the other food. In inflammation of the kidneys, bladder and bowels, it may be used in the form of a tea, which is made by pouring a gallon of boiling water on a quart or two of the meal, stirring it for a few minutes, then leaving it to cool and settle, after which it is drawn off and given to drink instead of water, any quantity being allowed.

Ginger, Powdered.—Valuable constituent of colic drenches. When a dose of physic is given, one or two drams of ginger should be given to prevent griping, and to assist action of purgative. It is usually one of the constituents of condition powders. A drench with one-half pint of cold gruel or ball of the following is good:

Gentian, powdered .... 2 drams.
Aloes .... 1 dram.
Ginger, powdered .... 2 drams.

Gentian, Powdered.— A most valuable tonic; it increases

the appetite and stimulates digestion. The dose is four to five drams, repeated in from two to six hours.

Glycerine.— Used principally for external application. A liniment made of—

```
Carbolic acid .............................. 1 dram,
Glycerine.................................. 8 drams,
```

is much used for scratches, sore heels, chafes, wounds and sores exposed to the air. It is applied once or twice a day. As a dressing for bandaged wounds or sores take—

```
Carbolic acid .............................. 1 dram.
Glycerine ................................. 2 drams.
Water ..................................... 6 to 8 ozs.
```

This solution is also used to remove dirt or scurf from the skin, to kill lice, mange and ringworms, and to inject into the rectum to remove pinworms.

Chloride of Lime.— Used internally in cases of wind colic, fermentation of the food and indigestion, accompanied by the formation of gas. Particularly where the stomach is affected, make of—

```
Gentian, powdered....................... 2 drams,
Flaxseed meal .......................... 4 drams,
Chloride of lime ........................ 2 to 4 drams,
```

a thick paste out of the first two drugs; shape into a hollow cylinder about two inches long, closed at one end; then introduce the lime, close the open end, and administer at once; or drench with lime as above in half a pint of cold gruel or milk. A four-dram dose of lime may be repeated two or three times in the course of two hours. Its action should also be supplemented with full doses of charcoal. Solution of chloride of lime one part, and water four to eight parts, is used in foul sores of the feet or other parts. The lime may be mixed with two parts of charcoal, finely powdered, and sprinkled over the diseased tissue. It is also used as a disinfectant.

Iron, Sulphate of, Desiccated.— A valuable tonic; should never be used during the height of disease, where there is fever, or when the digestion is weak and the appetite poor.

A mixture of —

Sulphate of iron . . . . 1 dram,
Ginger . . . . 1 dram,
Alcohol . . . . 1 to 2 ozs.,

diluted with half a pint of cold gruel, and repeated two or three times daily, makes a good tonic for weakness.

Externally, a solution of iron, one dram to one or two ounces of water, may be used to stimulate the healing of old wounds, or the powdered drug may be sprinkled over the surface of the wound.

Lunar Caustic, or Nitrate of Silver.— Is used for destroying tissues and for stimulating the healing of wounds. The point of the stick is dipped in water and then touched to every part of the unhealed flesh. A white surface is formed, under which the healing process progresses. Before a wound receives an application of lunar caustic, carefully clean the exposed parts with water. Application should be made every day or every other day.

Oil, Linseed.— Used internally as a physic; dose, eight to sixteen ounces. A drench of —

Linseed oil . . . . 8 ozs.,
Aloes . . . . 4 drams,
Ginger . . . . 2 drams,

is good. It is used in connection with aloes when the latter does not operate.

Oil, Olive.—Used internally for diluting irritating medicines; externally for oiling blistered surfaces and for making liniments and ointments. It should not be used as a purgative.

Tincture of Opium (Laudanum).—A poison used to allay pain. Dose, half an ounce to two ounces. For spasmodic colic, as a drench, diluted with six ounces of gruel, use—

Tincture of opium . . . . 2 ozs.
Sweet spirits of niter . . . . 2 ozs.

Give half of above every half hour. For wind colic dilute with one-half pint of gruel—

Tincture of opium . . . . 1 oz.,
Aromatic spirits of ammonia . . . . 2 ozs.,
Aloes . . . . 2 drams,
Tincture of Cayenne pepper or ginger . . . . ½ oz.,

and give as above. No more than four doses of this should be given.

Pepper, Cayenne, Ground.—This drug creates a feeling of warmth, acts as an appetizer, and, in frequent doses, stops the watery discharges of diarrhea and excessive purging. Dose, one-half to two drams, given in a ball, oil or gruel. In colic it is added to the usual drench of ammonia, opium or niter. As an appetizer give twice a day in a ball—

Cayenne pepper . . . . 1 dram.
Aloes . . . . 2 drams.
Gentian . . . . 2 drams.
Salt . . . . 3 drams.

If to above one dram of the sulphate of iron is added, it may be used for mild cases of staggers.

Potassa-Nitrate (Saltpeter).—A stimulant for the kidneys, and a reducer of fevers. When given to act on the kidneys the dose is one-half to one ounce, made into a ball, or dissolved in half pint of water, and repeated once or twice a day for three or four days. As a remedy for founder this drug has probably no equal. Dose, two to three ounces dissolved in a pint of water, and repeated every six hours. This treatment may be continued for three or four days without danger. Externally used as a cooling lotion, one ounce dissolved in a pint of water and applied at once. Niter is a common ingredient of condition powders.

Soap, Castile.—May be used in making balls, liniments and ointments. In the absence of other remedies it may be given to stimulate the kidneys.

Soda, Bicarbonate.—Serves to correct acidity of the stomach. When corn is the sole food, causing an interference with digestion, soda frequently sets matters aright. It is made into a ball, and repeated once or twice daily, of

```
Cayenne pepper ..................... ½ dram.
Gentian or ginger .................... 2 to 4 drams.
Salt ............................... 2 drams.
Bicarbonate of soda .................. 2 to 4 drams.
```

In fevers it may be combined with niter in doses of two to four drams each. Externally used as a cooling lotion.

Sulphur, Washed.—One of the constituents of condition powders. Externally, sulphur destroys mange and ringworm. An ointment made of—

```
Sulphur ............................ 2 drams,
Lard ............................... 1 oz.,
```

well rubbed together, the skin cleaned with soap and water, and ointment well rubbed in, or a liniment of —

Sulphur .... 1 part,
Linseed oil .... 6 parts,
Tar .... 1 part,

may be used.

Oil of Turpentine.— For constipation of long standing give —

Aloes .... 7 drams.
Turpentine.............................. 1 oz.
Linseed oil............................. 2 ozs.

To remove seat worms inject two or three times —

Turpentine............................. 1 part.
Linseed oil............................ 12 parts.

Externally for liniments for rheumatism —

Turpentine .... 1 part.
Opium, tincture of .... 1 part.
Linseed oil .... 3 parts.

To destroy lice take —

Linseed oil .... 4 parts.
Turpentine .... 1 part.

Apply once a day.

Sulphate of Zinc.— A solution of five to ten grains to the ounce of water, applied once a day; good for wounds, and stimulates the healing. Useful in wounds of the feet, scratches, burns, frost bites, fistula, sore backs, etc. Good disinfectant. Sometimes given internally as a tonic and astringent in doses of one to three drams, diluted with gruel. Use as an eye wash, five grains to an ounce of distilled or filtered water.

Drenching Horn (Tin).— For giving medicines in form of drenches.

Fleam.— Used for bleeding. Open one blade till it is on a straight line with the handle; place the point on the skin over the vessel to be opened, and then strike a short, quick stroke with a stick. The lance should be kept sharp and disinfected. The lance is used for opening abscesses. (Fig. 2, Plate XXXVI.)

Probang.— Used for removing objects lodged in the throat or gullet, the animal being cast before the operation, and three or four ounces of linseed oil poured down the throat. Indiscriminate use of this instrument is injurious. (Fig. 5, Plate XXXVI.)

Speculum, Mouth.— For holding mouth open for examinations, balling, etc. (Fig. 6, Plate XXXVI.)

Ball Forceps.— Used for extracting bullets and other foreign substances from the tissues, located by means of a probe. (Fig. 7, Plate XXXVI.)

Bistoury (Straight).— Used in cutting deep tissues. The parts of the wound at the bottom are protected by the probe point. (Fig. 4, Plate XXXVI.)

Catheter.— Used for drawing water from the bladder. (Fig. 1, Plate XXXVI.)

Trocar.— Is used for tapping the abdomen when filled with gas, as in wind colic. (Fig. 8, Plate XXXVI.)

Oakum.— Used as a dressing for wounds or sores. Balls are made of the fiber, and soaked in solution of carbolic acid, chloride of zinc, and applied to wound, being kept in place by a pad of oakum and bandage. It should never be used a second time for dressing. It may be used to arrest bleeding. It should be kept clean and free from dust, and closely packed to prevent the drying out of the tar which is in it.

Silk, for Ligatures.—Two sizes of the silk should be supplied, one for sewing up small wounds, the other where considerable strain will come on the stitches. It may be used as a ligature on small warts or tumors, when it is desired to remove them by sloughing off. Silk should be kept clean, and disinfected with a weak solution of carbolic acid.

Sponges.—For cleaning wounds, washing sores, etc. They should always be washed after being used, and dried to prevent rotting.

The following are some of the useful prescriptions which may be prepared with medicines from the supply table:

BLISTER OINTMENT.

Cosmoline .... 4 parts.
Cantharides .... 1 part.

CARBOLIC LOTION.

Carbolic acid .... 1 part.
Glycerine .... 9 parts.

CARBOLIZED OIL.

Carbolic acid .... 1 part.
Linseed oil .... 7 parts.

CARBOLIC OINTMENT.

Cosmoline .... 7 parts.
Carbolic acid .... 1 part.

SPASMODIC COLIC MIXTURE.

Ether, sulphuric .... 1 oz,
Opium, tincture of .... 1 oz.
Ginger, powdered .... 1 dram.

FLATULENT COLIC MIXTURE.

Ammonia, aromatic spirits of .... 1 oz.
Opium, tincture of .... 1 oz.
Ginger, powdered .... 1 dram.

DIARRHEA MIXTURE.

Alcohol .... 1 oz.
Cayenne pepper .... 2 drams.
Ginger .... 1 dram.
Opium, tincture of .... 1 oz.

DIURETIC POWDERS.

Potassa, nitrate of .... 4 drams.
Gentian, powdered .... 2 to 4 drams.

FOUNDER POWDERS.

Potassa, nitrate of .... 3 to 4 ozs.
Gentian, powdered .... 4 drams.

HARTSHORN LINIMENT.

Ammonia, solution of .... 1 part.
Olive oil .... 2 parts.

HOOF OINTMENT.

Cosmoline .... 4 ozs.
Turpentine .... 1 oz.
Charcoal .... 1 oz.

ANODYNE MIXTURE.

Opium, tincture of .... 99 parts.
Aconite, tincture of .... 1 part.
  For inflamed bowels, etc.

SORE THROAT MIXTURE.

Belladonna, fluid extract of .... 20 drops.
Aconite, tincture of .... 10 drops.

TONIC POWDERS.

Gentian, powdered .... 2 drams.
Ginger, powdered .... 2 drams.
Sulphur .... 2 drams.
Aloes .... 1 dram.

TURPENTINE LINIMENT.

Turpentine, oil of	1 part.
Ammonia, solution of	1 part.
Olive oil	3 parts.

IRON TINCTURE POWDERS.

Iron, sulphate of, desiccated	½ dram.
Gentian, powdered	2 drams.
Aloes	1 dram.

ANODYNE LINIMENT.

Belladonna, extract of	2 drams.
Aconite, tincture of	2 drams.
Alcohol	6 ozs.
Camphor	4 drams.

One of the most important astringent lotions, called the "white lotion," is composed of—

Sulphate of zinc	1 oz.
Acetate of lead	1 oz.
Water	1 quart.

For antiseptic use add carbolic acid, 1 dram. Acetate of lead is not on the supply table.

CHAPTER XIV.

DISEASES AND INJURIES.

Common Cold.—Influenza.—Strangles.—Glanders.—Pneumonia, or Lung Fever.—Lampas.—Constipation.—Spasmodic Colic.—Flatulent Colic.—Diarrhea.—Lockjaw.—Profuse Staling.—Retention of Urine.—Bloody Urine.—Poll Evil.—Sore Back.—Mange.—Scratches.—Spavins.—Curb.—Capped Hock.—Broken Knees.—Splint.—Ringbones.—Windgalls.—Interfering.—Swelled Legs.—Pricking of the Foot.—Punctures of the Frog.—Corns.—Quittor.—Sand Cracks.—Seedy Toe.—Thrush.—Navicular Disease.—Laminitis.—Side Bones.—Calking.—Flesh Wounds: Gun Shot; Stabs; Cuts; Lacerations and Contusions.

COMMON COLD.—This is an acute inflammation of the mucous membrane which lines the nostrils. It is the same affection as cold in the head in the human subject.

Symptoms.—A snorting cough, loss of appetite, dullness of the eye, rough coat, redness of the mucous membrane lining the nostrils, followed by a thin discharge, gradually becoming thicker and more profuse, characterize this disease.

Sometimes a light fever exists, the bowels are more or less constipated, and the throat becomes sore; the glands under the jaw may become inflamed.

Treatment.—Put the animal in a loose box, with plenty of fresh air without draughts. If the weather is cold, cover with blankets. Give plenty of water, and feed on bran mashes and hay.

If the running at the nose be considerable, and the cough troublesome, relief may be given by steaming the head frequently. This is accomplished by holding the head over a pail of hot water, which is stirred gently with a whisp of hay.

The steaming may be done over a nose bag or gunny sack into which some chopped hay or sawdust has been placed, over which hot water is poured. If the patient becomes feverish, give a dose of nitrate of potassa, one to two drams, daily for two or three days. If constipated use an injection of warm water.

In all diseases of the respiratory organs, active purgative medicine should be avoided.

If neglected the disease may terminate in pneumonia, or become chronic, and is then known as nasal gleet.

INFLUENZA.—This disease has its origin generally in dirty stables, bad ventilation, or when animals are crowded together in damp, ill-ventilated situations. Severity is much increased by poor forage and overwork.

Symptoms.— Loss of appetite, prostration, respiratory organs become involved, and nervous system is affected. Often complicated with diseases of the liver, lungs and mucous membranes generally.

Under various names, such as pinkeye, epizootic, etc.,

this disease at times becomes very general, and is considered contagious.

Treatment.— The aim should be to support the animal through the disease, and enable nature to throw off the morbid material in the system. Good nursing and food, mostly of a laxative character, are prime requisites. Water should be kept where the animal can help itself.

STRANGLES.— This is a disease, usually attended with an eruptive fever, to which young horses are especially subject. The disease generally manifests itself in the glandular structures, particularly the submaxillary and parotid glands, which become inflamed, followed by suppuration in the connective tissue.

Symptoms.— The horse looks sick, is off his feed, and has perhaps a slight discharge of a catarrhal nature. The coat becomes harsh and staring, and the animal hidebound. In a day or two the glands under the jaw, or behind the ear, begin to swell, and the throat becomes sore. Hesitation and difficulty in swallowing, with unusual slobbering, the water frequently returning through the nostrils, and acceleration of breathing occur. The animal may be unthrifty for some weeks before the disease manifests itself. Increase in temperature and pulse take place.

Treatment.— When the tumor forms regularly in the submaxillary space, and is of the ordinary size, the abscess generally comes to maturity without much trouble or inconvenience. If, however, it is situated high up towards the parotid glands, the distress in the breathing will often be very great, and the fever run high. The great object is to assist nature to develop the eruption fully and quickly, as strangles runs a specific course; hence, good nursing and soft food, on account of the attending sore throat, are the principal things. The appetite must be watched, and tempted with grass, if to be had. Sick animals soon tire of bran mash, so that linseed meal should be on hand to add to the mash or make a separate gruel. Cut hay, steamed, and oats softened with boiling water may be given as soon as the animal can eat.

Blankets and leg bandages should be used, and if the legs are cold they should be hand rubbed. No purgative medicine should be given.

As soon as the tumor has headed it should be freely opened with a lance, for it may be opened at a favorable point, and the incision is not so apt to leave a blemish as a ragged natural opening. The abscess must be kept open, if necessary, by a piece of tow, and warm water should be occasionally injected into it.

The tumor does not always form favorably, but sometimes comes on the shoulders, front of the chest, etc., and occasionally on some of the internal glandular structures.

GLANDERS.—This is a contagious, malignant and fatal disease, communicable to human attendants. Is caused by a specific germ, which gains entrance to the system most easily when the animal is debilitated.

Symptoms.—May be looked for in cavalry commands after hard, debilitating work, accompanied by bad food and miasmatic surroundings, if previously exposed to the germ. The horse refuses food, coat appears rough, perspiration is induced by the slightest exertion, and a generally unhealthy appearance exists. There is a discharge of a gluey material from one or both nostrils, sometimes tinged with blood. The mucous membranes are pale and unhealthy, and that covering the nasal chamber, from which the discharge issues, is studded over with deep, pit-like ulcers. The ulcers are characteristic, being excavated as if cut with a punch, but after a time they become ragged at their edges, irregular, enlarged in all directions, and finally confluent. The spaces between the ulcers are covered with hard, yellowish pimples, which soon ulcerate. The eye is affected, and an unhealthy discharge often issues over the face. The glands under the jaw enlarge and form a tumor.

Chronic glanders is the common form. When acute glanders appear the temperature rises as high as 105° to 109°. The animal fails rapidly, and death ensues. In many cases of chronic glanders the ulcer is undiscoverable, but if glanders is known to exist in a stable or vicinity, any suspicious symptom becomes at once significant.

Farcy is a lighter manifestation of glanders, characterized by "farcy buds," or nodular swellings.

Treatment.—An animal in which glanders or farcy is suspected should be at once isolated, and when the disease is clearly manifested there should be no hesitation about destroying the animal, since no known methods of treatment avail to do more than prolong for a time an unhealthy existence.

PNEUMONIA, OR LUNG FEVER.—This is an inflammation of the lung structure.

Symptoms.—The attack, at times, comes on imperceptibly, and again it appears suddenly without any premonitory symptoms. The attack is generally ushered in by sudden fits of shivering, followed by coldness of the ears and extremities, and other usual signs of inflammation, and a staring coat. The coldness of the extremities is a marked sign throughout the disease. The horse is evidently uneasy, and turns his head frequently around to his chest. The pulse is accelerated, and generally averages about eighty beats to the minute. The temperature in the early stage will be 103° to 106° F.

The respiration becomes disturbed as soon as the disease is established. The nasal linings are paler than usual, but as the disease progresses they become purplish, and then of a leaden hue.

The horse will stand persistently with his fore legs wide apart, and his elbows out, to afford greater expansion to his chest. Horses affected with this disease never lie down except for a moment at a time, until extreme exhaustion comes upon them, when death from suffocation rapidly ensues.

Cough may or may not be present. If it accompany the disease it is sharp at first, but as the attack progresses it becomes dry and of a dull character.

The disease may attack only one lung, or both. If, during the early stage, the ear be applied to the chest, a confused, humming noise, accompanied with a harsh, dry murmur, instead of the gentle, respiratory sound peculiar to health, will be heard. With increase of the disease the breathing becomes quicker and more labored. The fever lasts from five to ten days.

Convalescence is indicated by the return of the pulse to something like its normal condition, restoration of warmth in the extremities, a moist state of the nostrils, and a disposition to lie down for rest.

Treatment.— Laxative food, entire rest, blankets, and flannel bandages should be provided at once; plenty of fresh air in the box stall, but no draughts. The condition of the animal has much to do with the treatment accorded. If the animal is in good condition, and the attack arises from some well marked cause, give ten to fifteen drops fluid extract of aconite every four hours in first stages, and as much nitrate of potassa, in two dram doses, as the animal will take in his drinking water. Blankets or cloths wrung out in hot water should be applied to the sides of the chest and covered over with dry cloths or rubber cloth. This should be continued for some time, and when stopped the skin should be dried thoroughly, and liniment of soap and ammonia gently rubbed in, and this covered with dry cloths.

When the crisis is reached, or the febrile stage checked somewhat, tonics and stimulants are used. Whisky or pure alcohol, in one ounce doses, well diluted with water, may be given, and in many cases carbonate of ammonia, in two dram doses, in the form of a ball, may be advantageously used.

If the animal is distressed with cough, a dram each of gum camphor and extract of belladonna, should be given four or five times a day.

If the attack is the sequel of influenza or catarrh, or occurs in a horse of low vitality, aconite should not be used, but the tonics and stimulants at once resorted to. When the animal begins to convalesce, encourage his appetite with such stimulating food as can be procured, but no corn should be given.

LAMPAS.— This is an active inflammation and swelling of the ridges of the roof of the horse's mouth. It is a trifling ailment.

Symptoms.— The soreness of the palate prevents the animal from eating for a few days, and the inflammation sometimes causes feverish symptoms.

Treatment.— A few days of feeding wet bran and other soft food will cause the inflammation to subside. The brutal practice of burning the palate with a hot iron should never be allowed. If marching where it is necessary to keep up the horse's strength, an early recovery may be induced by scarifying the swollen roof of the mouth in front of the third ridge with a knife or lancet.

CONSTIPATION.— This exists when the fæces are wholly retained, or are scanty, hard and small.

Symptoms.—When of long standing the coat is rough and staring. There is a slight swelling of the extremities, sometimes a distended condition of the belly, and loss of appetite. In all cases the animal strains in voiding the fæces, which are usually, though not always, small, hard and dry. There is not usually any sign of pain.

Treatment.— In mild or recent cases the diet should be laxative, and as varied as convenient. An injection of tepid water and sweet oil twice a day for a few days will be useful. In prolonged cases a good purgative may be necessary.

SPASMODIC COLIC.—This is a griping or spasmodic contraction of the muscular coat of any part of the intestines. The usual seat of trouble is the small intestine, although impaction of food in the large intestine may cause it.

It is always accompanied by pain of an intermittent character.

Symptoms.—The early sign of colic is sudden pain in the region of the intestines, indicated by the horse looking anxiously around to his flanks. As the pain increases, the animal becomes more restless; paws; kicks at his belly; lies down and gets up frequently; wants to roll over when down. After a time the spasm passes away, to return again after a brief interval with the same signs.

During the paroxysm of pain the pulse is much quickened and the breathing accelerated; during the intervals they return to the normal. During the attack there may frequently be a passage of hard, angular dung pellets. Ineffectual attempts to pass urine are frequently made.

Favorable indications are an increase in the intervals of time between attacks, and each attack becoming slighter than the preceding one. If the animal passes wind and soft dung, it is a favorable sign. The increase or decrease of the attack is also indicated by the tenseness of the belly, or the reverse. The symptoms are only those of pain, no inflammation being present, and the extremities and skin continuing normal.

Treatment.—The spasms being caused by an irritant of some sort in the bowels, the treatment is directed to removing this as soon as possible. For this purpose administer about one pint of raw linseed oil. If a light case, where overloading of the stomach does not exist, give an anti-spasmodic compound—a minimum dose—of one ounce of sulphuric ether, one ounce of tincture of opium, and one dram of powdered ginger, in cold water.

There are many other simple remedies useful in relieving this trouble. An injection of warm soapsuds may be used with the other remedies.

Rubbing the belly and legs gives comfort, but some

horses are very violent, and must be handled with care. A favorable sign of relief is the free passage of urine. The horse should be watched for several hours after the attack has passed.

FLATULENT COLIC.—This is more to be dreaded than the spasmodic colic. It is apt to be chronic, resulting at times from imperfect digestion.

Symptoms.—There is distention of the belly, which is resonant on percussion. The expression of pain is not so acute as in spasmodic colic, but more constant; there is more or less delirium; the animal is unsteady upon his feet, and his extremities are cold.

Treatment.—Give as a drench two ounces of bicarbonate of soda, one to two ounces of sulphuric ether, and one to two ounces of tincture of opium, dissolved in cold water. Also use oil and injections, as in spasmodic colic.

In both spasmodic and flatulent colic, if relief is not obtained, the dose should be repeated at intervals of an hour.

In some cases it may be necessary to puncture the animal on the right side, in the triangular space bounded by the vertebræ, the hip bone and the last rib; puncture with a trocar, and leave the canula in the opening temporarily. The trocar should be directed downward and inward.

DIARRHEA.—This is a scouring of the bowels, resulting from a natural effort to expel some irritating substance, or from change from dry forage to green grass. If unchecked the animal loses flesh rapidly at times.

Treatment.—Give a laxative of one-half pint of raw linseed oil. Give an infusion of gentian, one ounce, and one to two ounces of tincture of opium; feed dry food.

Other remedies recommended are tannic acid, prepared chalk, catechu, or powdered opium.

LOCKJAW.—This is a persistent spasm of the voluntary muscles. The immediate cause is some abnormal condition of the nerves and their centers. A part of the brain, and the spinal cord in particular, become involved.

The disease is most commonly induced by picking up rusty nails or other bits of iron, causing an injury to the sensitive portion of the foot, but it arises not infrequently from a punctured wound or a sudden chill to the back or loins, such as that caused by a horse being left to stand in a draught whilst sweating, after the saddle has been removed.

Symptoms.—The attack is characterized by more or less closure of the jaws; sometimes the teeth are firmly fixed together; also great difficulty in swallowing, rigidity of the limbs, and extreme difficulty in moving. The animal pokes out his nose as if suffering from sore throat. As the disease advances the jaws become so tightly locked that neither food nor medicine can be introduced through them. The ears are held erect and turned to the front, the eyes are retracted, and the haw partially protrudes; the nostrils are dilated. The animal spreads his legs wide apart, and stands persistently with tail erect. The belly is tense and tucked up, and the muscles everywhere stand out prominent and rigid. Obstinate constipation and torpidity of the bladder form a marked feature of the symptoms, which, in general, reach their height in three or four days.

Treatment.— The exciting cause should be sought for. If it is a wound of the foot the offending substance must be removed, and the opening enlarged to give free passage for the pus which has accumulated. The hoof should be pared down quite thin about the hole to make an easy exit for the pus, and a flaxseed poultice applied, to which belladonna is added.

Perfect rest and quiet are necessary; the stable should be darkened, and the horse disturbed as seldom as possible, even by the attendant. A pail of water should be left within reach of the horse at all times.

As soon as the attack is recognized, a purgative should be administered. Solid extract of belladonna may be given twice daily; the medicine may be placed in the mouth and allowed to dissolve slowly. Oatmeal gruel in liquid form should be left so that the horse can suck it from a bucket without opening his mouth. During convalescence provide laxative, nutritious food, and give tonics.

PROFUSE STALING.—This disease, as its name indicates, is characterized by great increase and peculiar alteration of the urine. It is accompanied by excessive thirst, and the body becomes emaciated. The presence in the system of the poison of glanders, indigestion, or feeding on musty hay or oats, or boiled grain, all tend to produce this condition.

Symptoms.—Excessive thirst and unusual urination, accompanied by depraved appetite, characterize the disease. The mucous membranes are pale and dirty-colored, the breath offensive, and the pulse thin and weak. A rough coat and a disposition to perspire on slight exertion, are accompanying symptoms.

Treatment.—The food should be changed, grass being given, if procurable. If the water is hard, it should be boiled. If the horse can be induced to drink linseed tea, he should have it freely. As great prostration accompanies this disease, a liberal diet should be allowed, preferably of a laxative nature.

RETENTION OF URINE.—This may result from inability of the animal to rise to its feet on account of some other trouble. Anything which may impede the flow of urine, such as a spasm of the neck of the bladder, cancer of the penis, or dirt in the sheath, may cause the condition.

Symptoms.—These are frequent and ineffectual attempts to urinate, although the animal strains and groans with his efforts.

Treatment.—Apply hot cloths to the loins and hand rub the belly; put on blankets and shake up the bedding, which sometimes causes so much desire to urinate that the horse overcomes his difficulty.

If these fail, and a catheter is at hand, relieve the bladder by mechanical means.

BLOODY URINE.—This generally arises from a sprain of the muscles in the neighborhood of the kidneys. It may also be due to an escape of the coloring matter of the blood, without any inflammation being present.

Treatment.—Linseed tea, a laxative diet, grass if available, and rest, are what is required.

LACERATION OF EYELID.—This occurs from being bitten by another horse, striking against nails or splinters while rubbing against the stall.

Treatment.—No part should be cut away unless it is so badly lacerated as to make reunion improbable. There is a strong natural tendency to reunion of these parts, and with judicious management a successful result is often obtained even in very severe injuries. The parts may be brought together with two or three stitches. A wet cloth should be hung over the eye, and care taken to prevent the animal rubbing against the manger.

FOREIGN BODIES IN THE EYE.—These are generally seeds, particles of hay or straw, or small grains of dirt.

The trouble usually occurs at night, and is indicated by tears more or less profuse running from a closed eye.

Treatment.—The particles will be generally found under the upper eyelid, which may be gently turned back over a pencil or other smooth article, and the irritating substance removed; afterward bathe the eye in lukewarm water, and cover it with a wet cloth.

FISTULOUS WITHERS.—This is the presence of an abscess more or less formidable at the withers, caused by pressure of the saddle or other bruising injury.

In most cases the mischief is at first slight, and a few days abstinence from work, with a little alteration of the saddle, if that caused the trouble, will generally effect a cure and prevent recurrence. If the skin is tender a salt and water dressing may be applied.

When, however, the cause is continued or repeated, the tissues under the skin become inflamed, and the cartilaginous pads of the ends of the spinous processes may be injured. If such be the case fomentations must be applied in the first instance to reduce the inflammation. If these fail, matter will probably form under the skin.

Unless a free opening is made for its escape it will burrow in, under, and among the muscles, tendons and ligamentous tissues which lie on each side of the spine or withers, and will form sinuses. A seton should be introduced to enable the pus to escape, and prevent caries of the spinous processes, which sometimes occur. In the latter case the diseased bone must be removed. The parts frequently heal over nicely, with perhaps a slight hollow, but a serious case is apt to subject the horse to suspicion, as not being suitable for hard service with packed saddles.

POLL EVIL.— This is a fistulous abscess situated on top of the head immediately behind the ears, and is usually caused by accidental violence or pressure of the head stall.

At the first stage it may be recognized as a soft, fluctuating tumor, surrounded by inflammatory swelling, and attended with stiffness of the neck.

From the peculiar position of the injury, the matter has no depending orifice, and unless artificial assistance by free incision is given for the escape of the matter, it will burrow downwards among and under the ligaments which support the head. Among these it is apt to form large and deep sinuses, which often extend down to the bone.

Treatment.— Before pus is formed, reduce the inflammation by the application of cold water to the part, and by administering purgatives internally. If suppuration becomes established, the abscess must be opened at once to its base, so that the pus may escape from the lowest point. The opening must not be allowed to close too soon; fomentations should be repeatedly applied. In some cases, a seton inserted from the original opening, following the fistula and brought out on the opposite side of the poll, are very successful.

SORE BACK.—This may take the form of slight tumors, sitfasts, or saddle galls. They are generally caused by friction or undue pressure of the saddle, and in the case of team horses, of the harness or collar. Improper saddling, or poor riding with good saddling, have the same effects.

Treatment.— The most essential thing is to remove the cause of the irritation, and the animal should, if possible, be spared from work for a few days. Such alteration as is necessary in the equipment should be made. The blanket may have holes cut in it over the swelling, or the corners turned under to raise the saddle bars, when the tumor or abrasion is near the edge of the saddle. With pack animals, the hay or stuffing must be altered, hard lumps removed, and, if necessary, a chamber or hole left over the affected spot. The aparejo is the best pack saddle in existence for heavy loads in the hands of experts, but if not continually watched, will, in the hands of poorly instructed troops, ruin all the mules in a few days marching.

The tumor, or swelling, will be best treated at first by an application of salt and water. If the irritation is not removed, and there is sign of suppuration, it must be treated according to its nature and degree, by application of poultices of linseed meal mixed with boiling water, and sweet oil stirred in afterwards.

Fluctuating tumors sometimes require to be laid open through the center from end to end, and injected with a weak solution of one part carbolic acid and fifty parts water, and cold dressings applied afterward until healed.

When one of these swellings, either through neglect or repeated recurrence of the cause, has become hard and insensible, and the skin is permanently injured, it is then known as a "sitfast," because of the difficulty of removing it or effecting a cure. The skin becomes thickened and half dead, and is often adherent to the bottom of the sore. The sitfast will frequently be found to be partially separated all around from the living skin.

The surest treatment then is to cut it out. Remove every particle of the hard, horny skin, after which it may be carefully touched with nitrate of silver, to remove any of the disorganized part which has been left by the knife.

True elastic skin of the orginal quality is never reproduced when once destroyed, either in the case of sitfasts or of any other injuries; a substitute is formed which answers sufficiently well in most cases, and the parts will frequently contract in such a way as to leave only a small scar. Care should subsequently be taken not to bring undue pressure on the part.

Sometimes the saddle or harness will abrade the skin; If not attended to, these "galls" may run into ulcers. As soon as observed, the saddle or harness should be shifted so as not to rub on the sore spot. If the skin has not been broken, it may be hardened by rubbing with a weak solution of salt and water.

If a scab be rubbed partly off, trim away the edges, and if necessary, poultice it until it all comes away.

In warm weather the woolen saddle blanket produces

much heat, and care should be taken to cool off the horse before exposing the back. This will tend to reduce swellings arising from ill-fitting saddles. The back should be carefully examined when the saddle is removed, and the salt and water immediately applied to any swelling. If the skin has been rubbed off and a raw spot formed it should be treated with cosmoline, or carbolized oil. If necessary to continue the horse in use, the open wound should be covered with the cosmoline, and if it is possible to remove part of the load it should be done, and a hole cut in the blanket as before mentioned.

MANGE.—This disease depends upon the presence of a parasitic insect, which is so minute as to be seen only with much difficulty. The attacks cause itching of the skin, and the hair falls off in patches. Any horse affected should be isolated, and other animals should not be groomed with the same brush and currycomb. It generally commences at the roots of the hair of the mane and tail. Minute pustules appear, whose summits gradually expand, burst, and coalesce with one another, and the united discharge from them forms patches of crusts upon the skin. It is under these crusts that the hair loosens and falls out.

Treatment.—The treatment of mange must be thorough to be effective. The parts affected should be washed with soap and water, and be dressed with a solution of carbolic acid in the proportion of half an ounce of the acid to a pint of water, going over a part of the horse each day. In slight and recent cases the skin will recover its tone when the mites have been killed, and in most cases the hair will grow out again.

SCRATCHES.— This is a condition of the skin in and about the hollow of the heel akin to chapped hands, and is frequently called cracked heels. It is usually produced by exposure to wet and cold. Clipping of the long hair or fetlocks, which is the natural protection of the parts, is apt to produce it.*

Symptoms.— Lameness, more pronounced when starting off. Dry, inflamed condition of the skin about the heel, and formation of small crusts, from which a thin, watery discharge exudes.

Treatment.— Keep the parts dry, if possible. If necessary to wash, do so with warm water and castile soap, and dry thoroughly. If the skin be unbroken, rub with fresh lard and vaseline. Dust with powdered alum twice a day. If cracked, rub with sulphate of zinc and lard, one dram of the former to six of the latter, mixed, or one part sulphur to six of cosmoline. It is a troublesome affection, and if the animals are in camp, and exposed to standing on muddy picket lines, it is very difficult to cure.

---

*In preparing his troop for the annual visit of the Inspector-General during the spring, the author was misled by a spell of warm weather, and premature shedding of the horses, and in consequence had all the fetlocks trimmed. On the day of the inspection a cold rain set in, and almost the entire troop broke out in a few days with clearly defined cases of scratches.

BONE SPAVIN.— This disease generally appears on the inner side of the hock, and usually involves two or more of the weight-bearing bones. Spavins once fully formed cannot be removed by any remedial agent, but in common with most abnormal growths, become less as age advances. The common causes are undue concussion, pressure, or sprain. Hereditary influence has much to do with production of spavin.

Symptoms.— During the formation of the bony deposit some degree of abnormal heat may be detected, but usually the disease first makes its presence known by the prominence of the bony growth, which destroys the symmetry of the hock. Some stiffness of the hock and an occasional tripping of the toe may be noticed. Peculiarities will be observed when the animal is trotted on hard, smooth ground, especially when turning, for the horse is apt to flinch perceptibly. Exercise for a few minutes greatly diminishes the symptoms, but after exercise and the horse has cooled off, the stiffness will recur, probably in an increased degree.

If the horse is worked during the formation of a spavin, the inflammation will greatly increase, and an enormous deposit of bone may be the result. The deposits may be on both hocks, but they are rarely similar; therefore by comparing one hock with another it can be determined if anything abnormal exists.

If spavin is suspected and any doubt exists, lift the hind leg and forcibly flex it up to the thigh several times.

After this trot the horse slowly, and if he has spavin he will probably show lameness.

Treatment.—If incipient spavin be suspected, rest is the great essential. Cold applications are useful, and tincture of iodine may prove beneficial, a dram being injected under the skin in each of from two to four places. If the inflammatory action does not subside, and the horse continues lame, it will be well to use a blister.

If properly performed, firing is regarded as an efficacious remedy.

BOG SPAVIN.—This is a distention of the capsular ligament of the true hock joint. The swelling, which is tense and fluctuating, shows itself primarily in front and the inner side, because in that part the capsule is large and loose. It is always a defect commonly occurring in weak hocks, and may become serious.

Treatment.—This should be directed toward allaying pain and reducing its size, but the swelling should never be punctured. A wet bandage covered with oil silk, and the whole covered with a flannel bandage, often acts favorably.

If these measures fail a stimulating ointment may be used, but as a rule blisters do not prove permanently beneficial in this disease.

BLOOD SPAVIN.—This is a distention of the veins in the vicinity of the hock. No great harm results from the dilitation of the vein, although it is both a blemish and a defect.

CURB.—This is an inflammation of the ligament, accompanied by a hard and painful swelling at the back of the hock, usually caused by a sprain. In the earliest stages it shows itself as a small, hard lump or ridge upon the lower part of the back of the hock. As the disease progresses, it is sometimes accompanied by lameness of a severe character.

Treatment.—Reduce the inflammation by fomentations; use a high heeled shoe, and apply a blister to stimulate absorption of the exudation. If the inflammation subsides and the lameness continues, firing may be tried.

CAPPED HOCK.—Synovial capped hock is a firm, fluctuating swelling on and about the point of the hock, causing lameness and sometimes decay of the bone.

Treatment.—Either applications of hot water or cooling lotions may be used to reduce the swelling, then apply a blister.

THOROUGH PIN.—This is a bursal enlargement which occurs at the upper and back part of the hock, and in a medium form is very common in cavalry horses. Unless very pronounced, no treatment is required. Cold applications, pressure, or counter irritation, are used in bad cases.

BROKEN KNEES.—Under this name are included all injuries to the knees, from a simple scratch to serious fractures of the bones, and which usually arise from a fall.

Treatment.—If the skin is simply bruised, the hair scraped off and a little blood oozing from the surface of the skin, a dressing of white lotion will probably heal it, and the hair will soon grow again.

When the skin is cut, wash it thoroughly to remove dirt and foreign substances, clip away the hair, and bring the edges together, and fasten with plaster. Put a muslin bandage around the knee, and tie up the horse's head so that he cannot lie down for a few days. If the tendon is crushed the case may become so serious as to call for the destruction of the animal, as is done in case the accident has been sufficiently severe to fracture one or more bones of the knee.

In all cases the limb must be kept as free from motion as possible. If inflammation sets in free exit must be allowed for pus, and hot fomentations applied until it subsides, after which the healing process may be encouraged by cold applications.

A pledget of wool or tow, covered with white of egg and placed on the wound, and a wet pad bandaged lightly over this, will exclude air and dirt.

The horse should be tied where he will not be apt to strike his wounded knee against the manger.

SPLINT.—This is a deposit of bone, either between one of the two small bones and the cannon bone, or upon any of the three bones of the fore leg. The deposit generally develops on the inner side, and usually a little above the center of the bone between the knee and fetlock.

A simple splint in a position removed from either articulation or tendon is not looked upon as serious, or classed as an unsoundness; all other forms are liable to cause lameness, and are indicative of more disease than is apparent. Under this head may be classed those close to the knee; double or pegged splints; that is, those which are found on both sides with a communicating bar running from one to the other; two or more on the same side connected, and finally, little bony deposits involving the knee joint.

Treatment.—If it does not cause lameness it should be left alone. When once fully formed it cannot be removed, but often becomes absorbed as the horse grows older. A bandage wet in cold water, and rest, will usually be sufficient, but if the horse continues to go lame after a rest of a month or six weeks, and the splint is still sensitive, it may be advisable to apply a blister.

RINGBONES.—These are bony deposits upon either the upper or lower pastern bones, forming a more or less complete ring around the bone. True ringbone is serious, and the degree of lameness does not always depend upon the size of the deposit. It occurs more often on the hind than the fore fetlocks.

Symptoms.—Lameness is more perceptible on hard than soft ground. The peculiarity shown in this case is a stiffness, or want of flexion, in the fetlock joint, and a consequent snatching up of the foot in action. Swelling and heat are generally apparent. If lame in the fore leg, the horse is apt to put his heel down first, but if the deposit be upon a hind leg, the toe is usually put down first. Lameness from ringbone is sometimes confounded with laminitis, or seedy toe, but an examination of the foot will speedily determine if these exist.

Treatment.—If the horse puts his fore feet down heel first, put on a shoe worked very thin behind. If, on the contrary, he walks on his toe, shoe with a high-heeled shoe. Reduce the inflammation, and blister, or fire, if necessary, but only as a last resort.

WINDGALLS.—These are soft, pulpy swellings in the neighborhood of the fetlock joints. They vary from very small to the size of a hen's egg. They are quite common with old cavalry horses, and arise from over-exertion and irritation, rather than from sprain. As they are very apt to return, and they do not specially inconvenience the horse, it is not customary in the military service to subject them to any treatment.

INTERFERING.—This is striking the fetlock with the opposite foot, causing a contusion, often abrading or scratching the surface, and commonly occurring with the hind feet only. Horses when much fatigued are apt to interfere, particularly if badly shod. This sometimes is occasioned by a poorly clinched nail. The occurrence is generally indicated by the horse flinching, and if badly struck he may carry the injured leg off the ground for several steps. Proper shoeing is the best remedy.

SPEEDY CUT.—This is an injury caused by a fore foot wounding the opposite leg immediately below, and sometimes even above the knee. It is usually inflicted at a gallop when the horse has begun to tire. The blow frequently causes the formation of pus.

Treatment.—If pus is present open the abscess freely to give it vent; bathe with warm water and a weak zinc wash.

SWELLED LEGS.—This is commonly called stocking, and is usually occasioned by want of exercise. It will generally disappear when the animal is exercised or worked.

THE FOOT.—Considering the hard, horny nature of the outer crust of the hoof, and the provisions made by nature in the way of a cushion on the bottom of the foot, it would seem hardly necessary to have any anxiety about that part of the horse, but this is not so.

The foot is subject to many injuries and some diseases. Prevention is much better than cure, and hence too many precautions cannot be bestowed upon this part of the horse. Upon the manner in which the blacksmith performs his work the success or failure of an expedition may depend, and owing to the scarcity of well trained men for these positions, it is essential that officers should make themselves acquainted with all that pertains to this part of the animal.

PRICKING OF THE FOOT.—This is caused by nails actually penetrating the sensitive laminæ which line the interior of the horny substance of the foot, or by their being driven into the soft horn which surrounds them. In the latter case it may be a week or two before the lameness disappears. Picking up a nail produces a similar wound, and is liable to occur at any time a horse is in use. An injury of this kind should be promptly treated, as it may result seriously, even producing lockjaw.

When the sensitive sole is injured, inflammation almost always occurs, terminating in the formation of pus, which, unless aided to escape, may burrow its way up and form an opening upon the coronet, producing quittor. In any case the horse shows lameness.

Treatment.—If not readily seen, the exact point of the lameness may be detected by pinching around the foot with a pair of pinchers, one branch being against the outside of the hoof while the other presses the sole inside of the shoe. The injured spot being found, draw the nails from the shoe, carefully watching each as it comes out. If one appears wet, it is probably the cause of the trouble.

In all cases it is essential to pare out freely, not merely the seat of puncture, but the surrounding sole for a considerable distance, with the view of affording an easy exit for any matter which may form. The foot should then be soaked in hot water for at least an hour.

Having taken these precautions in cases treated immediately after the occurrence of the injury, that is, before inflammation has begun, close the puncture at once with tar and tow, to exclude the air and lessen the chance of inflammation. Perfect rest should be given.

As a rule, inflammation will set in and the formation of pus commence before the injury is noticed. In addition to paring the sole, recourse must be had to poultices of linseed meal.

When prompt measures are taken, injuries of the sensitive sole seldom prove serious. The insensitive sole having been pared off, the horse will not be fit for work until nature has resupplied enough of it for the protection of the foot, unless an artificial covering such as a leather shoe is provided.

PUNCTURES OF THE FROG.—These are similar in character to those of the sole, and require similar treatment. They nearly always arise from picking up a nail.

When taken in time they yield to treatment more readily than prick of the sole.

If neglected, however, they are apt to lead to extensive disease of the frog, and canker may be the result. In rare cases the navicular bone may be punctured, when perfect recovery need not be expected.

CORNS.—Corns are bruises of the sole, usually occurring in the angle formed by the bars and the crust in front of the heel. They are rarely found on the hind feet. Corns are very similar to blood blisters on the human skin, and are probably formed suddenly by a bruising blow. An indirect cause of corns is bad shoeing, the practice of filing off the crust to make a good looking foot from the blacksmith's point of view, and also from the senseless and brutal practice of cutting out the bars. Sometimes they are probably caused by stepping on a stone. When the horse goes lame from no other known cause, apply the pinchers, as before described, to various points, with firm pressure, until the flinching of the horse shows that the right spot has been found.

Treatment.—The treatment usually consists in removing the cause, which is nearly always undue pressure of the shoe.

Paring out corns gets rid of them for a time, but it should be borne in mind that the only means of preventing a recurrence of them consists in the maintenance of a good, sound, unrasped crust and unpared bars, in order that properly fitted shoes may have a correct bearing.

QUITTOR.—This is a fistula of the coronet, which burrows in various directions, with usually several openings upon the quarters and heels of the coronet. The most common cause is a severe tread or bruise on the coronet. It may also arise from a neglected corn or prick of the sole.

Treatment.—The first thing is always to afford an easy exit for the pus. Pare the sole clean, to see if the trouble has been caused by a wound in that part. If it has, cut down into the sole and open a channel for the pus to escape downward. If no sinuses have formed, apply a linseed poultice, followed by a zinc and lead lotion.

Great care must be taken, as in all cases of confined pus, to prevent the external sore from healing over before the internal disease is entirely eradicated.

SAND CRACKS.—These are longitudinal divisions in the fibres of the hoof wall, amounting sometimes only to a flaw, and at others to a fissure entirely through the substance of the horn. It is caused by brittleness of the crust, often arising from the practice of cutting away the sole and rasping off the hoof. The brittleness may be constitutional, some horses being evidently predisposed to it. The fissure may also be traced at times to contracted heels, aggravated, if not produced, by cutting away the bars or opening the heels.

These cracks do not ordinarily cause lameness until sufficiently deep to expose the sensitive laminæ, or until they reach the coronary band. They then become very painful, and the lameness is extreme. They become so bad at times as to open and close as the horse raises and puts down his foot.

Treatment.—With a knife scrape the sharp edges of the crack to its bottom, until a clean groove has been formed.

Wash out with zinc and lead lotion, and blister the coronet, rubbing it in every two or three days, to stimulate the formation of new horn.

If the crack does not extend the entire length of the hoof, draw a deep furrow with a red hot iron at either end or both, sufficient to stop the crack from extending, but not deep enough to cause pain.

Toe cracks usually extend the entire length of the foot, and expose the flesh, which is apt to become granulated. These granulations should not be removed with caustic, which only inflames the tissues more than before. When they have appeared, cut them away with one stroke of a sharp knife. The loss of blood which follows will be of advantage to the parts. Bathe with white lotion twice a day.

When the inflammation has subsided, the fissure may be drawn together by cutting a niche about a quarter of an inch deep, half or three-quarters of an inch from the crack on each side, and driving a flat horseshoe nail through from one to the other; the ends should be drawn together and clinched with pinchers. It should be kept in mind that the horn of the hoof is thick below, and thin towards the coronet, so that nails cannot be driven very high up.

Clasps are manufactured for drawing together quarter cracks, owing to the difficulty of using nails advantageously on the thin quarters of the hoof.

Shoeing with tips, and also with three-quarter bar shoes is advantageous in treatment of toe and quarter cracks.

SEEDY TOE.—This term is applied to a separation of the outer wall or crust of the hoof from the inner layer of soft horn derived from the laminæ. It is caused by an unhealthy secretion of the lower portion of the laminæ, which is incapable of maintaining the union between the structures. The disease always commences in the lower portion of the laminæ, and extends upward and laterally. Though called seedy toe, the disease frequently affects the quarters.

Treatment.—Cut away all that portion of the crust which has become detached from the laminæ, and if the disease shows signs of extending, such further portions as may be necessary. Apply a bar shoe with a toe clip, blister the coronet every other day, and cover the exposed surface every day with an ointment of melted lard and beeswax, into which turpentine is stirred. This will keep out moisture. Feed liberally, and keep the foot dry.

THRUSH.—This is a disease of the frog, usually occurring in the hind feet, accompanied by a foul discharge. As the disease advances fissures occur in the side of the frog close to the heel, from which fœtid matter exudes. The condition is generally brought on by wet, unclean stalls, or dirt of some kind, such as stopping the feet with dung. In contracted feet the sole is lifted off the ground to such an extent that from want of use the frog frequently becomes diseased. Paring the frog has a similar tendency.

Treatment.—If it originates from dirt remove the cause,

and keep the frog clean and dry. Any ragged parts should be removed with a knife, so as to open the cracks in and around the frog. Having removed the cause, endeavor to absorb the discharge. This will be best effected by inserting pledgets of tow, greased with calomel and lard. The process of drying may be assisted by the application of powdered burnt alum.

If thrush be long neglected the neighboring parts become affected, and in bad cases the whole of the sensitive sole becomes involved.

CANKER.—This is a morbid secretion of the sensitive frog and sole, involving the corresponding insensitive parts. It usually has its origin in neglected thrush, but it may be due to constitutional causes.

Symptoms.—These consist of an abundant, fœtid, and colorless discharge from the frog, which is large, spongy, and covered by a fungoid growth, intermixed with offensive matter.

Treatment.—This consists in the complete exposure of the diseased surface, in the application of pressure, and in thorough dryness. The diseased portion, including the sole, must be removed, and the surface dressed with nitric acid; the sole is then covered with dry tow, and the foot enclosed in a leather boot. The nitric acid may be mixed with tar.

NAVICULAR DISEASE.—This, in its primary stage, is inflammation of the lower side of the navicular bone. After a time the tendon which passes under the bone, and its cartilage and bursa become involved. The navicular bone acts as a roller for the tendon which passes under it, and is attached to the coffin bone, and hence is peculiarly liable to suffer from the effects of concussion. It rarely affects the hind feet, and is most frequently seen in fore feet with narrow and high heels.

The inflammation once set up in the bone leads to a variety of changes both in its external and internal structure.

Symptoms.—Lameness may appear suddenly and without any apparent cause. It may disappear, and after a time reappear, either in the same or in the other foot, and thus go on for some time. In time the symptoms become more marked, and in most cases the first sign is pointing of the foot in the stable, or when at rest outside, followed by shortness in the step and lameness. The foot and the horse may be examined and nothing wrong be found. The animal may appear sound one day and have a return of the lameness the next.

A horse may point his foot as a habit, but if so, he usually points a fore and the opposite hind at the same time, whereas, only the fore feet are pointed in navicular disease.

With the symptoms described, if no other cause such as corns or laminitis can be found, and there is no external heat or injury, it is quite safe to diagnose the case as navicular disease.

Treatment.— The shoes should be taken off and the frogs allowed to touch the ground. The feet should be placed in a cold water bath for some hours during the day, and a linseed meal poultice applied at night. The animal should be encouraged to lie down so as to get the weight off his feet, and he is likely to do so if isolated in a dark stall. At the end of a couple of weeks, blister the coronet mildly. Sometimes it is well to insert a seton in the frog.

Horses are sometimes "nerved" for this disease, but such animals soon break down, and are obviously unsafe for military service.

LAMINITIS.— This is an inflammation of the sensitive laminæ which cover the outer and upper surface of the coffin bone, and is known more commonly as "founder." The original attack is always acute. It may be entirely relieved, but often a change of structure results from the effects of the acute attack. It is very painful and is attended with much lameness. The pain is due to confinement of the products effused by the inflammation within the outer hard case of the foot, and the pressure thereby caused on the sensitive structures of the interior.

The immediate cause most frequently is concussion. It may occur in all the feet, but the fore feet are more often affected than the hind ones. Excitement, overexertion and indigestion are frequent causes.

Symptoms.— The attack occurs very suddenly. The horse can hardly be got to move. He seems as if all his body were cramped. There is heat in the feet affected.

As the seat of the disease is in the front portion of the feet, the animal will save that portion of his feet as much as possible by throwing his weight on his heels. On account of the pain the pulse is always accelerated.

Treatment.—Endeavor to relieve the local inflammation within the feet. Mild purgatives should be given, and if the bowels are torpid, injections of warm water. Aloes or strong cathartics should not be given.

Remove the shoes, and rasp the wall down level with the sole, so as to allow it and the frog to bear the weight. Do not pare the sole.

Give laxative food, and plenty of water. Give two ounces of the bicarbonate of sodium twice a day in the food, and if the fever be high give a drench of from fifteen to thirty drops of tincture of aconite in water, and repeat at intervals of four hours. Put the feet in a tub of warm water, and also apply poultices for a few days. Give plenty of bedding, as the horse should lie down as much as possible.

SIDEBONES.—This consists in ossification of the elastic lateral cartilages, or wings of the bone of the foot. Nature supplied cartilage instead of bone in this part, in order to give elasticity toward the heels, and any alteration, such as conversion into bone, interferes with elasticity, although it may not occasion lameness. In light horses they are seldom visible to the eye, but their existence may be ascertained by feeling the wings of the bone of the foot.

Treatment.— There is no cure, but if the cartilages are still undergoing change, blistering the coronet will hasten the process.

CALKING.— This is an injury of the coronet, generally inflicted by the shoe of the other foot, or by the foot of another horse in the herd, or in ranks.

Treatment.— Remove any jagged ends and apply tincture of arnica. Keep the wound clean, and bathe three times a day with white lotion. If neglected it may terminate in quittor.

FLESH WOUNDS.— These may be gunshot; incised or clean cut; lacerated, where the skin is torn and broken, with edges more or less ragged and uneven; punctured, or those whose depth is much greater than the entrance aperture; and contused wounds, or those produced by concussion without perforation of the skin. They are more or less the result of accident, except those inflicted in battle.

There is a greater disposition in the horse than in man to suppurative action. Wounds of any extent seldom heal completely in the horse by direct union or by adhesion.

Wounds healed by granulation must fill up from the bottom gradually, and they should be prevented from closing outside. This may be done by inserting a piece of dry lint or tow between the edges of the wound.

For wounds to be healed by granulation there is no better dressing than lint steeped in cold water. This may be covered with oil silk, to retain the moisture.

Unhealthy granulations or proud flesh, must be kept in check by application of some caustic, such as sulphate of copper, nitrate of silver, or chloride of zinc.

In all wounds it is an object of much importance to keep the parts in a state of rest. In some parts a certain degree of motion cannot be avoided, but an endeavor should be made to lessen it as far as possible. In some cases the animal will have to be tied up to prevent his moving, and in others a cradle will be needed to prevent his gnawing the wound with his teeth.

Sutures are useful in bringing together the edges of the skin in parts where there is but little flesh, such as on the forehead and the nose, but they do not answer so well for fleshy parts, where the needful apposition of the parts is best maintained by bandages.

Sutures are best applied by means of a curved needle. Interrupted sutures answer better than continuous ones. The twisted suture, made by two needles and a skein of silk twisted over them, answers very well in small incised wounds.

Bandages should be adjusted very evenly, and not so tight as to obstruct circulation. When circumstances admit of it, the bandage should be applied above and below, but not over the wound.

If there is any hemorrhage it should be stopped at once by the application of styptics, cold or pressure. Oakum, tow, etc., bound over a wound will often stop hemorrhage.

In the general treatment of wounds, attention should

first be directed to cleansing the injured parts from all foreign bodies, by allowing lukewarm water to fall in a stream over it, one per cent. of carbolic acid being added to the water. Abraded surfaces should be touched as little as possible. Splinters, gravel, and all foreign substances, if not too deeply imbedded, may be removed with forceps.

GUNSHOT WOUNDS.—If a wound has been made by a bullet, a careful examination should be made to ascertain if the ball has passed through or out of the body. If not, the probe should be introduced, and if located it should be cut out if possible. Sometimes a ball may be so lodged that it cannot be removed, and it may become encysted and remain without giving rise to any inconvenience. It is often difficult to locate a bullet, as it is very readily deflected by resistances met with after entering the body. Should bones be struck by a ball, they are frequently shattered and splintered to such an extent as to warrant having the animal destroyed.

Apply hot fomentations, or poultices to which carbolic acid has been added, to the wound until suppuration has been fairly established. Should pus accumulate in the tissues, openings must be made at the most dependent parts for its escape.

INCISED WOUNDS.— Under this class come those made by some sharp instrument or body. The edges of the wound are smooth, as though cut with a knife. If they occur in fleshy parts, and blood vessels, tendons or joints are not injured; they soon recover, often with little or no special treatment. Bleeding is more apt to occur in wounds of this kind than any other. If from arteries, the blood is bright red or scarlet in color, and flows in jets or spurts; if from veins, it is darker, and the flow is regular. If the bleeding is from an artery, pressure should be applied between the wound and the heart; if from a vein, between the wound and the extremities. The bleeding stopped, the wound should be cleansed, but an incised wound should never be rubbed with any coarse substance.

If the wound is parallel to the muscular fibres, it does not open to any extent, but if the incision be across the muscles, gaping ensues. In the former case stitches may be taken to hold the parts together; in the latter they do harm, a properly applied bandage, bringing the edges of the wound together, being preferable. The bandage should be applied so as to encourage union from the bottom, and prevent accumulation of pus. An antiseptic wash should be applied, and if necessary, the wound may be gently cleaned with a soft sponge, and castile or carbolic soap and hot water. Meddling with and frequent dressings of such wounds do more harm than good.

LACERATED AND CONTUSED WOUNDS.—These may be described together, although in contused wounds there is no break of the skin. Lacerated wounds are usually also bruised or contused to a greater or less extent. Such wounds may not at first seem as serious as incised wounds, but they are commonly very much more so. In severe contusions, infiltration of blood takes place into the surrounding tissues; mortification follows, often involving deeper seated structures, and frequently resulting in abscesses.

In lacerated wounds the amount of hemorrhage is generally small; the edges of the wound are ragged and uneven. These wounds are commonly produced by some blunt object, as where a horse runs against fence posts, corners of buildings, trees, wire fences, etc.

After a thorough exploration, such wounds should be carefully fomented with warm water, to which has been added three parts of carbolic acid to one hundred of water. Free exit for pus must be secured. If the orifice is found to be too high, or if pus is found to be burrowing in the tissues, an opening low enough to drain it must be made.

There is usually soreness and considerable inflammation in lacerated wounds, and warm linseed poultices may be used effectively in many cases.

PUNCTURED WOUNDS.—These are produced by the penetration of a pointed substance, sharp or blunt, such as a thorn, fork or nail, and are apt to be neglected or remain undiscovered, by reason of the opening being insignificant as compared to the depth. They are very common in the feet and legs, and in board stalls where nails work loose from the rubbing and kicking of the horse, they occur in the face, neck, and all over the exposed parts of the body. Treatment is the same as in simple gunshot wounds.

Punctured wounds in the fetlock, knee, hock, stifle or other joint, are always serious, and frequently result in stiffening or anchylosis. These must be looked for in winter campaigns, when horses are shod with ice calks. After the wound has been examined and cleaned, if inflammation has not set in, apply a cantharides blister over the joint. This treatment operates to prevent ingress of air by swelling of the skin and tissues underneath, and also the superficial inflammation established acts to check deep-seated inflammation. If the joint fluid is escaping it must be stopped; treat with cooling lotions and a paste of flour and alum, or ten grains of chloride of zinc to an ounce of water. Medicine should be applied on pledgets of tow held in place by bandages. Such wounds require much time and perfect rest for a cure. Slings are very useful in many cases.

It may be remarked that in all injuries where the true skin is destroyed it is not reproduced. Its place is supplied by a cicatrix, which differs from true skin in not containing hair follicles.

The description of diseases and injuries, and methods of treatment, by no means includes all those known to veterinary practice, but is quite ample for the average experience in cavalry service. To fix a knowledge of diseases and remedies in the mind, it is absolutely necessary to watch the progress of such animals as may be attacked from time to time, and note the effect of various modes of treatment.